MW00680234

# Global
# Strategies for
# Emerging Asia

The Jossey-Bass
Business & Management Series

# Global Strategies for Emerging Asia

Anil K. Gupta
Toshiro Wakayama
U. Srinivasa Rangan

Editors

JOSSEY-BASS
A Wiley Imprint
www.josseybass.com

Copyright © 2012 by John Wiley & Sons, Inc. All rights reserved.

Published by Jossey-Bass
A Wiley Imprint
One Montgomery Street, Suite 1200, San Francisco, CA 94104-4594—www.josseybass.com

No part of this publication may be reproduced, stored in a retrieval system, or transmitted in any form or by any means, electronic, mechanical, photocopying, recording, scanning, or otherwise, except as permitted under Section 107 or 108 of the 1976 United States Copyright Act, without either the prior written permission of the publisher, or authorization through payment of the appropriate per-copy fee to the Copyright Clearance Center, Inc., 222 Rosewood Drive, Danvers, MA 01923, 978-750-8400, fax 978-646-8600, or on the Web at www.copyright.com. Requests to the publisher for permission should be addressed to the Permissions Department, John Wiley & Sons, Inc., 111 River Street, Hoboken, NJ 07030, 201-748-6011, fax 201-748-6008, or online at www.wiley.com/go/permissions.

Limit of Liability/Disclaimer of Warranty: While the publisher and author have used their best efforts in preparing this book, they make no representations or warranties with respect to the accuracy or completeness of the contents of this book and specifically disclaim any implied warranties of merchantability or fitness for a particular purpose. No warranty may be created or extended by sales representatives or written sales materials. The advice and strategies contained herein may not be suitable for your situation. You should consult with a professional where appropriate. Neither the publisher nor author shall be liable for any loss of profit or any other commercial damages, including but not limited to special, incidental, consequential, or other damages. Readers should be aware that Internet Web sites offered as citations and/or sources for further information may have changed or disappeared between the time this was written and when it is read.

Jossey-Bass books and products are available through most bookstores. To contact Jossey-Bass directly call our Customer Care Department within the U.S. at 800-956-7739, outside the U.S. at 317-572-3986, or fax 317-572-4002.

Wiley publishes in a variety of print and electronic formats and by print-on-demand. Some material included with standard print versions of this book may not be included in e-books or in print-on-demand. If this book refers to media such as a CD or DVD that is not included in the version you purchased, you may download this material at **http://booksupport.wiley.com.** For more information about Wiley products, visit **www.wiley.com.**

Cover images by Thinkstock

**Library of Congress Cataloging-in-Publication Data**

Global strategies for emerging Asia / Anil K. Gupta, Toshiro Wakayama, U. Srinivasa Rangan, editors. – 1st ed
    p. cm.
  Includes bibliographical references and index.
  ISBN 978-1-118-21797-9 (hardback); ISBN 978-1-118-28235-9 (ebk.);
  ISBN 978-1-118-28322-6 (ebk.); ISBN 978-1-118-28440-7 (ebk.)
  1. Asia–Commerce.  2. International business enterprises–Asia.  3. Asia–Foreign economic relations.  4. Asia–Economic policy–21st century.  5. Asia–Economic conditions–21st century.  I. Gupta, Anil K.  II. Wakayama, Toshiro.  III. Rangan, U. Srinivasa.
  HF3752.3.G55 2012
  337.5–dc23

                                         2012008075

Printed in the United States of America
FIRST EDITION
*HB Printing*           10  9  8  7  6  5  4  3  2  1

*Dedicated to our children—the creators and shapers of the future:*
*Anjali, Meili, and Rahul Gupta*
*Naomi Wakayama*
*Raghu and Sridhar Rangan*

# Contents

# Preface

The idea for this book originated at Leveraging Megatrends for Global Advantage: Delivering High Impact Executive Insights Grounded in Academic Rigor, a conference held in Tokyo in December 2010 and organized by the Center for Global Communications (Glocom), International University of Japan. A central theme of the conference was that the rise of emerging markets is changing the structure of the global economy more profoundly and more rapidly than at any other time in human history. Within this broader phenomenon, the rise of emerging Asia forms the center of gravity of the structural changes under way.

The conference was aimed at both managers and scholars. The intent was to open a dialogue between senior managers wrestling with immense global business challenges on the ground and academics trying to make sense of them. Given the high quality of the papers presented at this conference and the high quality of the discussions they generated, we concluded that some of the papers could constitute a wonderful book targeted at managers and business students. This book is the product of significant further work by the selected authors toward making each chapter not only richer (with more detail and deeper analysis) but also easier to read.

The book consists of nine focused chapters, each addressing a central question, plus a concluding chapter that pulls together and summarizes the central ideas emerging from the nine chapters as a set.

In Chapter One, Anil Gupta and Haiyan Wang argue that given the size and growth rates of emerging economies, ignoring or even giving peripheral treatment to these markets is no longer a viable option for most companies. They do so at grave peril to their own future. Rooted in this premise, the authors discuss how the changing structure and dynamics of the global economy will determine the characteristics of the global enterprises that emerge as the new winners or survivors ten years from now. The four building blocks of their analysis are the need to rethink global strategy, the need to rethink global innovation, the need to rethink global organization, and the need to keep globalizing the corporate mind-set.

In Chapter Two, Niraj Dawar and Charan Bagga start by highlighting two broad trends in today's global economy: domestic consumption in the emerging economies is gathering steam, and trade between emerging markets is ready to boom. Building on this observation, they ask: Can the conventional business model serve the new consumers in emerging markets? If not, what needs to change? They go on to examine the implications of these two trends and set out an agenda to prepare multinational corporations for the new world trade order.

In Chapter Three, Toshiro Wakayama, Junjiro Shintaku, Tomofumi Amano, and Takafumi Kikuchi present a detailed analysis of Panasonic's evolutionary history in China. They note that in its nearly twenty-five years of presence in China, Panasonic has gradually developed local capabilities through multiple phases, having increasingly addressed deeper localization enabled by more extensive cross-border integration of its home-grown resources and capabilities. Based on this analysis, they conclude that the best way to manage the apparent tension between the need for local adaptation and that for global integration is to view the two as synergistic rather than antagonistic. Deeper localization invites greater global integration, which in turn enables yet deeper localization.

In Chapter Four, Junjiro Shintaku and Tomofumi Amano examine how developed country multinationals can successfully compete against low-cost competitors in emerging markets. Starting with a number of examples that illustrate what they term the "emerging market dilemma," Shintaku and Amano present a detailed analysis of how Honda took on and beat low-cost competitors from China in the Vietnamese motorcycle market. One of their important conclusions is that, in emerging markets, cutting prices regardless of other considerations is not always a good idea. Reducing prices without trying to understand the market is unlikely to lead to long-term success. Customers gradually learn about the products and the technologies, and their buying behavior follows not only their budget but also their level of product knowledge.

In Chapter Five, Akira Tanaka and Yue Wang present a longitudinal case study of the joint venture between Toyota Motor Company and Tianjin Automotive Group in China, with a particular focus on how Toyota transferred its supply chain practices to the joint venture. They demonstrate that China's macroinstitutional environment provides important insights into the differences between the Chinese and Japanese parts supply practices and the problems that Japanese firms faced during the transfer of their supplier management practices to China. They also assess the Toyota way of resolving these difficulties in China's unique institutional environment and offer advice to multinationals on how to manage the transfer of their home-grown management practices to their China operations.

In Chapter Six, Aneel Karnani looks at the case of companies from emerging Asia that are spreading their wings abroad. He notes that megadeals involving acquisitions by emerging economy firms (such as Tata Steel buying Corus, Tata Motors buying Jaguar Land Rover, and Lenovo buying IBM's PC business) have attracted much adulatory attention from the business press. Instead of getting caught up in the rhetoric, Karnani presents an empirical analysis of the stock market performance of all large foreign acquisitions by Indian companies from 2000 to 2009. He also analyzes the three largest acquisitions using a case study approach and concludes that foreign acquisitions from India have not created shareholder value. The causes of this underperformance are too little integration, agency problems, and easy capital. A successful approach to foreign acquisitions will require significant synergies, reasonable price, and deep integration.

In Chapter Seven, Srinivasa Rangan and Sam Hariharan also analyze the emergence of aspiring global champions from China and India. They outline the various conceptual frameworks that might explain why there has been a quantum jump in acquisitions by Chinese and Indian firms. Using aggregate and anecdotal data, they show that the current growth in acquisitions abroad marks a significant departure in the behavior of Chinese and Indian firms. Building on this conclusion and using a series of case studies, they look at how Chinese and Indian firms' global acquisitions pose a strategic challenge to established developed country multinationals. They conclude by offering suggestions on how multinationals from Europe, Japan, and the United States might address the strategic challenge that Chinese and Indian firms pose.

In Chapter Eight, Srikanth Kannapan and Kuruvilla Lukose look at India as a platform for innovation. They examine three companies in detail: the Indian operations of IBM, the technology giant; Sasken, a publicly listed Indian company in the software and services sector employing thirty-five hundred people spread across India, Europe, and the United States; and Strand Lifesciences, a privately held computational life sciences organization headquartered in Bangalore. They conclude that companies must now learn what they refer to as "vortex leadership"—a new leadership practice for recognizing and realizing business opportunities in emerging economies like India. Leaders need to learn how to exploit new vistas that get uncovered as in a kaleidoscope, with small patches of light transforming to something much larger with a turn. They need to be able to see opportunity in complexity and transcend apparent opposites of agility and patience. Finally, leaders need to be at ease at combining an unhurried sociocultural sensitivity with the urgency demanded by business pragmatism.

In Chapter Nine, Andreas Schotter and Mary Teagarden focus on theft of intellectual property (IP), a widely recognized challenge, especially for companies operating in China. Intellectual property theft in China is a much bigger problem than simply knockoffs of Gucci purses, North Face jackets, or Rolex watches. The challenge ranges from copying toys and luxury goods to copying automotive and aircraft parts, pharmaceuticals, and other cutting-edge high-tech products like medical X-ray machines. It also includes copying business processes and even business or service models. They start their analysis with why there is such widespread IP theft in China. Based on a study of what companies are doing to combat this challenge, they then offer a set of best practices that a company can deploy to minimize the risk of IP theft.

In Chapter Ten, the editors of this book reflect on the totality of the advice that all nine chapters collectively offer to multinationals about how to compete in emerging Asia. In this conclusion, we reinforce the validity and relevance of the overall framework proposed by Gupta and Wang in Chapter One: the imperative to rethink global strategy, global innovation, and global organization and, above all, the need to keep globalizing the corporate mind-set.

We hope that you will find this book interesting to read and useful. Since no book can ever be the last word on anything, we also invite you to share your feedback and your own experiences with us. The book's Web site is
www.globalstrategiesforemergingasia.com.

University of Maryland and INSEAD      Anil K. Gupta
agupta@umd.edu
International University of Japan      Toshiro Wakayama
wakayama@iuj.ac.jp
Babson College      U. Srinivasa Rangan
rangan@babson.edu

# Acknowledgments

The idea for this book originated at Leveraging Megatrends for Global Advantage, a conference held in Tokyo on December 16–17, 2010, and organized by the Center for Global Communications (Glocom), International University of Japan. We, the editors of this book, are indebted to Akira Miyahara, director of Glocom, and the staff at the center for their support and encouragement for holding this conference and for support toward the development of this book. We are also grateful to Ji Soo Kim at KAIST Business School and Steven White at Tsinghua University for their tireless efforts in co-organizing the conference. We thank the following corporations for their generous sponsorship of the conference:

DAIKIN INDUSTRIES, LTD.

Fuji Xerox Co., Ltd.

Hitachi, Ltd.

Honda Motor Co., Ltd.

Kikkoman Corporation

Nippon Express Co., Ltd.

NIPPON TELEGRAPH AND TELEPHONE
  CORPORATION

ORIX Corporation

Panasonic Corporation

SAMSUNG JAPAN CORPORATION

Yokogawa Electric Corporation

Anil Gupta would also like to acknowledge his deep appreciation for the ongoing collaboration and support offered by Jossey-Bass/Wiley and Kathe Sweeney, its executive editor. This is Anil's sixth book with Jossey-Bass and John Wiley & Sons (and the third book during Kathe's role as executive editor). Many thanks, Kathe, for your ongoing friendship and support. Many thanks also to Dani Scoville, editorial program coordinator at Jossey-Bass, for your wonderful support in all aspects of this book's production.

Finally, Srinivasa Rangan would like to acknowledge the support of Babson College while working on this book. In particular, he is most appreciative of the support and encouragement received over the years from Len Schlesinger, college president; Shahid Ansari, provost; Deans Fritz Fleischmann, Carolyn Hotchkiss, and Raghu Tadepalli; Management Division chairs Bill Nemitz, Ashok Rao, James Hunt, Keith Rollag, and Nan Langowitz; and his colleagues, especially Stephen Allen, Allan Cohen, and Sam Hariharan. He is also grateful to Andronico Luksic, who funded his endowed chair professorship, which allowed him to devote time to work on this book. He is deeply appreciative of the support and help of his wife, Sudha, while he was immersed in working on this book.

# Part One

# GEARING UP FOR THE NEW GLOBAL REALITY

# 1

# BUILDING THE NEXT-GENERATION GLOBAL ENTERPRISE

## Anil K. Gupta, Haiyan Wang

The rise of emerging markets, with emerging Asia at the center of them all, is rapidly changing the structure of the global economy. Many of the emerging markets are no longer small. They already constitute nine of the world's twenty-four largest (and four of the twelve largest) economies (see Table 1.1). Within the next ten to fifteen years, emerging markets will account for half of the world's gross domestic product, up from about a third today and less than 10 percent in 1980. Emerging markets are also becoming the launching pads for a new generation of global competitors. According to *Fortune* magazine, of the world's five hundred largest corporations by revenue, sixty-seven are now headquartered in the BRIC (Brazil, Russia, India, and China) countries, up from just seven in 1995. Given the likely growth rates of emerging economies (three times that of the developed ones), it is all but certain that the shift in the world's economic center of gravity will accelerate over the coming decade. For most companies, ignoring or even giving peripheral treatment to emerging markets is no longer a viable option. They do so at grave peril to their own future.

As evolutionary theory tells us, when the environment changes, one must adapt—or die! Rooted in that premise, in this chapter, we look at how the changing structure and dynamics of the global economy will determine the characteristics of

### Table 1.1 The World's Twenty-Four Largest Economies in 2010

| Rank | Country | 2010 GDP (US$ billion) | Rank | Country | 2010 GDP (US$ billion) |
|------|---------|------------------------|------|---------|------------------------|
| 1 | United States | 14,582 | 13 | Mexico[a] | 1,040 |
| 2 | China[a] | 5,879 | 14 | South Korea | 1,014 |
| 3 | Japan | 5,498 | 15 | Australia | 925 |
| 4 | Germany | 3,310 | 16 | Netherlands | 783 |
| 5 | France | 2,560 | 17 | Turkey[a] | 735 |
| 6 | United Kingdom | 2,246 | 18 | Indonesia[a] | 707 |
| 7 | Brazil[a] | 2,088 | 19 | Switzerland | 524 |
| 8 | Italy | 2,051 | 20 | Poland[a] | 469 |
| 9 | India[a] | 1,729 | 21 | Belgium | 467 |
| 10 | Canada | 1,574 | 22 | Sweden | 458 |
| 11 | Russia[a] | 1,480 | 23 | Norway | 414 |
| 12 | Spain | 1,407 | 24 | Venezuela[a] | 388 |

*Note:* All data at market exchange rates. These twenty-four economies comprise 62 percent of the world's population and 83 percent of the world's GDP in 2010.

[a]Denotes an emerging economy (defined as any economy categorized by the World Bank as either middle income or low income).

*Source:* World Bank.

the global enterprises that emerge as the new winners or the survivors ten years from now.

There are four building blocks to our analysis: rethinking global strategy, rethinking global innovation, rethinking global organization, and globalizing the corporate mind-set (see Figure 1.1). We assign a central role to corporate mind-set because the cognitive biases of senior leaders have a decisive impact on resource allocation and corporate direction.

## Rethinking Global Strategy

The new global reality requires a fundamental rethinking of the answers to three of the most central questions pertaining to global strategy:

**Figure 1.1 Building the Next-Generation Global Enterprise: Analytical Building Blocks**

1. *What market position must we achieve and sustain within our industry on a worldwide basis?* Some of the questions that follow from this broader one are: What should we consider to be our strategic markets? What target opportunities in these markets must we go after? What business models must we design and implement to realize these opportunities?

2. *How should we globalize our resource base?* For any particular resource (research laboratories, production centers, or sales units, for example), globalization refers to the number and choice of locations where the resources will be based.

3. *How should we manage the tension between the need for global integration and the need for local responsiveness?* At one extreme, the choice may be to offer a globally standard mix of products and services (say, commercial aircraft by Boeing). At the other extreme, the choice may be to offer locally tailored products and services for every market (say, ice cream by Unilever).

These questions lead to the following three imperatives for a rethinking of global strategy.

## Robust Emerging Market Strategies

We believe that less than one-tenth of the world's five hundred largest companies have even close to a robust strategy for the key emerging markets of Asia, Latin America, Eastern Europe, and Africa. By "robust strategy," we mean a strategy that is fundamentally market driven (What do the customers in China and India need?) rather than product driven (How can we sell our current products and services in China and India?).

Consider the case of a Fortune 500 company with over $10 billion in 2010 revenues. It derives over 75 percent of its revenues from the United States and Canada. Yet by most estimates, over 80 percent of the market for this company's products and services is outside North America. Whereas the U.S. market is largely mature, that in emerging markets (especially China and India) is growing at over 20 percent a year. When senior executives at this company analyze the global market, the question they ask is, "How large is the market for our U.S.-based products and services, especially those that provide the bulk of our revenues and profits?" What they overlook is that, within their industry, much of the opportunity in emerging markets is for ultra-low-cost products and services that must be conceived, designed, and manufactured within these markets. Cloning or mere adaptation of U.S.-based products and services does little more than skim the surface of the vast opportunities in these emerging epicenters.

Contrast that case with the approach taken by Deere & Co. A few years back, Deere's Agricultural Equipment division initiated a zero-based redesign of its strategy for India and other emerging markets. Until then, Deere had viewed India predominantly from the lens of its existing U.S.-based products: large, technologically advanced, and very expensive machines designed for large American farms. Not surprisingly, executives had concluded that the market for their products in India was very small and had assigned India a relatively peripheral role in the company's global strategy.

Our discussions with a senior-level strategy group focused on two central questions: (1) How does Deere define its business: as a supplier of "large 100+ horsepower tractors" or as a supplier of "agricultural equipment"? (2) How large is the current and future market for agricultural equipment in India that may be smaller in size and horsepower and may not look anything like the company's machines for the U.S. and other developed markets? Discussions around these questions revealed that the company's global strategy had been driven too much by a product-centric mind-set and not enough by a market-centric mind-set. These discussions also led to Deere's decision to upgrade its engineering center in India and give the Indian subsidiary the autonomy and resources to design and manufacture products for the Indian as well as other emerging markets. Since then, Deere's India-made tractors (the 5003 series) have proved to be popular with farmers in India and other emerging markets. To its surprise, Deere has discovered that these small, very basic, low-horsepower, highly maneuverable, and inexpensive tractors (with a starting price of $14,400) are also proving to be popular with hobby farmers in the United States.

Emerging markets are not just large and rapidly growing; they are also radically different from those in developed countries. Selling the same or defeatured versions of existing products and services does little more than skim the surface of the market opportunities. The winning corporation of tomorrow will have a robust strategy that stays within the bounds of the company's business domain ("beverages" for Coca-Cola, "hospitality" for Marriott, and "agricultural equipment" for Deere) but is market rather than product driven.

## Atomization of the Value Chain

Go back only about thirty years, and for most firms, "global expansion" meant a clear choice between either of two strategies: export from home (for example, Toyota, Sony, or IBM) or produce locally to sell locally within each foreign market (for example, Procter & Gamble or Unilever). The former strategy made sense if scale economies were very high and tariff and transportation costs low relative to total costs. In such cases, virtually all elements of the value chain were concentrated in the home country. The latter strategy made sense when scale economies were low or tariff and transportation costs were prohibitively high, or both. In such cases, virtually the entire value chain was replicated in each market. Either way, other than sourcing of raw materials and distribution of finished goods, virtually all elements of the value chain were colocated in the same country and often on the same corporate campus.

Today's reality is already very different. For a Hong Kong–based apparel supplier, fulfilling an order for a U.S. or European retailer can mean that the fabric may be woven in China, the fastenings may be sourced from South Korea, and the actual sewing may be done in Guatemala or Vietnam. A PC company can now source hardware and software components from twenty countries, conduct assembly operations in five countries, and sell the finished laptops in over two hundred countries. A doctor in Boston can now order a magnetic resonance imaging scan on a patient after midnight and, if needed, have a highly experienced radiologist based in Bangalore send back his or her reading of the image within minutes. An architectural firm based in New York can now do the overall design for a building in Manhattan but have the engineering details of the piping, plumbing, and electrical wiring drawn up by a subsidiary in Shanghai.

This trend toward atomization of the value chain will continue and become more finely grained. Communications technologies are becoming more user friendly and less expensive at a very rapid rate. High-fidelity video telephony by mobile phone is already a reality. These developments will make it increasingly crucial for companies to push the envelope in terms of an increasingly finer disaggregation of the value chain and an optimization of the choice of locations for individual activities, subactivities, and even sub-subactivities. Also, as the relative competitiveness of different locations shifts over time, companies will need to be increasingly flexible in shifting the operational base of specific activities. William Amelio, Lenovo's former CEO, termed this approach to running the company "worldsourcing." An ever-greater commitment to worldsourcing will indeed be one of the defining features of tomorrow's global corporation.

## Global Platforms, Customized Solutions

Some of the earliest literature on globalization argued that the future would belong to companies that offered globally standardized products. The assumption was that the world was moving toward a converging commonality and that a strategy of global standardization would enable the company to deliver products that were advanced, functional, reliable, and low priced.[1]

We disagree completely and predict that the end game in globalization will be extreme customization and not extreme standardization. Ask any serious observer (the World Bank, International Monetary Fund, or Goldman Sachs, for example) to define *globalization*, and the answer will be that globalization refers to integration across countries.[2] Integration is a fundamentally different concept from homogenization. As we look ahead, the world economy will be far more integrated than it is today. At the same time, however, people will demand and be able to buy, at reasonable prices, more not fewer, customized products and solutions than we do today.

The Left Shoe Company, based in Helsinki, Finland, provides an interesting example of the shape of things to come. A customer of this company can get a pair of made-to-measure shoes, manufactured from a choice of several high quality materials, delivered to his/her door. Once the customer's feet have been scanned at a company-designated outlet and the customer has received an identity number, new shoes can be ordered directly from the company's Web site. The company relies on assistance from a shoe design firm based in Italy, sources the scanner from Germany, has a factory in Estonia, and sells through affiliated stores in several countries within and outside Europe, including Japan, Hong Kong, and Malaysia. This approach to selling customized shoes would be impossible without the combined power of technology and globalization.

Our prediction regarding extreme customization as the future reality rests on two premises. First, heterogeneity within and across countries (in buying power, cultural norms, habits, language, geographic climate, body shape and size—you name it) will remain an enduring feature of humanity for many decades to come. Even as buying powers converge across countries, given the side effects of capitalism, large income and wealth disparities within countries will remain a permanent feature of virtually all societies. Aside from buying power, look also at the cultural reality of societies. With each passing day, the United States, Europe, India, and China are becoming more (not less) multicultural with a growing number of subcultures.

Second, as illustrated by the Left Shoe company (and as depicted in Figure 1.2), developments in information, communications, and manufacturing technologies are rapidly reducing the cost of customization. This is already evident in the ability of individuals to customize, at near zero cost, the PC they buy, the first Web page they see, the apps they download, and the news they get. Over the next decade, it will also start becoming evident in other goods and services such as the medicines they take, the clothes they wear, and the cars they drive.

Large emerging markets such as China and India are not just very different from the United States and Europe; they are also vast and internally very diverse. There is no such thing as the

## Figure 1.2 How Technology Reduces the Cost of Customization

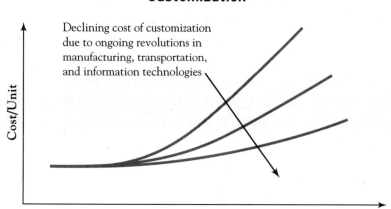

Declining cost of customization due to ongoing revolutions in manufacturing, transportation, and information technologies

Cost/Unit

Degree of Customization

average Chinese consumer or the average Indian consumer. Thus, the winning corporation of tomorrow will have to be a master at the art and science of fine segmentation and mass customization. Technologies and platforms are becoming increasingly global. In a seeming paradox, it is the very globalization of technologies and platforms that will enable companies to offer extremely customized and yet low-cost products, services, and solutions that will vary not just across individual customers but also from today to tomorrow.

## Rethinking Global Innovation

Innovation is best defined as the "production or emergence of a new idea."[3] We use this term to stand for both an outcome (the new idea) as well as a process (how the new idea emerged). It is hard to imagine any issue more central to society than innovation. All adaptation, whether evolutionary or revolutionary, requires innovation.

How companies must think about and manage innovation over the next ten years is unlikely to be similar to what they have done over the past ten. We focus on three of the major differences: (1) the rapidly growing need for pervasive innovation in all activities and at all levels of the organization; (2) the rapidly growing need for innovation that economizes on raw material and energy use, minimizes the environmental impact of the company's products and processes, and yields products and services that are ultra low cost; and (3) the rapidly growing need for companies to work across interfirm boundaries, that is, in collaboration with other firms, to develop new products, processes, and solutions.

## 360 Degree Innovation

At least three major forces are causing a steady decline in the half-life of technologies, products, services, processes, and even entire business models. The first is the ongoing march of technology, which continues to advance at an exponential rate. In 1990, if you needed to buy a book, you walked to a brick and mortar store. By 2000, you could order a book over the Internet and it would be delivered to your home in three to five days. Today you can order it as an e-book and have it delivered instantaneously to your PC, tablet, or a cell phone. The very idea of what we mean by "a book" is undergoing transformation, from today's static product that is updated, if at all, once every few years by the author, to a dynamic product where readers become ongoing cocreators of and even characters in the story. The impact of rapid technological advancement is evident all around us, from autos, pharmaceuticals, and clothing to even the lowly toothbrush.

The second force is the all-around transparency imposed by the Internet. A company's actions are becoming increasingly visible to almost every stakeholder—customers, competitors, suppliers, shareholders, employees, alliance partners, the community, governments, and social activists—in real time. A direct result has been that barriers to competitive imitation have rapidly gone down even as companies are now scrutinized and held more accountable by more stakeholders more frequently. Not surprisingly, the tenure of CEOs the world over is on a steady decline. As the Internet continues to become more powerful, the ability to hide will decline even more. The only salvation will be an accelerated pace of innovation.

The third force is the emergence of new competitors from nontraditional countries: competitors that bring very different capabilities (such as significantly lower-cost structures and larger pools of R&D talent), are very ambitious, and are comfortable moving at great speed. The processes that have resulted in the emergence of such new champions (SABMiller, Tata Motors, Suzlon, Huawei Technologies, and Alibaba Group) are still in the very early stages. As these processes gather momentum, we should see a cascading effect.

Given these trends, tomorrow's global enterprise will have to figure out how to make innovation an always-on and 360 degree pervasive activity. It will not be confined to the company's R&D labs. Even mundane activities such as cleaning the office floor and ensuring security at the office entrance will require a passion for innovation. Might we put carpets or vacuum systems at the entrance that remove well over 90 percent of the dirt from people's shoes as they enter the building? What newer technologies could we invent or acquire that reduce security risks while also cutting waiting times and making the entrance to the building a more pleasant experience? Given the pressure to save every penny and every ounce of raw material, asking questions such as these will need to become a central responsibility of not just people in the skunkworks but also everybody else, including the janitor, the receptionist, and the sales rep.

## A Passion for Frugal Innovation

By "frugal innovation," we mean innovation that strives to create products, services, processes, and business models that are frugal on three counts: frugal use of raw materials, frugal impact on the environment, and extremely low cost. The rapid rise of emerging markets, with China and India as the central players, is once again the prime mover behind the critical need for all three types of frugality.

Consider global warming. Two of the biggest contributors to global warming are emissions from cars and, perhaps surprisingly, buildings that need to be kept well lit and comfortable (cool in the summer and warm in the winter). Look now at the impact of China and India in these two areas. In 2000, motor vehicle production in China was barely 16 percent of that in the United States. By 2010, it was twice as large as that of the United States. Between 2006 and 2010, China added more square meters of urban floor space than all of the developed countries combined. India is behind China by about fifteen years, but it is following a similar path. As economic development in both countries spreads to the countryside, these trends are not likely to abate. In fact, the numbers will become much larger. No wonder, then, that the price of almost every commodity has risen sharply over the past ten years and that China and India have become two of the biggest contributors of greenhouse gases into the air that the world breathes.

It is unlikely that, for the sake of lifestyles in the developed world, China and India will decide to put brakes on their own growth. Instead, what we will witness is a rapid shift from products, services, and processes that are energy inefficient, raw material inefficient, and environmentally inefficient to those that are efficient. Companies that take leadership on these fronts on a worldwide basis are likely to find it easier to preserve and increase their global market shares at the expense of those that spend their time lobbying governments to ease up.

Note also that, over the next twenty years, the bulk of the absolute growth in market demand for most products and services will occur at the middle- and low-income levels in the big emerging markets. Winning these megamarkets will require that products and services also be ultra low cost.

A passion for frugal innovation will become increasingly essential not just for companies that sell consumer products and services but also for those that are purely in business-to-business domains such as Nokia Siemens Networks (NSN), Ericsson, and IBM. Bharti Airtel, the world's lowest-cost provider, is India's market leader in cell phone services. The company's ingenuity lay in devising a new-for-the-industry business model for mobile telephony that relied heavily on outsourcing all network operations (to NSN and Ericsson) and all business support services (to IBM). However, for this business model to succeed, it was essential that companies such as NSN and Ericsson depart from their traditional practices and agree to get paid for network operations on a per minute basis rather than for selling and installing the equipment. In short, the Bharti Airtel model works because all of the players (NSN, Ericsson, IBM, and Bharti Airtel itself) are committed to frugal innovation.

Over the coming decade, companies such as GE, which must help hospitals in Beijing and Kolkata provide better care at a lower cost; Otis, which must provide lower-cost and more energy-efficient elevators and escalators for tomorrow's Mumbai; and Carrier, which must keep buildings in Guangzhou and New Delhi cool in the summer, will have no choice but to become ever more passionate about frugal innovation. Otherwise the market will move to companies that are.

## Collaborative Innovation

The disaggregation of value chains coupled with greater outsourcing means that even as companies become more global and more diversified, they are becoming more focused regarding what they manage within their own boundaries. In short, companies are becoming embedded in ever larger interfirm networks.

The growth in outsourcing is being fueled by a combination of more intense competition plus developments in information technology. As companies become subject to the transparency brought about by the Internet and as barriers to imitation and new entry decline, companies find themselves facing more intense competition. Consequently the penalties from internalizing any activity that somebody else can do better, cheaper, or faster have gone up. As a complementary development, the growing power of information technology is making it possible to accurately measure and effectively coordinate increasingly complex interfirm transactions.

The trend toward disaggregation will continue. Companies will find that the features, quality, performance, and price of their end products will depend increasingly on the decisions and actions of their business partners on all sides of the value chain. Thus, unless companies become masters at the art and science of collaborative innovation, they will find themselves playing just a commodity game within some other player's differentiated business system.

Disaggregation of the value chain is not the only factor that will make collaborative innovation increasingly important. Other factors are the rapid integration of multiple technologies into the same product, service, or process, and a growing external market for proprietary intellectual property. Look at the integration of multiple technologies. Today's tablet computer is not just a computing and office productivity device; it has also become a source of multimedia communication, information, and entertainment. Today's cars have largely become computers on wheels. Today's books need to be published and made accessible not just in paper-based formats but also in many different types of digital formats. And it will not be long until contact lenses may come embedded with medications so that you can not only see better but also become healthier in the process. As disparate technologies come together into a single product, service, or process, companies will find that no matter what their size, they do not have the mastery of all of the essential technological puzzles. Directly relevant innovation increasingly will take place outside the firm's boundaries or collaboratively at the interfaces between firms.

The final driver of the move toward reliance on external innovation is the emergence of increasingly sophisticated markets for proprietary intellectual property such as patents and trademarks. Consider Intellectual Ventures, a company founded in 2000 by Nathan Myrvhold (until then, chief strategist and chief technology officer at Microsoft) and Edward Jung (until then, chief architect and advisor to the executive staff at Microsoft). Intellectual Ventures has emerged as one of the major players in creating a liquid market for patents that often remain buried and unused in corporate vaults.

## Rethinking Global Organization

Every company's organization is an ecosystem that consists of complementary elements such as structure, processes, and culture that work together to drive the company's decisions and actions. We identify three of the most important ways in which tomorrow's global corporation will need to be different from that of today: (1) a reengineering of the company's worldwide corporate headquarters from a single location to a network of global hubs that are situated in a small number of carefully selected locations; (2) a shift in how the company is managed, from a command-and-control model to a connect-and-coordinate model; and (3) an ever greater need to cultivate a strong one-company culture that provides the intellectual, social, and psychological glue to bind a geographically dispersed staff into a cohesive body.

### Network of Global Hubs

Cisco Systems is one of the world's leading-edge companies in trying to figure out what the global enterprise of tomorrow must look like. Here is what Wim Elfrink, chief globalization officer and executive vice president of Cisco Services, has said about the impending "virtualization of the corporation":

> The tradeoff between the intimate but inefficient old-world organization and the hyper-efficient but impersonal modern organization is on the verge of extinction. Today, the increasing pervasiveness of broadband networks have facilitated the slicing and dispatching of corporate functions around the globe. . . . The ability to be both dispersed and close will encourage a transformation from today's typical client-server corporate model, in which a central headquarters is linked to various satellite offices, to more of a peer-to-peer network. This translates into an extraordinary cultural shift . . . and possibly from the very idea of a corporate headquarters.[4]

We agree entirely with Elfrink. Legacy notions of corporate headquarters will undergo a transformation over the next ten years. Even for most U.S.-headquartered companies, where the historical home market might remain the world's largest for the next decade, the locus of market opportunities and major functions is shifting rapidly. For any company that wants to emerge or stay as one of its industry's global leaders ten years from now, it is imperative that the center of gravity of its marketing and sales efforts, its manufacturing operations, and even its R&D activities shift sharply from the United States to other countries. We do not suggest that the role of the United States will somehow cease to be unimportant. Far from it. We do believe, however, that even for today's so-called American companies, the U.S. operations will have to be viewed not as the mother ship but as one of five to ten major global hubs. Similar transformations will be required of companies such as Toyota, Nissan, Siemens, and Daimler that we view today as Japan-centric or Germany-centric. Companies that resist such transformation will do so at their own peril.

What will replace the old-fashioned mother ship based in Armonk, New York, or San Jose, California? Some observers have proposed that the new global architecture will consist of regional hubs (say, North America, South America, Asia, Europe, and so forth); in such an architecture, each regional hub would have all of the resources and decision-making power to manage all operations within its region. With due respect to the proponents of such a view, we beg to disagree. The world economy is becoming not only increasingly multipolar but also ever more globally integrated. IBM's procurement operations in China serve the company's global needs, not just those in Asia. Similarly, IBM's global delivery centers in India serve the needs of its clients worldwide and not just those in Asia. Microsoft's research center in Beijing is a global hub for the development of next-generation user interfaces for the global market and not just China. These are only a few of countless examples that will multiply over the coming ten years. The last thing that the global enterprise of tomorrow should do is to become a federation of regional fiefdoms.

Instead, what will be needed is the creation of a small number of global, not regional, hubs, each situated in a carefully selected location. Some of the central criteria for these locations will be physical proximity to the global epicenter of that particular function or line of business; attractive and safe living conditions for senior executives and their families, who will spend much of their time living in and working out of these global hubs; and world-class connectivity in terms of both telecommunications infrastructure and airports and flights so that the executives based at these hubs can stay connected with their peers as well as external partners in other locations with the least amount of wasted time, effort, and frustration.

IBM, Honeywell, Cisco, and Infosys serve as examples of companies that are transforming the central corporate headquarters into a network of carefully dispersed global hubs. In October 2006, for example, IBM moved the office of its chief procurement officer, John Paterson, to Shenzhen, China. As the company noted in its announcement of the move,

> The decision . . . marks the first time the headquarters of an
> IBM corporate-wide organization has been located outside
> the U.S. This move illustrates a shift underway at IBM from
> a multinational corporation to a new model—a globally
> integrated enterprise. . . . In a multinational model, many
> functions of a corporation were replicated around the world—
> but each addressing only its local market. In a globally
> integrated enterprise, for the first time, a company's worldwide
> capability can be located wherever in the world it makes the
> most sense, based on the imperatives of economics, expertise
> and open environments.[5]

## From Command and Control to Connect and Coordinate

How the emergence of the commercial Internet has transformed markets and enterprises has been well documented.[6] We focus here on how the more recent Web 2.0 (social media) technologies will reshape the way global enterprises are managed.

For corporations, Web 1.0 was mainly about making transactions more efficient. Companies could book an increasing proportion of orders over the Internet largely through self-service by customers themselves. Employees too could engage in a greater degree of self-service, particularly for routine matters such as checking the company's policy about annual vacations or keeping track of their stock options. And suppliers could engage in more real-time coordination between customer needs and their own production and logistics schedules.

The thrust of Web 2.0 developments (such as Facebook, Twitter, Wikipedia, podcasts, and blogs) is predominantly about collaboration. On top of these Web 2.0 innovations, there have been major developments in communications technologies.

Examples on the consumer side are Skype and Google Talk, which permit zero-cost real-time audio-video communication between any number of individuals in the world as long as they are connected to the Internet. Examples on the corporate side include technologies such as Cisco's TelePresence, which enables people to interact and collaborate with others in remote locations using life-size, high-definition video and audio with fidelity so high that one can almost "feel" the other person's presence.

Given the pace of advances in communications technologies, it is hard to speculate about what Web 3.0 and Web 4.0 technologies may look like. However, looking at the collaboration capabilities already unleashed by Web 2.0 technologies, it is clear that the global enterprise of tomorrow will have to be managed predominantly through a horizontal connect-and-coordinate model rather than a hierarchical command-and-control model. The impact of the new collaboration technologies is likely to be particularly profound on knowledge-intensive and creative tasks where coordination is not constrained by the delays currently inherent in the movement of physical goods.

Combining the growing power of collaboration technologies with the fact that knowledge workers are becoming almost like free agents who stay with any particular organization for increasingly shorter tenures (or who may literally be free agents who sell their services on a contractual basis to any buyer) leads to some interesting insights. Could it be that as key knowledge workers become free agents, the competitive advantage of the enterprise will derive less from the individuals who "work for it" than from the technological and social mechanisms that the company deploys to transform individual knowledge and skills into a collaborative product, service, or solution?

## A Strong One-Company Culture

As companies become geographically more dispersed, the need for tight integration across organizational subunits will increase rather than go down. No CEO ever wants to have things go out of control and let chaos reign. It is only when leaders are confident that the company would not fall apart that they are comfortable in pushing the envelope in creating a distributed organization with roots in many countries. GE, IBM, Cisco, and P&G are some of the leading examples of how a global enterprise that is ready for tomorrow ought to be run. Each of these companies has a strong culture that defines what they believe in, who they are, and what makes them different and superior to their competitors.

Building a strong one-company culture—one that has widely shared and internalized core values, beliefs, and behavioral norms—does not mean a lack of diversity. P&G operates in almost every country and has a large portfolio of brands, none of them called "P&G." Yet you could go to any corner of the P&G empire and you are likely to get the same answer to key questions such as these: "What is the job of a brand manager?" "Why should we win in the marketplace?" "What are the two moments of truth?"

The push for a strong corporate culture while operating in a world of enduring heterogeneity across national cultures requires deliberate and sophisticated decisions about what constitutes the core and the context with regard to corporate culture. Consider Toyota. As Toyota set up factories in the United States, it wisely concluded that most aspects of the manufacturing culture in its Japanese factories were a core part of its corporate culture and that the last thing it should do is to emulate the historical manufacturing culture of the U.S. auto industry. At the same time, however, it knew that it would be ridiculous to have each day in a San Antonio factory start with Shinto prayers. The four basic rules (pertaining to how people work, how people connect, how the production line is constructed, and how to improve) that guide Toyota's production system are part of the core.[7] What religion people believe in, what food they like to eat, or what language they speak are part of the context.

Cultivating a strong one-company culture requires paying particular attention to investing in corporate infrastructure: the communications and information technology (IT) infrastructure, the human resource (HR) infrastructure, the intellectual infrastructure, and the emotional infrastructure. A strong corporate-wide communications and IT infrastructure ensures that people have easy access to and the ability to communicate with others within the enterprise. A strong HR infrastructure ensures that there are no glass ceilings and that anyone anywhere in the world has an equal chance for training, development, and career advancement. A strong intellectual infrastructure ensures that people share the same worldview, the same strategic priorities, and the same corporate lingo (which may be jargon to outsiders but enables people within the company to communicate with each other efficiently without loss of content). Finally, a strong emotional infrastructure ensures that people take pride in the global enterprise, identify with it, and are willing to engage in voluntary extra-role behavior that goes beyond what is minimally required by formally defined job specifications.

It is the reality of a strong infrastructure that makes it easy for a company such as P&G to appoint an Indian man as the general manager of its beauty care business in China without fear of failure or to take a high-end facial cream, SK-II, developed by its Japanese subsidiary, and roll it out globally.

## Globalizing the Corporate Mind-Set

The term *mind-set* refers to the cognitive lenses through which people make sense of the world around them. To understand the power of mind-sets, look at the following examples.

In 1927, Harry M. Warner, the founder of Warner Bros., observed, "Who the hell wants to hear actors talk?" In 1943, Thomas Watson Sr., the architect and chairman of IBM, speculated, "I think there is a world market for maybe five computers." In 1977, Ken Olsen, chairman and founder of Digital Equipment, noted, "There is no reason for any individuals to have a computer in their home."[8] More recently, in 2003, Seth Godin, one of the foremost Internet marketing experts, observed that while Google provided a terrific search service, it was not the foundation for a great business.[9]

What is going on here? These are really smart people. The problem is that, like Harry Warner, they were looking at the future from the lens of the past. When movies were silent, actors were selected for how they looked and not how they spoke. And many of them had terrible voices. Harry Warner was right in asking why in hell anybody would want to hear them talk. What he overlooked, however, was that a new business model might emerge—one based on actors who not only looked good but also had great voices. Think now about whether you and your colleagues might similarly be looking at the global reality from the mental prison of past business models.

Companies and business leaders can be said to have a global mind-set when they reflect two characteristics: an openness to and awareness of diversity across cultures and markets, combined with a propensity and ability to integrate across this diversity. Becoming a prisoner of diversity is just as bad as being blind to it.

Most business leaders still view foreign markets as an add-on supplement to the domestic market. Very few have internalized the fact that even for U.S.-headquartered companies, 75 percent of the world's GDP is outside the United States and that emerging economies are growing three times as fast as the U.S. economy. Thus, it may well be more prudent to view opportunities outside the United States as more central to the company's future than those within the United States.

The primary explanation for why most companies lack global mind-sets is that leaders with the power to shape the company's future direction are far removed psychologically, cognitively, and physically from the new epicenters of global change. The net result is that they rely primarily on information that is not merely several months old but has been filtered and processed to make it palatable—in other words, information that may well be useless or even misleading. Given the vastness, complexity, dynamism, and importance of emerging markets, there can be no substitute for gut-level judgment based on direct observation and deep immersion within these societies.

What steps must a company undertake in its moves to globalize the sensing and decision-making capabilities of the corporate leadership? The starting point in cultivating a global mind-set is to deepen people's knowledge of major cultures and markets other than their own home country. The key here is to build knowledge that is deep rather than superficial. Deep knowledge comes not from short visits but from on-the-ground immersion over a longer duration. It comes not from observation but from problem solving within the new culture. This requires that the career paths of fast-track employees must involve cross-border on-the-ground experience in at least a couple of the major economies. Of course, it's crucial to make sure that the identification of fast-track employees is blind to nationality or cultural background.

Another mechanism to deepen knowledge of different cultures and markets is to rotate the locations of key meetings and, when a particular group meets in a location, to make sure that the agenda includes addressing not only the immediate task at hand but also learning through field experience, even if the field experience is for only half a day.

Deeper learning of other cultures can also be fostered by building interpersonal networks that cut across borders. Deployment of technologies such as Facebook within the company is making it easier by the day. Evolution has programmed human beings into social animals. As each of us knows from personal experience, people like to interact with others, and they interact more frequently, more openly, and more helpfully with others whom they know and like. The idea here is not that the company should mandate the formation of cross-border interpersonal networks. Rather, what the company should do is to eliminate every barrier that prevents such networks from emerging spontaneously.

The final and perhaps most potent mechanism for cultivating a global mind-set is to globalize the company's leadership architecture. On this issue, the first question to ask is: Where should the leaders come from? Having studied strategic leadership over the last twenty years, we have come to the firm belief that the best leaders are not those who are supposedly objective but those who are biased—but with an important caveat that those biases reflect the reality of the future rather than that of the past. The best leaders are those who have a sense for where the future is headed and are passionate about this vision. Vision and passion reflect a biased view of the world, a bias that propels the company forward rather than holds it back. Some questions to ponder are: How many of the top three hundred people in your company today reflect a deep knowledge of geographies that represent your future markets and sources of your future talent pool? What about the executive committee? And what about the board of directors?

The second major question pertaining to the globalization of the leadership architecture is this: Where should people with decision-making power sit? In far too many companies, there exists a gap of five thousand to ten thousand miles between the location of major opportunities and the location of decision-making power. The typical outcome is that people in the field often find themselves banging their heads against a wall. Business leaders who spend most of their time in New York City, Tokyo, or Munich have a difficult time looking at the world from anything other than American, Japanese, or German eyes. If you are passionate about transforming your company into a next-generation global enterprise, you need to start decoding why companies such as Cisco, IBM, and GE have started to relocate some of their most powerful executives to the new epicenters of the global economy. It is instructive to take note of a favorite expression of Cisco's Wim Elfrink: "You can't think out of the box while sitting in the box."[10]

The winning global enterprise of tomorrow will be one that figures out how to take advantage of three realties: the rapid growth of emerging markets and the increasing multipolarity of the world economy; enduring cultural, political, and economic differences across countries and regions; and the rapidly growing integration of national economies.

# 2

# IS YOUR BUSINESS MODEL READY TO DRILL INTO THE CORE OF THE DIAMOND?

Niraj Dawar, Charan Bagga

In the year 2020 will cricket players in India be wearing Nike or Li Ning? Will their uniforms be sporting the Pepsi or the Wahaha logo? In the FIFA World Cup in Brazil, will the billboards be advertising Huawei, Gazprom, Haier, and Tata Motors brands? Will Chinese banks be buying their enterprise software from IBM or from Infosys? Answers to these questions have profound implications for the strategies of many traditional Western and Japanese multinational companies that have built their business models on assumptions about who their principal customers are and where they source manufactured products.

Starting in the early 1990s, the most pressing global business question in the boardrooms of traditional multinational companies has been, "What is our strategy for emerging markets?" More often than not, it meant, "What is our strategy for sourcing products from China and other low-cost manufacturing centers?" More recently, its meaning has expanded somewhat to include other emerging markets, as well as to examine the opportunity for selling products to consumers in the emerging economies. But the business model that this question spawned remains relatively unaltered: to find low-cost labor and manufacturing sources to make the products, brand them, and market them to consumers in developed markets willing to pay several-fold the production cost.

Two-thirds of China's current manufacturing exporters are multinational companies, which together account for half of all of China's merchandise exports. Most of those exports are intended for consumption in the developed markets of the West and Japan. A pair of branded athletic shoes manufactured in China retails for between ten and twenty times its manufacturing cost in the markets of North America, Europe, and Japan. Similar economics drive multinationals' selling strategies in other product categories and sourcing strategies in other emerging markets. The resulting high returns have customarily been ascribed to the multinationals' value-adding activities in R&D, design, management, and branding capabilities. They have allowed these companies to carry heavy marketing and administration overheads in their home markets and still provide a comfortable return to shareholders.

Multinationals that sell to consumers in emerging markets have typically defined their target market as the tip of the income pyramid. In socioeconomic terms, consumers at the tip are similar to those that multinationals serve in developed markets. They have the means to buy the product and brands the multinationals sell and an awareness of global brand positioning that justifies their premium prices. In other words, rather than develop value propositions that would fit consumers in emerging markets, multinationals have been actively seeking out consumers who fit the value propositions they have developed for their traditional markets. As a result, multinationals are locking themselves into gilded cages in the emerging markets, barely scratching the surface of the emerging countries' population and market potential.

It is not that they do not want to address a larger market, but that often they cannot. They are unable to drill beyond the tip of the pyramid because they are hindered by their high-margin business models that place great value on branding, packaging, positioning, design, expensive R&D, and display. But with slowing growth, overindebtedness, aging populations, and declining currencies in developed markets, multinationals are turning their attention to the emerging markets where a two-decade-long uptrend in growth is now being reinforced by booming intra–emerging market trade. In this new environment, the conventional emerging market business model as developed in the boardrooms of multinationals over the past two decades is looking increasingly obsolete. But the signs of an incipient business model are already present. Two broad trends make it so.

First, domestic consumption in the emerging economies is gathering steam. Emerging market consumers are becoming one of the drivers of global growth. Savvy multinationals around the world now expect more than half their global growth for the next decade to come from the large emerging market economies. Most of this growth can be traced to the middle-class consumers whom multinational corporations (MNCs) are not accustomed to serving.

Second, emerging market to emerging market (EM2EM) trade is set to boom. Companies from emerging markets, not burdened by the overheads that MNCs carry, are well placed to serve emerging market consumers around the world.

Both trends call into question the entrenched business models and emerging market strategies of traditional Western and Japanese multinational companies. The question before boardrooms today is this: Can the conventional business model serve the new consumers in emerging markets; if not, what needs to change? In the following sections, we examine the implications of these two trends and set out an agenda to prepare MNCs for the new world trade order.

## Domestic Consumption

The emerging market growth story is by now well established. The share of global gross domestic product (GDP), measured in purchasing power parity (PPP) in 2010 dollars, accounted for by the large emerging economies (particularly, the

### Figure 2.1 GDP in Billions of U.S. Dollars, PPP Adjusted, 2000-2010

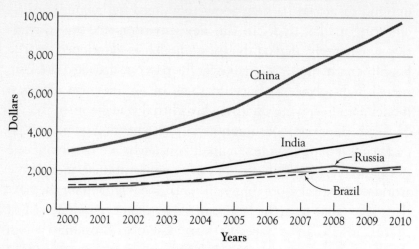

*Source:* International Monetary Fund, World Economic Outlook Database, 2010.

four BRIC countries: Brazil, Russia, India and China), as a percentage of global output increased from around 16 percent in 2000 to almost 25.2 percent in 2010. In the same period, the GDP share of the United States in the global pie shrank from 23.4 percent in 2000 to 19.1 percent in 2010. China has been the spectacular locus of growth even among the BRICs. Figure 2.1 shows the growth of overall GDP of the BRIC economies (PPP adjusted) between 2000 and 2010.

Despite the great recession gripping the rest of the world, each of these countries has seen a continuation of the dramatic rise in domestic consumption. Boosted by government programs to support local consumption, including lower taxes, rebates, trade-in programs, and easier loans, Chinese consumers have been buying like never before. China is now both the world's largest car market (by unit sales) and its largest carmaker; the average size of the flat-screen TV sold in China is now larger than that in the United States. And yet private consumption in

**Table 2.1 Percentage Growth of Key Consumption Indicators 2000–2009, PPP Adjusted**

| Country | GDP | Total Domestic Consumption | Household Consumption | Household Consumption per Capita |
|---|---|---|---|---|
| Brazil | 63% | 67% | 69% | 51% |
| China | 191 | 138 | 131 | 120 |
| India | 131 | 113 | 113 | 86 |
| Russia | 88 | 121 | 152 | 159 |
| United States | 43 | 50 | 50 | 37 |

Sources: Data are based on International Monetary Fund, World Economic Outlook Database, 2010, and U.N. statistics division. Data for China are for mainland China (People's Republic of China) only.

China is still only 40 percent of GDP, compared with almost 60 percent of GDP in India and over 60 percent in Brazil. The growth rates of domestic consumption in both China and India are double that of the United States (in PPP terms; see Table 2.1) and more than double the rate in the European Union member states or Japan, which have grown at a slower pace than the United States.

Looking beyond aggregate growth in consumption, it is even more instructive to see who is now buying. Table 2.2 is derived from an analysis that classifies the emerging market population in economic classes based on (PPP adjusted) household income criteria.[1] This analysis suggests that the consumption distribution has transitioned from a pyramid to a diamond-shaped structure over the past decade. The top and bottom brackets of the diamond have a consumption share of 17 percent and 28 percent, respectively, while the middle now accounts for a 55 percent share. The potential of emerging markets may reside not at the base of the pyramid but at the core of the diamond.

Much of the growth in domestic private consumption in the emerging markets can be traced to increased earning and

**Table 2.2 Emerging Markets: Population Classification by Economic Segments**

| Socioeconomic Class | Household Income (PPP adjusted) | Population Percentage | Percentage Consumption | Global MNC Presence |
|---|---|---|---|---|
| Upper class | Above $56,500 | 2% | 17% | Pioneer Global MNCs have made inroads into this socioeconomic segment. |
| Middle class | $13,500 to $56,500 | 37 | 55 | Segment neglected by global MNCs; this is the segment driving the real growth of emerging markets. |
| Lower class | Below $13,500 | 61 | 28 | Segment unviable for most Global MNCs. |

*Note:* Emerging market economies include Argentina, Brazil, Chile, China, Colombia, Egypt, India, Indonesia, Iran, Malaysia, Mexico, Nigeria, Pakistan, Peru, the Philippines, Poland, Romania, Russia, South Africa, Thailand, Turkey, Ukraine, Venezuela, and Vietnam.

*Source:* D. Court and L. Narasimhan, "Capturing the World's Emerging Middle Class," *McKinsey Quarterly*, July 2010. http:/www .mckinseyquarterly.com/Capturing_the_worlds_emeging_middle_class_2639#.

spending by consumers at the core of the diamond—the emerging market–middle class (EM-MC)—defined as the 1 billion consumers with an annual household income between $13,500 and $56,500. This segment of the market has been mostly neglected by the global multinationals. But it is becoming increasingly clear to both the global multinationals and local firms that this is where the action is going to be over the coming decade or longer. We reason that if MNCs remain wedded to their conventional business model, they will miss out on the opportunity of the middle-class consumer in emerging markets.

## EM2EM Trade

A closer look at Asia, where for the past decade intraregional trade has been booming, carries instructive lessons. The most dramatic bit of news here is that China in some ways has replaced the United States as the top trading nation of the world. In 2000, the United States was the unchallenged top trading nation in the world. It was consistently one of the top three trading partners for eight of the top ten trading countries. Compared to this, China featured among the top three trading partners for only three of the top ten trading countries. By 2009 (see Figure 2.2), the picture was very different: China now features in the top three trading partner list for seven of the top ten trading nations, while the United States has slipped out of the list for three of the top ten and is now in the list of top three trading partners for only five of the top ten trading nations. China replaced the United States over the previous decade as one of the top three trading partners for leading the key European trading economies: the United Kingdom, Germany, and Italy. Not only has China become the top trading partner of countries in the developed world, but by 2009 China also featured among the top three trading partners for each of Brazil, Russia and India.

So, is the multinationals' business model already obsolete? Not quite yet—much of the increase in intra-Asia trade is

## Figure 2.2 Top Three Trading Partners for the United States and China, 2001 and 2009

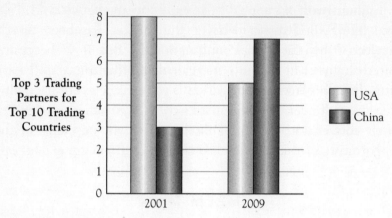

Top 3 Trading Partners for Top 10 Trading Countries

*Source:* The analysis is based on data from the Trade Competitiveness Map, International Trade Center.

business-to-business (B2B): iron ore from India to China, oil from Russia to China, and agricultural products from Brazil to China, for example. Within Asia, a good chunk of the increases in intraregional trade is accounted for by multinational companies' supply chains transferring parts, components, and semifinished products from factories in one country to those in other countries. The end products from those factories are still bound for developed markets. That kind of intraregional trade between emerging markets will continue to grow. But it is the trade that is now beginning to grow on top of this B2B trade that will challenge MNCs' business models. The next few years will witness a substantial increase in business-to-consumer trade as domestic demand takes off, lifted by growing standards of living, stronger currencies, and relatively easy credit (by historical standards). Already, Chinese toys account for 70 percent of the toys sold in India. And plastic Chinese toys, as we know from other markets, are the canary in the coal mine.

Big as the China growth story is, it is not the only phenomenon driving intra–emerging market trade. Just as revealing is
the comparison of trade growth rates between the BRICs and the
developed world versus EM2EM (in this case intra-BRIC) trade.
Trade between the BRIC countries and the developed world (the
United States, European Union member countries, and Japan)
grew by 289 percent from around $525 billion in 2001 to $2.04
trillion in 2010. During the same period, the nascent intra-BRIC
trade that was a paltry $29 billion in 2000 grew by a staggering
1,004 percent to around $319 billion by 2010 (Figure 2.3). The
relevance of emerging markets in the global trading landscape is
placed in further relief when compared with overall global trade,
which grew at a more modest compounded annual rate of around
9 percent during the same period.

## Figure 2.3 Trade Data (Billions of U.S. Dollars)

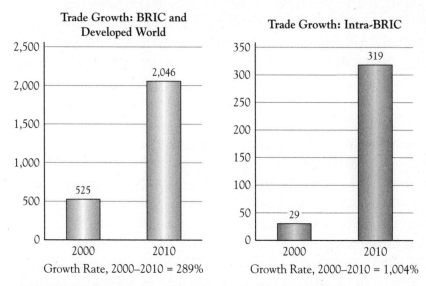

*Source:* The analysis is based on data from the Trade Competitiveness Map,
International Trade Center.

## Figure 2.4 Drivers of Global Trade Growth, 2000-2010

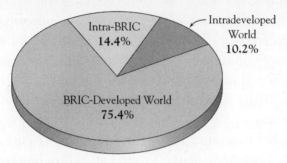

Drivers of Global Trade, 2000–2010

Intra-BRIC
14.4%

Intradeveloped
World
10.2%

BRIC-Developed World
75.4%

*Source:* The analysis is based on data from the Trade Competitiveness Map, International Trade Center.

Almost 90 percent of the new global trade growth over the past decade has been attributable to the emerging economies at one end of the trading equation, the other end of the equation being either the developed world or increasingly (and importantly) other emerging economies. Figure 2.4 shows the slices of global trade growth attributable to the trading blocs—the developed world (the United States, the EU member countries, and Japan) as well as the major EM economies (BRIC economies). The substantial growth of trade between or with the emerging economies creates a new playing field with new rules. The trillion-dollar question is: What kind of business model is best suited to serve the emerging market middle class?

The MNCs have the organization, the infrastructure, and the know-how to capture large opportunities. But emerging market firms are better placed to understand the needs of local consumer and address them. Will Indian consumers be wearing Nike, Gola, or Li Ning?

Multinationals will confront the need for a new business model, driven primarily by two changes in their environment: new consumers and new competitors. The questions multinationals urgently need to address are these: Who are the new consumers and competitors? What are the consumers' needs, requirements, and aspirations? How do we develop value propositions that fit those needs, while maintaining the advantages of scale and standardization that we have established? A particularly pressing question for multinational companies is: Where (in which geographies and which segments) will value be generated and captured, and what role can we play? These questions are pressing because if the target market is the emerging market middle class, then there is little room for the high-margin business models to which multinationals are accustomed, for two reasons.

First, while the conventional business model has been devised to sell Chinese tools, toys, and trinkets to affluent consumers everywhere, it breaks down when the buyers are not-so-affluent consumers in other emerging markets. Consumers in those markets cannot afford the R&D, design, branding, and management overhead built into the business model. All of the tasks that those overheads pay for will now need to be performed cheaply. This is where the new competitors come in. Emerging market companies, with their razor-thin margins and low overhead costs, may well be better placed to compete for the emerging market opportunity. Increasingly, Indian information technology companies such as Wipro, Infosys, and TCS are developing direct access to the Chinese market. They have already shown they can grab market share from Accenture, EDS, and IBM in the smaller Southeast Asian markets. Like Chinese toy manufacturers, Indian software and services firms have the advantage of low costs and relatively low overheads. More important, they also understand emerging market customers better than the multinational companies that have spent the better part of their history serving affluent global customers.

If emerging market companies do indeed seize the opportunity of driving the EM2EM trade, the multinationals' business model will come under further strain. The economies of scale that local players can build serving both their domestic market and the markets of other emerging market giants will give them a formidable cost advantage in global markets. It will not be long before these advantages are deployed to challenge the R&D-, design-, and branding-based advantages of the multinationals in their traditional developed country markets. In preparing for these long-term shifts, what are multinational companies to do?

## Implications for Marketing Programs of MNCS in Emerging Markets

We turn to a case study of Hyundai India to draw implications for the strategy and marketing programs of multinationals aiming to serve the consumers in the rapidly expanding emerging markets middle class.[2] We then generalize to an outline of an emerging market business model designed to address the middle-class consumer, and demonstrate how this is distinct from the conventional marketing practices of the MNCs.

### The Indian Car Market

The Indian passenger car market was estimated at around 2.5 million cars in 2011. Sales have grown by over 62 percent in the last two years between March 2009 and March 2011, and the trend shows little sign of abating.[3] With auto penetration rates a mere 13 cars per 1,000 people (compared to 1,200 in the United States, 445 in Japan, and 45 in China), there is room to grow. The Indian auto industry today is a product of the economic liberalization that the Indian government instituted starting in the early 1990s. Under these policies, global car companies set up shop in India, and local companies were encouraged to invest in product and market development. Global players that entered the market included Toyota, GM, Honda, Fiat, Peugeot, Ford, and later Volkswagen, BMW, and Mercedes. All of them were attracted by the promise of millions of consumers with rising disposable income.

Most of these global brands decided at the outset to introduce stripped-down versions of their midsize and premium models that they had phased out in the developed markets. Their reasoning was that after decades of enduring the 1950s car models that domestic manufacturers had continued to produce, Indian consumers' expectations were not terribly high. So they minimized costs by transplanting models they were phasing out elsewhere. Local competitors included Maruti Udyog Limited (a joint venture between the government of India and Suzuki Motors), a formidable volume player that held more than a 50 percent market share, and a host of smaller players.

Almost a decade and a half later, most of those global entrants are struggling. As of 2010, none of the big four (Toyota, GM, Honda, and Ford) had more than 5 percent of the market, and collectively their share stood below 13 percent; Maruti still held a 45 percent market share, more than three times larger than the big four combined. The global players came to the realization that it was difficult to compete with Maruti's incumbent advantages of a vast service network, its well-known brand, and its popularly designed and targeted cars. But one multinational entrant stood out for its success. Hyundai has a larger market share today than the big four combined. The Korean company started its India operations at about the same time (1996) as the others: Toyota (1997), GM (1994), Ford (1996), and Honda (1995). By 2010, Hyundai's market share by volume was more than 25 percent and more than 16 percent of domestic sales by value. It also accounted for a staggering 64 percent share of India's automobile exports.

## What Did Hyundai Do Differently?

A key difference between Hyundai and the big four was Hyundai's superior understanding of the EM-MC segment. Hyundai knew that to succeed in the Indian market, it could not afford to waste time testing the market with models it was retiring elsewhere.

Nor could it position its brand at the top of the market before gradually moving down toward the middle-class market. It went for the jugular. While the focus of the big four was on the midsize and premium car segments that accounted for 18 percent of market in 2000 (Figure 2.5), Hyundai immediately decided to take Maruti head on in the compact segment.

Hyundai's compact car, the Atos (locally branded as Santro), was aimed directly at the incumbent Maruti Suzuki's best-selling models. But it offered more contemporary design and a modern and comfortable interior. This appealed to all consumers and helped build equity with the internationally traveled and well-informed Indian middle-class consumer. Hyundai built its strategy on the bet that what the market wanted was not stripped-down hand-me-downs. Instead, its products and marketing were designed to appeal to the aspirations of the upwardly mobile Indian middle-class consumer. The purchase of a first car was a step up, not a letdown. And upgraders who had already owned a car were lured to the Hyundai Ascent, a contemporary model sedan sold at a significantly lower price than older model cars from the big four. Marketing for Hyundai's cars engaged the A-list of Bollywood stars.

The distinct strategies of Hyundai versus those of its big four rivals reveal a crucial strategic dilemma that all companies face as they consider serving the emerging market consumer. If they look at the initial size of the market for the value propositions they already sell elsewhere, they inevitably consider the market too small to justify large investments. This is the position that the big four initially took: they wanted to limit their entry risk. In contrast, Hyundai flipped the question on its head and asked: What will it take to become a major player in this market? So while its foreign rivals were limiting their initial investments, dipping their toes in the water, Hyundai jumped in with both feet. The company realized that to serve middle-class customers in the low-margin compact car segment (where cars typically retail for less than $10,000) would require massive investments

# Figure 2.5 The Changing Landscape of the Indian Auto Industry, 2000 and 2010

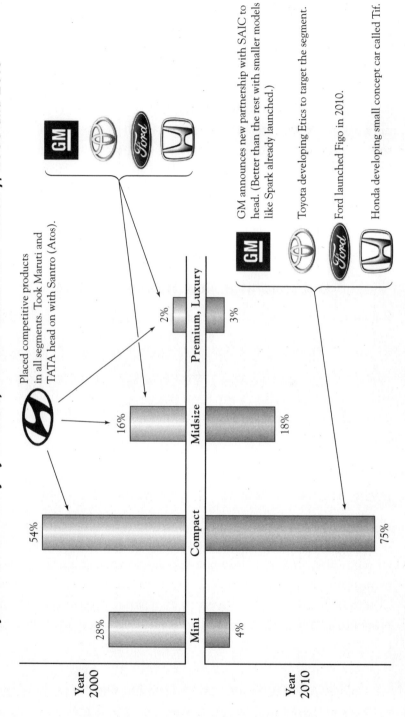

Placed competitive products in all segments. Took Maruti and TATA head on with Santro (Atos).

GM announces new partnership with SAIC to head. (Better than the rest with smaller models like Spark already launched.)

Toyota developing Etics to target the segment.

Ford launched Figo in 2010.

Honda developing small concept car called Tif.

Year 2000

Year 2010

Mini — 28% / 4%

Compact — 54% / 75%

Midsize — 16% / 18%

Premium, Luxury — 2% / 3%

in scale and efficiency. The company now has the capacity to make 600,000 vehicles a year in India.

Hyundai's production capacity serves more than Indian consumers: it is also used to export cars to other emerging markets. On the distribution front, Hyundai has built a large distribution and service center network covering 290 cities (the largest network after Maruti). In keeping with its long-term focus on the emerging market consumer, Hyundai also invested in a sophisticated R&D center in India intended "to inject local understanding and talent to customize product design that suits the need of Indian customer."[4] Fifteen years after the entry of global players, it is clear which strategy paid off.

## Outlines of a New Business Model

Business models and assumptions developed for traditional affluent markets do not work well when targeting the emerging market middle-class consumer.[5] In this section, we look at how strategy can be recalibrated to fit emerging market opportunities. We look at emerging market strategies along five dimensions: market segmentation, product, communication, distribution, and pricing. Table 2.3 summarizes the strategies.

### Implications for Market Segmentation Strategy

A critical aspect of strategic positioning is proper segmentation of the market. To succeed in emerging markets, managers need to recognize that in those markets, market segmentation may have to be done taking into account that the market segmentation may be coarser, be driven by functionality and aspirational attributes, and call for new categories not seen in developed countries.

*Coarse Market Segments.* A defining feature of developed markets is their finely grained segments, predicated on the low

### Table 2.3  Strategic Tool Kit for Success in Emerging Markets

| Strategy Element | Conventional Developed Market Wisdom | New Strategic Tool Kit for Winning Over Emerging Market Middle Class |
|---|---|---|
| Market segmentation strategy | Well-defined sophisticated segments. | Market segments are large and coarse—calls for creation of broad appeal products and brands. |
| | Segments tend to be lifestyle driven. | Segments tend to be driven by functionality and aspirational attributes. |
| | Mature market: majority of consumers are familiar with a large array of categories. | Gaps exist in market; new categories are still being created. |
| Product strategy | Standardized products for global markets. | Sturdy, functional products that also meet EM middle-class aspirational needs. |
| | Advanced functionality products that cater to high per capita consumption. | Product design and packaging to meet price sensitive EM customers. |
| Communication strategy | Targeted communication for fine segments. | Broad messaging that appeals to large, coarse segments. |
| | | Mass media typically better suited to reach EM-MC consumers. |
| | | Persuade consumers to consume more and nonconsumers to adopt. |
| Distribution strategy | Well-organized, highly concentrated retail and well-established distribution system. | Highly fragmented retail requires large sales and service feet on the ground. |
| | | Trade promotion plays an important role—retailers are an important personal service and information delivery channel. |

(continued)

**Table 2.3  Strategic Tool Kit for Success in Emerging Markets *(continued)***

| Strategy Element | Conventional Developed Market Wisdom | New Strategic Tool Kit for Winning Over Emerging Market Middle Class |
|---|---|---|
| Pricing strategy | Multiple pricing and promotion formats. | Large volume and low margins drive profitability. |
| | | Consumers gauge prices in relation to a local basket of purchases. |
| | | Saturate price points—price promote to discover demand elasticity. |

*Source:* Adapted from N. Dawar and A. Chattopadhyay, "Rethinking Marketing Programs for Emerging Markets," *Long Range Planning,* 2002, *35,* 457–474.

costs of and high returns on segmentation. Consumers are both able and willing to pay for specialized products that better meet their needs. In contrast, mass market consumers in emerging economies are unable to afford a fine level of segmentation. Segments there tend to be larger and coarser. Consider the fine segmentation of the soap marketing in developed markets: cream soap, antiaging soap, hypoallergenic soap, natural soap, and so on. In contrast, in Indonesia, 88 percent of the soap market is classified as regular soap, with another 11 percent accounted for by deodorant soap, and the remaining 1 percent is moisturizing soap.

In the hair care category, the segmentation contrast is even starker. In a mature market like the United States, the category consists of benefit segments such as antifrizz, hair shine, higher hydration, gloss content, herbal content, antidandruff, enhanced hair thickness, and color care, among others. The consumer goods giant P&G segments the hair care market into twelve segments in the United States, four in China, and three in India. In China and India, the segments focus on utilitarian benefits such as hair strength, hair smoothness, or antidandruff.

*Segments Driven by Functionality and Aspirational Attributes.* Segments in the developed markets tend to be lifestyle driven. The proportion of consumers purchasing a product for its functionality alone is limited. The segmentation basis for the EM-MC is primarily functional or aspirational (for example, a desire for upward mobility). The passenger vehicle purchase decision in developed markets begins with whether to buy a car or van or cross-over, or SUV, or sports car, or hybrid, or truck. Choice is primarily driven by life-cycle stage and lifestyle considerations. A typical EM-MC consumer primarily buys a car for its functional utility (reliability, economy) and secondarily for status. The best-selling car in India is Suzuki's Maruti Alto. With a base price as low as $5,000, it is very popular on congested Indian roads.

*Market Gaps Suggest New Categories for EM-MC.* Global MNCs are well placed to fill gaps in the market by creating entirely new segments or building a place for product categories not yet part of the consumption habits. In many emerging economies, beverages such as iced tea, energy drinks, and wine are not part of the store shelf. Consider diapers in China. When P&G launched diapers there in the late 1990s, the category was fairly novel.[6] Baby disposable diapers, a necessity in Western baby care markets, were not used in China, where cloth diapers, or no diapers at all, were the norm. Toilet training for babies began as early as six months, and many children wore what is called *kaidangku*—*butt-less* baby pants that let them squat and relieve with ease. So when P&G first launched Pampers in China in 1998, it tried to meet a price point that would encourage consumers to switch. The lower-quality version of the diapers was not as soft and had a more plastic feel to it. It was not a success.

Eventually P&G redeveloped the product, acting on its new product development philosophy to "delight and not to dilute." The diaper still needed to be economical to fit EM-MC consumers' budget, but it also had to do what other cheap diapers did not: keep a baby dry and at least as comfortable as cloth. So P&G reintroduced the product with added softness, reduced the plastic feel, and strengthened the absorption capacity. The revamped diaper was priced for an equivalent of ten cents, less than half the retail price in the United States. Now that P&G had the right product at the appropriate price point, it still needed to convince consumers to adopt the product.

P&G launched the Golden Sleep Campaign in 2007 that included carnivals and in-store campaigns in some of China's largest urban areas. As part of the promotion, parents were asked to upload pictures of their babies asleep. The resulting 200,000 pictures were used to create a 660-square-meter photo montage in a Shanghai megastore. At the same time, with the help of Beijing Children's Hospital's Sleep Research Center, P&G researchers conducted two research studies that used Pampers instead of cloth. The research demonstrated that babies who wore the disposables fell asleep 30 percent faster and slept an extra thirty minutes every night. The study further linked the extra sleep to improved cognitive development. The scientific and functional nature of the messaging, coupled with heavy advertising spending, ensured that Pampers became a top-selling brand in a burgeoning Chinese disposable diapers market.

## Implications for Product Strategy

As all marketing managers recognize, choosing the right product plays a critical role in market positioning. Again, as in market segmentation, managers need to recognize that emerging markets pose some interesting challenges for product strategy as well.

*Product Localization.* Kellogg, the U.S. cereals giant, ventured into India in the mid-1990s. Indian consumers at that time were not sold on breakfast cereals: most either prepared breakfast from scratch every morning or grabbed some biscuits with tea at a roadside tea stall. Over time, Kellogg India has widened its product portfolio and expanded its range to include Frosties, chocolate-flavored flakes, and other taste variants of Corn Flakes. Kellogg India also adapted its products to address local need gaps. For example, it launched a range of breakfast biscuits under the Chocos brand name and enhanced its focus on iron and calcium fortification with products like Iron Shakti and Calcium Shakti. The localization of the product strategy helped reverse its fortunes, and Kellogg's has contributed to the rapid growth of the breakfast cereal market in India.

Another successful example is the customization of the McDonald's menu.[7] The challenge for McDonald's in India was that beef and pork are unacceptable considering religious sentiments. A suitable vegetarian menu along with an alternative to beef and pork was necessary. McDonald's responded by creating the McAloo Tikki burger, a potato patty with spices. It also made chicken and fish options available for nonvegetarian consumers. McDonald's even separated the nonvegetarian and vegetarian cooking process to assuage the apprehensions of the devout vegetarian customer base. The localization is indicative of a flexibility of approach not readily evident among MNCs.

***Reengineer Products for Income and Environmental Variability.*** Variability in consumer incomes and income flow requires a product portfolio that addresses the needs of various value segments without adding to costs. Offering a variety of pack sizes at different prices is one solution. Cooking oil, for example, is sold in single-use 5 milliliter sachets for the daily purchaser, as well as in large 10 liter containers. In several emerging markets, Unilever's brands are available in small sachets, offering a small amount of shampoo or detergent priced at ten cents. Pepsodent toothpaste is sold in a 30 milliliter tube, enough for a family of five to brush their teeth once a day for a week. It is priced at around fifteen cents.

The variability of the infrastructure tangibly affects the quality of products that arrive on the shelf. They have been through a sourcing, production, and delivery system that is subject to nonstandardized treatment at every stage. Delivering on the central promise of branding—consistent quality over time—is a difficult task in such an environment. But it is precisely this variability in the environment that puts a premium on brands that are able to deliver consistency. Marico, an Indian edible oil company, has found that rural consumers willingly pay a reasonable price premium for branded cooking oil over commodity oil because they are certain of its consistent quality. Unbranded products are often of uncertain quality, while products from developed markets are designed for fairly standardized use and handling conditions and do not tolerate wide environmental variance. To deliver consistent quality, products need to be designed to cope with variability. For example, washing machines in emerging markets need to be designed to cope with unexpected interruptions of power and water supplies. Whirlpool found that its machines needed to be designed to restart from the point in the washing cycle where they had left off when the power or water was interrupted rather than return to the start, as they are designed to do in developed markets, where reliable power and water supplies are taken for granted.

## Implications for Branding and Communication Strategy

Branding and communication strategies need to be adapted for the emerging markets as well. This need for adaptation naturally follows from the differences in market segmentation and products in emerging markets.

*Broad Messaging That Appeals to Large, Coarse Segments.* Broad-based brand positions that are likely to appeal to a variety of people are more cost-effective than finely differentiated niche positions. Broad-based positions often need to be targeted to consumers who have not previously consumed the product or are unfamiliar with the benefits of the product. For example, offering the benefit of a shampoo-and-conditioner-in-one is of little relevance where consumers have never used conditioner or, for that matter, shampoo. The task of communication is to position these products on the basis of broad-based consumer needs. Kellogg, for example, has developed a "nutritious breakfast" positioning in India, based on research on school children that shows they are not getting their recommended daily doses of some ingredients.

***Mass Media Typically Better Suited to Reach EM-MC Consumers.*** The four BRIC countries are among the seven largest countries in the world and home to almost half of the world's population. Unlike developed markets where online and digital media are now mainstream, Internet advertising penetration among EM-MC consumers is still low. Television, coupled with endorsements by mass celebrities who represent national passions, are usually more effective. This mass strategy is complemented with focused regional strategies, considering the multiplicity of languages and varying levels of illiteracy. Unilever pioneered the concept of the video van. Its video vans travel from village to village screening films in the local language, interspersed with advertisements for Unilever products. The company also provides product-use demonstrations to the captive audience because written instructions on the pack are of no use to consumers who are illiterate or do not understand the dialect.

***Selling Users and Nonusers on Product Benefits.*** Once brand positioning is established, the communication focus shifts to increasing the traditionally low rates of product use in emerging markets. A key communication decision therefore is whether to target existing consumers to consume more or to draw non-consumers into the market. Typically multinationals choose to target existing consumers. International brewers in China, for example, are focusing on urban markets where per capita consumption is already high. The reasoning is that it is easier to convince an existing beer drinker to have another beer than to convert someone who has never had beer to try one. The existing product portfolios of multinationals, however, often drive this reasoning. It is easier to sell more of an existing product to current consumers than to develop new products and brands to appeal to nonconsumers. But some multinationals are not averse to seizing local opportunities. Just as Kellogg realized that biscuits were the way into Indian consumers' breakfast diet, Coca-Cola has found that to gain what the company refers to as "share of throat" in China and Russia, products that fit with local consumption habits are required. It has therefore introduced fruit-flavored tea in China and low-priced carbonated fruit-flavored drinks in Russia.

## Implications for Pricing Strategy

An important challenge in emerging markets is pricing. Since emerging markets comprise a wide range of consumers with different purchasing powers, getting the pricing correct is critical for competitive success.

*Large Volumes and Low Margins.*  Pricing logic drives marketing programs. Strategies that favor thin margins and rely on large volumes tend to succeed. Unilever's Lifebuoy brand of soap, popular in Africa, India, and Indonesia, is priced low and made using inexpensive local ingredients and packaging material. By volume, Lifebuoy is the largest-selling soap in the world, and large volumes can make even trivially priced products profitable. Cadbury's knows that Indian consumers are willing to pay the equivalent of four cents for an impulse purchase candy like Eclairs, a single-wrap toffee. The company delivers large packs of these candies to retailers, who then break the bulk and sell the candy by the unit. Cadbury's international managers question why their company should spend time, effort, and money selling products that retail at four cents. But in this market, it is the enormous volume, not the margin, that drives profitability. If 10 percent of the population were to buy just one candy a week, annual sales would exceed $220 million. An added advantage is that the inexpensive candy maintains a shelf presence for the brand and provides an entry-level item that converts some consumers to higher-priced and higher-margin products.

*Purchasing Power Parity–Based Pricing.*   Prices need to be established in the context of local consumers' purchasing power rather than in relation to international standards. Purchasing power parity (PPP) exchange rates estimate the value of a currency in terms of the basket of goods that it buys (compared with the cost of a similar basket in a reference country and currency) rather than in terms of the existing market exchange rates. By this measure, most emerging market currencies are undervalued relative to hard currencies, meaning that they buy more than one would expect given the market exchange rate. Successful firms that capture a share of wallet of the EM-MC consumer typically do so by adopting a PPP-based pricing approach versus pricing based on market exchange rates. Consider South African Breweries (SAB), one of the most profitable foreign breweries in China today. Although it truly gained size (almost 21 percent of the Chinese beer market) through a series of acquisitions after 2000, its initial approach in the mid-1990s to capture the Chinese market was markedly different from that of the fifty other international brewers operating in China. It started brewing and selling local brands of beer, consciously targeting the mass market and avoiding the crowded premium urban segments. The price of its brands was up to 70 percent lower than that of international brands such as Budweiser or Carlsberg. This initial success gave SAB a strong foundation in China and set the course for its future success.

*Saturating Price Points.* In an occasional effort to capture volume sales or simply move inventory, multinational brands use price promotions that often yield dramatic, if temporary, sales increases. Large volume increases reveal a potentially large market that remains untapped, just below the actual price points. It suggests an opportunity for a permanent product entry at the lower price point. Not addressing this latent demand can even place the premium branded business at risk. By the mid-1990s, Sony and Matsushita had captured 75 percent of the top end of the Chinese market for televisions with sales of 1.5 million units. But this left the door open to local manufacturers Changhong, Konka, and Panda, each of which achieved significant economies of scale by catering to the mass market. Together these manufacturers sold over 5 million units and were then able to use their strong position to move upmarket.

## Implications for Distribution Strategy

Perhaps the most challenging aspect of emerging markets is getting the product to the consumer. Since emerging markets have wide disparities in income, infrastructure weaknesses, and multiplicity of channels, getting the distribution strategy right is critical for success in emerging markets.

*Distribution Strategy to Manage a Highly Fragmented Retail Trade.* In contrast to the highly concentrated retail and distribution industry in developed markets, the retail trade in emerging markets is extremely fragmented. While major international retail chains such as Carrefour, Metro, and Walmart operate in many emerging markets, they have yet to develop a retail format that fits the mass emerging market consumer. Overall, chain stores account for less than 5 percent by value of the retail market in China. Some multinationals still rely on these chains as their primary channel. But it is unlikely that chains will provide access to mass markets where high population density, small homes with little space for storage, lack of refrigeration, and low automobile ownership mean that consumers buy daily and locally. As a result, retail outlet density is very high. Retail formats from developed countries cannot deliver economically under these conditions, and so foreign distributors cannot be the sole pillar of any mass market distribution strategy. At the same time, using small, independently owned stores poses a serious challenge to many international firms, because they lack the expertise to deal with a fragmented trade. Estimates are that there are 9 million small, independently owned grocery shops in China that have limited working capital and typically occupy fewer than three hundred square feet. To access even the first tier of these outlets and establish a brand presence on the shelf, large, dedicated sales forces and large amounts of working capital are required. Beyond the first tier of retail outlets, many companies use multiple levels of wholesalers and distributors to capture shelf space one store at a time.

India is a nation of shopkeepers: over 7.7 million retail outlets account for an average of 6.8 stores per thousand people—the highest store density in the world. Unilever has built direct coverage of 1.5 million outlets and a total coverage of almost 6.4 million outlets.[8] It uses an array of approaches to reach customers. In urban areas, there are usually two formats of trade, referred to as modern trade and general trade. Modern trade (roughly 10 percent of all commercial transactions) consists of organized retail chains that Unilever services directly through dedicated account managers. General trade consists of the hundreds of thousands of independent retail outlets across the country, called *kirana* stores, that are typically in a mom-and-pop store format. This channel makes up the majority of Unilever's sales. Each of these stores is a distinct customer that is addressed individually. Unilever services these stores through a network of almost twenty-nine hundred stockists. Goods are sent to local warehouses or carrying and forwarding agents and are then dispatched to retail stores when they receive orders from Unilever's stockists.

The bigger challenge for Unilever is to tap the rural Indian market of almost 775 million people (1 of every 8 people in the world) spread across 638,000 villages. To overcome the challenge, Unilever India has a four-tier distribution system segmented on the basis of village accessibility and business potential. The first-tier (high potential and high accessibility) typically services towns with populations of under fifty thousand people. Unilever appoints a common stockist that services all outlets within a town. The second tier (low potential and high accessibility) targets retailers in accessible villages close to larger urban markets. Retail stockists are assigned a permanent route to service all accessible villages in the surroundings, usually once a week. The third tier (high potential and low accessibility), referred to as the streamline model, is used to reach markets inaccessible by road. Locally appointed wholesalers called star sellers purchase stock from a local distributor and then sell to retail stores in more remote villages using local means of transport such as rickshaws or two-wheelers. The fourth tier (low potential and low accessibility), called Project Shakti, is truly creative in its approach and reach. It targets small villages (with populations of fewer than two thousand) and appoints underprivileged rural women as direct-to-consumer sales distributors for Unilever products. These women distributors, called Shakti Ammas (meaning "strength mothers"), sell Unilever's home care, health, and hygiene products in their villages. By the end of 2009, Project Shakti network encompassed forty thousand Shakti Ammas covering 100,000 villages and cumulatively reaching over 3 million households daily.

***Channel Power by Trading as a Partner.*** Despite being fragmented, the trade has considerable power. Store formats do not allow consumers to browse. Typically the consumer interacts directly with the retail salesperson, often the owner, whose recommendations carry weight. The owner's relationship with consumers is based on an understanding of their needs and buying habits and cemented by the retailer's extending credit. These relationships give the trade clout in brand recommendations, making trade marketing an essential element of any manufacturer's program. Building relationships with a fragmented trade requires an understanding of their interests. For example, it is counterproductive to push inventory on them given their tight working capital positions. Rather, successful manufacturers creatively develop new revenue activities for the retailer. United Phosphorous Limited (UPL), an Indian crop protection company, realized that in its rural markets, small farmers were not applying pesticide at all or applying it inappropriately due to the lack of application equipment. The capital cost of the equipment (mounted pumps and dispensers that cost up to three thousand dollars) placed it out of reach of small farmers and most rural retailers. UPL designed a program in which it arranged for bank loans for its rural retailers to purchase application equipment and demonstrated to these retailers the additional revenue possibilities from renting this equipment to small farmers. The result was an added revenue stream for rural retailers and additional sales of pesticides for UPL.

## Conclusion

Two global trends over the past decade—the rapid expansion of EM2EM trade and the growth of domestic consumption fueled by a newly economically empowered emerging market middle class—call for global MNCs to reevaluate their emerging market business models. Traditional business models that rely on expensive innovation, fine segmentation, high margins, low-cost sourcing in emerging markets, and finely tuned global brands need to be rethought for emerging markets. This is not to say that the fundamental principles of scale and standardization need to be abandoned to tackle the emerging market opportunity. Rather, those economies of scale and opportunities for standardization need to be applied to serve common needs across emerging markets. This may require the building of a new business model.

In this chapter, we have described the pressing need for a reevaluation of the business models of MNCs to address the emerging market opportunity. We have outlined a general framework that firms can use to develop a business model for their particular market and industry.

# Part Two

# WINNING THE LOCAL COMPETITION IN EMERGING ASIA

# 3

# COEVOLVING LOCAL ADAPTATION AND GLOBAL INTEGRATION

## The Case of Panasonic China

Toshiro Wakayama, Junjiro Shintaku,
Tomofumi Amano, Takafumi Kikuchi

The tension between local adaptation and global integration is an age-old issue facing most multinational corporations (MNCs). This tension is drastically amplified when developed economy MNCs enter emerging markets due to the vast difference between developed and emerging economies. A prevailing view of the heightened tension among MNCs seems to be the trade-off perspective: one of the two competing themes can be pursued only at the expense of the other. We claim, however, that a more constructive perspective is to view the two themes as dynamically coevolving competitive dimensions. Deeper localization invites greater global integration, which in turn enables yet deeper localization. Central to this coevolution perspective is the ability of the organization to view the adaptation-integration tension as a driver for creating competitive advantage through innovative products, new organizational practices, and, eventually, new business models.

Panasonic China is a case in point. In its nearly twenty-five years of presence in China, Panasonic has gradually developed local capabilities in China through multiple phases, increasingly addressing deeper localization enabled by more extensive cross-border integration of its home-grown resources and capabilities. In a recent phase of this evolution, Panasonic created China Lifestyle Research Center in Shanghai in 2005. This milestone resource for deeper localization uncovered a hidden local need for a particular feature in a washing machine, and Panasonic Home Appliances in China introduced a model that met this need through a technology specifically developed in Japan for the new feature. Panasonic's market share in China for this category of washing machines (the front-loading drum type) jumped from 3 percent to 15 percent in less than one year. By adopting a coevolutionary perspective, any MNC should be able to exploit the tension, rather than simply tolerating it, for building global competitive advantage.

## Meeting the Challenge of Local Adaptation Versus Global Integration in Emerging Markets

Since local adaptation and global integration are two base concepts in this chapter, we start with their working definitions. We then discuss how the tension between these two themes is amplified in emerging markets.

### Local Adaptation Versus Global Integration

*Local adaptation* refers to the creation of competitive value relevant to local conditions and constraints. The competitive value of local adaptation might be captured in new products, marketing campaigns, managerial practices, human resource development, administrative autonomy, or any other aspects of a business aiming to boost local competitiveness. For instance, when Procter & Gamble introduced liquid detergent, it had to address various local conditions and constraints, such as hard water problems in some markets, the coldwater washes common in Japan, and the limited use of phosphates in some environmentally concerned markets.[1] *Global integration* refers to the creation of competitive value through effective management of networks of the firm's operations worldwide. The competitive value of global integration can be realized in a number of ways:

- *Resource transfer.* The firm can gain competitiveness by redeploying its global resources, that is, resources developed in specific locations of the network, often in its home country, that can be deployed in other locations. When the destination of resource transfer is a location new to the firm, the firm is expanding its network of operations. In other words, the firm is integrating a new location into its existing network.
- *Aggregation.* The firm can aggregate its functions such as production and procurement throughout the network, either partially or fully, for scale merit.
- *Cooperation.* The firm can gain competitiveness through cooperative relationships among its locations having complementary resources. Arbitrage is one form of the cooperative integration. Another is the creation of innovative products by putting together local market knowledge and global resources.

An example is Zara, one of the most successful global retail chains in the fashion industry.[2] When Zara opens new stores, it transfers its resources and capabilities for managing store operations through a variety of means such as information systems, selection know-how of store collections, and well-trained store managers (resource transfer). Zara is vertically integrated, and it centralizes the design and manufacturing functions in its home base; in principle, it offers no country-specific customization (aggregation). Zara's competitiveness rests on its unique and innovative form of cooperation between its home base and individual stores worldwide (cooperation).

Thus, local adaptation and global integration represent two rather distinct competitive themes. Local adaptation emphasizes local relevance in individual locations and tends to value independence and diversity. Global integration stresses the effectiveness of the whole network and tends to strive for cooperation and uniformity (which is important for resource transfer and aggregation). The tension between the two themes is fundamental, and most MNCs must cope with it. Procter & Gamble, for instance, despite the intrinsic pressure for local adaptation for its lifestyle-sensitive products, must also address the challenge of global integration in order to remain competitive (cost competitiveness through aggregation, for instance). Similarly, Zara, despite its strategic focus on aggregation, must also address the challenge of local adaptation; stores in places such as Tokyo and New York are likely to meet significantly different customer preferences.

## The Tension Amplified in Emerging Markets

The tension between local adaptation and global integration exists rather universally for MNCs, but when developed economy MNCs enter emerging markets, the tension is considerably amplified because of the vast difference between developed and emerging economies. For instance, when Walmart entered the Chinese market, it was challenged by a host of local conditions and constraints it had never faced in developed economies: the transportation and communication infrastructure in China was incompatible with Walmart's logistics model, consumer behavior was very different from the bulk purchasing that is common in the United States, and government regulations and guidelines often were at odds with the core of Walmart's business model.

Faced with this amplified tension between local adaptation and global integration, a prevailing view of the two themes seems to be the trade-off perspective: the view that one theme can be pursued only at the cost of not sufficiently addressing the other.

In the case of Walmart China, its initial strategy was largely driven by its effort to transplant its home-grown business model in China; it was not very willing to locally adapt its practices to local conditions in any substantial way (that is, it was mainly interested in global integration at the expense of local adaptation). Even after several years of struggling performance, Joe Hatfield, CEO of Walmart Asia, who was also overseeing Walmart China, stated, "We have the core beliefs and operating strategy of American stores, but it is critically important to let Chinese customers understand those. We should crawl, walk and eventually run."[3] The other trade-off option, the pursuit of deeper localization without substantial deployment of global resources, is not a sensible choice for developed economy MNCs because local rivals are likely to outperform them along this dimension of competition.

## Coevolution Perspective

In many specific situations such as the development of products for local needs while considering the benefits of global scale, the trade-off seems to be a reality one has to accept. However, the trade-off perspective fails to serve as an effective strategic framework that recognizes the competitive importance of both local adaptation and global integration. A more constructive perspective for MNCs is to view the two themes as dynamically coevolving competitive dimensions (Figure 3.1).[4] In other words, greater global integration enables deeper localization, which invites yet deeper global integration. Suppose, for instance, an MNC creates a local market research unit for deeper understanding of local needs (deeper localization). Unique local market needs, when identified, might represent an opportunity to build more extensive cooperative relationships with the product development group in the home country (greater global integration). Once the cooperative relationships are established, the local market research unit may have greater access to various technological enablers for

**Figure 3.1 Coevolution of Local Adaptation and Global Integration**

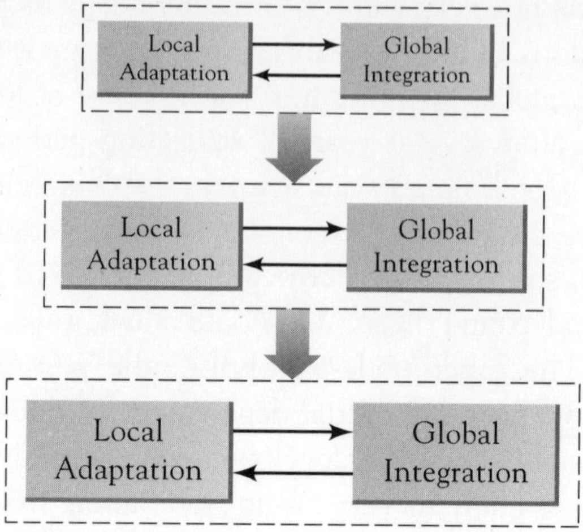

new product possibilities, which help it identify yet deeper local needs (yet deeper localization).

Of course, such coevolution of capabilities for local adaptation and global integration typically faces various organizational barriers and does not happen without a proper framework to nourish it. We call such a framework a *tension-embracing structure*. This structure manifests as a collection of organizational resources and capabilities that help individuals and organizational units embrace the two competing themes and views the tension as a driver for creating competitive value. Such resources and capabilities include

- Routines practiced by members of a local market research unit to extend their understanding of relevant global resources such as technological enablers available for new products

- An organizational unit with an active mission to address the challenges of both local adaptation and global integration

- A promotional policy that requires substantial managerial experience in a local subsidiary for promotion in its parent business division
- Human resources equipped with the mind-set of embracing the adaptation-integration tension
- Distribution of authority between a business division in the home country and its oversea subsidiaries
- Quality of trust relationships between a business division in the home country and its oversea subsidiaries
- Distribution of information in a network of relationships involving a business division in the home country and its overseas operations

The last three instances are examples of relational resources, defined as "qualities of relationships that enable people to work together."[5]

A tension-embracing structure enables individuals to engage in activities that address both local adaptation and global integration. We call such activities *tension-embracing activities*. Suppose a local market research unit has a mission of identifying local needs and proposing product concepts enabled by global technology resources. In pursuing the mission, the unit leader encourages his staff to consider technological enablers and cost consequences when they craft product proposals. He also sets up regular meetings between his staff and the technology group of the business division in the home country and maintains good cooperative relationships with the home base. Given this supportive environment, his staff is encouraged to go far beyond local market studies and seek out global resources that can be deployed for new product development. In fact, the very knowledge of available global resources, particularly technology enablers, might help the staff creatively articulate hidden local needs. Thus, the tension-embracing structure at the market research unit encourages and supports the research staff as it engages in tension-embracing activities (Figure 3.2).

**Figure 3.2 Dynamics of the Tension-Embracing Structure**

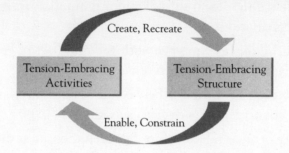

Now suppose that the tension-embracing activities of the staff have repeatedly resulted in successful introduction of new products in the local market. These successes are likely to alter the sense of trust between the business division in the home country and the local market research unit, thereby recreating the tension-embracing structure through renewed relational resources. In general, this dynamic of tension-embracing structure propels the coevolution of local adaptation and global integration.[6]

## Panasonic in China

Panasonic in China offers an interesting illustration of the coevolution perspective. In this section, we provide some background information relevant to this case.

In his historic visit to Japan in 1978, Deng Xiaoping met with Konosuke Matsushita, the founder of Panasonic, and asked him help China modernize its industries. Matsushita positively and passionately responded to the request, and Panasonic immediately followed the commitment through a large of number of technology licenses to China. In 1987, Panasonic established its first joint company in China, Beijing-Matsushita Color CRT. It was highly successful and represented the cornerstone of Panasonic's extensive entries in China that began in 1990. Around this time, Panasonic was organized around considerably independent business units (BUs) segmented at the level of product categories, such as washing machines, air conditioners, video players, and TV sets.[7] Panasonic had over one hundred BUs, and many of them established their own manufacturing companies in China—over forty of them, often in different locations, in the 1990s.

Between 2000 and 2006, Panasonic went through a radical transformation under the leadership of its CEO at the time, Kunio Nakamura. In 2003, as part of this transformation, Panasonic aggregated business units under higher-level units called "business domain companies" in order to minimize duplication of businesses and more effectively share resources such as R&D, product development, manufacturing, and marketing across related businesses. Through this reorganization, Panasonic created fourteen domain companies, and one of them was the Home Appliances Company. Home Appliances Company was headquartered in Kusatsu, a city about twenty kilometers east of Kyoto. Correspondingly, there was an increasing realization in China that the individual manufacturing subsidiaries of BUs were not competitive individually. With domain companies given the mission of creating cross-business synergies, there was a parallel effort in China to aggregate subsidiaries of related BUs. So, for instance, Panasonic Home Appliances China was established in 2003.

At the corporate level, Panasonic established Panasonic Corporation of China in Beijing in 2003, the regional management company for China, offering various higher-level shared services for manufacturing subsidiaries of BUs such as sales channel development, R&D, logistics, legal administration, and support for human resource management.

## Coevolution at Panasonic Home Appliances in China

Several manufacturing companies of Panasonic Home Appliances China are located in Hangzhou, a tier 1 city located about 180 kilometers southwest of Shanghai, with population of about 8 million. Hangzhou has an Economic and Technological Development Zone that houses a large number of foreign firms, including about eighty Japanese companies. Panasonic considers Hangzhou a key location for its home appliances operations in China and has gathered several of its home appliances manufacturing companies in the development zone. But due to the historical development of manufacturing plants by strongly independent BUs, some of its home appliances subsidiaries are not located in Hangzhou.

## Manufacturing-Centric Beginning

Panasonic entered China extensively in 1990s, establishing a large number of manufacturing subsidiaries. In the area of home appliance products, these companies include Panasonic Home Appliances Washing Machines Hangzhou, Panasonic Home Appliances Air Conditioners Guangzhou, Panasonic Home Appliances Refrigerators Wuxi, Panasonic Home Appliances Rice Cookers Hangzhou, and Panasonic Home Appliances Hangzhou Export (for dishwashers and vacuum cleaners). This extended network of operations was significantly motivated by labor arbitrage, and considerable portions of their output were for export. In fact, in the 1990s, Panasonic positioned China as its global manufacturing base, and its BUs transferred resources in a variety of forms to its subsidiaries in China, including manufacturing process know-how, quality management techniques, and supply chain management. Through arbitrage and resource transfer, Panasonic has solidly integrated its operations in China into its global manufacturing network. In the early 2000s, in the area of home appliances, a large portion of its global productions (often over 30 percent) came from China.

On the local adaptation side, the opening and subsequent development of manufacturing subsidiaries meant the creation of local competitive value in the form of manufacturing facilities operational under the local conditions and constraints as well as local human resource development. In particular, key people on the shop floor, such as those in charge of production lines, were given extensive training at respective BUs in Japan. Thus, in this beginning phase, many locations in China were integrated into the home appliances' manufacturing network, and in the process of this integration, the competitive value relevant to China's local conditions and constraints was created mainly in the area of manufacturing.

Notable also in this phase was the gradual buildup of factory design and development teams. Resource transfer in the design and development function was accomplished through extensive training of key local staff at the training site in Kusatsu as well as through on-site coaching by engineering expatriates sent from respective BUs in Japan. As in the case of the manufacturing function, the creation of local competitive value was mainly through this training of local personnel, who were presumably more familiar with local conditions and constraints. The product localization in this phase, however, was rather limited and did not go much beyond simple modifications of products developed in Japan. There were some attempts to design and introduce more uniquely local products, and product planning staff from Japan were stationed locally for a short period of time, but their effort did not result in products that were significantly successful in the local market.

## Development of Local Product Planning Capabilities

Panasonic in its home country has a strong commitment to extensive studies on how individual households and people use home electronics products and their general lifestyles related to the use of such products. Home Appliances Company, for instance, has a Lifestyle Research Center that offers such study services for all of its BUs. Each BU has its own product planning team, and the Home Appliances' Lifestyle Research Center closely works with product planning teams of the BUs.

Overseas, however, Panasonic did not have similarly extensive lifestyle research activities, and its products in markets outside Japan were largely modifications of base models developed for domestic markets. Although overseas sales were growing, top management at Panasonic were clearly aware in the early 2000s that without a deeper understanding of local markets, their competitiveness in oversea markets, particularly in emerging markets, would never reach a position critical for Panasonic's globalization agenda. This concern was particularly acute for China due to its size and rapid economic growth, as well as the long history of Panasonic's commitment in China that dates back to Konosuke Matsushita's promise to Deng Xiaoping.

Addressing this concern, Panasonic created the China Lifestyle Research Center in Shanghai in 2005, its first serious attempt overseas to gain a deeper understanding of local lifestyles. The center's director had extensive experience as a product planner at a home appliance BU and closely worked with the Home Appliances Lifestyle Research Center in Kusatsu. The director carefully hired local staff and personally gave them extensive training. Thus, the director was a powerful source of resource transfer. Through the center in Shanghai, together with the increasingly mature R&D team in Hangzhou, China was beginning to be integrated into the home appliances' product planning and development network, which represented the second wave of integration on top of the company's manufacturing network.

The Lifestyle Research Center in Shanghai has proved to be the cornerstone of resource creation in China for deeper localization. The well-trained staff at the center have begun to collect critical knowledge about and developed insight into local lifestyles related to the use of home appliances. In addition to group interviews and other conventional marketing research, the staff visit individual homes and study, for instance, their kitchens to gain information on such characteristics as the size of the kitchen, the height of the kitchen counter, the location of the refrigerator, and the size of the kitchen entrance. One of their findings was about the size of the space for the refrigerator: the typical refrigerator space in kitchens in Chinese households is fifty-five centimeters wide, while the standard size of Panasonic refrigerators is sixty-five centimeters wide. Based on this finding, Panasonic developed and introduced slimmer refrigerators to the Chinese market. The market enthusiastically responded to this localization, and sales increased tenfold.

Another key contribution of the China Lifestyle Research Center was the creation of an extensive local lifestyle database that covers many product categories for customer preferences specific to different income groups and regional characteristics. For instance, rice cookers must consider such regional preferences as short-grain rice in northern China, medium-grain rice in central China, and long-grain rice in southern China. Similarly, rice porridge is popularly served for breakfast in China, and many people use rice cookers to prepare porridge. But thin porridge is preferred in the north and much thicker porridge in the south. Detailed lifestyle information of this sort was systematically collected into the database and made available to BUs and their subsidiaries in China. The gathered information represents a value for local adaptation; in addition, its availability to all Panasonic BUs and their subsidiaries promotes resource sharing and hence strengthens cross-border integration.

## Local Autonomy for Home Appliances in China

The mission of the China Lifestyle Research Center goes beyond market studies: it aims to propose new product concepts based on systematically collected market data, knowledge of technological enablers, and cost considerations. A staff member at the center is usually assigned to a particular product category, such as washing machines or refrigerators. Staff members then have regular meetings with engineers of the corresponding BUs and their local subsidiaries, as well as the Home Appliances Technology Center in Kusatsu. Through repeated meetings of this sort, staff members of the center in Shanghai got to know their engineering counterparts in Kusatsu and local subsidiaries and established informal networks with them. Consequently staff members began to interact with these engineers more informally through telephone calls and e-mail exchanges. Through formal and informal networks, the center's staff in Shanghai have gained technological knowledge, and the engineers in home appliance bases in China (most prominently Hangzhou, Guangzhou, and Wuxi) and Kusatsu have developed a deeper understanding of local markets in China. In short, the Lifestyle Research Center has established effective cooperative relationships with BUs in Kusatsu and their local subsidiaries, made possible due to the center's ability to create deeper local knowledge. In other words, deeper local adaptation has led to correspondingly deeper global integration.

A host of successful product introductions in the local markets through the cooperative relationships has resulted in solid relationships between the center in Shanghai and the engineers in Hangzhou, on one hand, and the BUs and the Home Appliances Company in Kusatsu, on the other hand, that have altered the authority distribution leading to greater autonomy for local operations. Both as a placeholder and as an accelerator for this increasing local autonomy, Panasonic Home Appliances Hangzhou was established in 2003. In 2009, Panasonic Home Appliances R&D Hangzhou was established, with over two hundred engineers, mostly local staff members. This establishment also signifies the increasing local autonomy of China's Home Appliances.

With the local R&D building up its capabilities, decisions on new product introduction for local markets has, in effect, been under the local authority since around 2008. The final formal decision still belongs to respective BUs in Kusatsu, but this is to ensure global coherence for basic design elements such as the chassis of washing machines. Thus, the deeper integration enabled by deeper cooperative relationships has promoted local autonomy, a critical foundation for local value creation.

## Dynamics of a Tension-Embracing Structure: China Lifestyle Research Center

Another case of successful new product introduction initiated by the Lifestyle Research Center in Shanghai focused on washing machines. The research staff at the center visited and studied over three hundred households on how they use washing machines. One of their key findings was that over 90 percent of the households were hand-washing underwear despite the fact that they all owned a washing machine. Through in-depth interviews, the research staff identified several reasons, but the key reason was a concern about bacterial infection through underwear when it was washed together with outerwear, which was more likely to have been exposed to bacteria in the external environment. Based on these findings, the research staff came up with a product concept for a washing machine with a bacteria sterilization capability. They presented the product concept at one of the regular meetings with the Home Appliances Technology Center in Kusatsu. The feasibility of a washing machine with a bacteria sterilization device using silver ions was confirmed at the meeting, and the Technology Center in Kusatsu, in collaboration with Shanghai Jiao Tong University, developed the device. Washing machines with a bacteria sterilization function were introduced into the market in 2007 for front-loading drum types of washing machines. In less than one year, Panasonic's market share in China for this type of washing machine jumped from 3 percent to 15 percent.

In general, deeper localization exposes "missing resources" (for example, bacteria sterilization technology for washing machines), which then invites resource transfer and hence global integration (development and transfer of the bacteria sterilization device in this case). The market success of washing machines with bacteria sterilization is a superb example of the passage from deeper localization to missing resources revealed to more extensive integration, which we have observed in other firms as well.

At the same time, it is interesting to note that before Panasonic's launch, washing machines with bacteria sterilization were already on the market. But there were over eighty manufacturers of washing machines, and it was not uncommon for newly introduced functions not to work as well as their manufacturers claimed. As a result, the market did not always respond positively to product introduction with new functions. Panasonic was, however, the first major brand in China to introduce washing machines with bacteria sterilization. It also publicized its study data on the effectiveness of its bacteria sterilization device. In addition, Panasonic publicized that the device was developed in collaboration with Shanghai Jiao Tong University, one of the premier institutions in China. This collaboration with the university was likely to have contributed to the market acceptance of Panasonic's washing machines with this special feature.

Now we trace the dynamic development of the tension-embracing structure through a series of tension-embracing activities initiated or driven by the Lifestyle Research Center in Shanghai. First note that the most critical element of the tension-embracing structure at the establishment of the center was the director of the center himself. His strong conviction that product planning requires in-depth understanding of needs, seeds (technological enablers), and cost through his extensive experience at a BU product planning group was a primary resource in the initial tension-embracing structure. The director then established the center's mission as the creation of market-leading product concepts, going beyond mere studies of local lifestyles. Through this effort, the center's mission itself became a critical resource in the evolving tension-embracing structure.

The director created a rigorous hiring practice to identify people with proper talent that matched the center's mission. A large number of applications were screened, and about twenty applicants were invited for an in-depth interview for each position. At one of the tasks for the interview, applicants were given raw data and asked to interpret them. Some applicants gave superficial interpretations, yet others were able to extract some interesting insights, which is critical for conceiving market-leading product ideas. The hired applicants were given training on technology and the economics of product concept creation. In line with the center's mission, the director emphasized data interpretation, not data collection. Ultimately data interpretation is expected to culminate in new product concepts, and at this point, the very act of interpretation links the two themes of local adaptation (local lifestyle data) and global integration (transfer of global resources such as technological knowledge). Thus, hiring and training activities led to the further evolution of the tension-embracing structure through the center staff resources that can address the two competitive themes.

Note that the key contribution of the center's director was structuring the workplace environment so that people at the center and in its vicinity (the BUs and their subsidiaries in China that the center works with) could more effectively address both local adaptation and global integration. Most notable, the director's structuring included the development of the center mission, implementation of hiring practices, and regular meetings with Kusatsu for the center staff. Given this initial tension-embracing structure that the director nurtured, center staff were able to more effectively initiate tension-embracing activities. These staff were also able to rebuild and strengthen their capabilities for tension-embracing activities; for instance, they regularly participated in meetings with engineers in Kusatsu. Thus, the impact of the director's structuring was far-reaching and fundamentally of a recursive nature, kick-starting the snowballing chain of activity-structure reinforcement cycles (see Figure 3.2).

Now consider the relational resources involving the center in Shanghai and BUs in Kusatsu working with the center. We will show how the activities of people in the relationships alter the nature of relational resources (and hence the tension-embracing structure). Recall the case of washing machines with bacteria sterilization. The center's role was not so much of discovering a hidden lifestyle such as hand-washing underwear in China because there already were washing machines with bacteria sterilization. As the director of the center noted, the tough part of their task is not to collect data but to convincingly convey the interpretation of the data to Kusatsu. Thus, the more significant role of the center was to back up their product concepts with reliable, in-depth market data collected systematically in order to secure Kusatsu's approval and commitment for developing proposed products.[8] Consider the type of relational resource characterized by the distribution of information in the network of people working together. In light of the distribution of information in the network of relationships involving the center in Shanghai and the BUs in Kusatsu, we can say that a significant role of the center is to generate the bulk of information at a locus of the network closer to the competitive theme of local adaptation, thereby altering the configuration of information distribution in such a way as to strengthen the power of those involved in local adaptation. Here again, the activities of the center staff reshaped the landscape of the tension-embracing structure, this time through changes in the distribution of information in the network of Shanghai-Kusatsu relationships.

Finally, we consider another type of relational resource: trusting relationships between the center in Shanghai and the BUs in Kusatsu. The series of cases initiated by the center has improved the working relationships between the center and the BUs, which in turn had a positive impact on the development of trust between Kusatsu and its local operations. Given the increased local autonomy since around 2008, the tension-embracing structure has matured substantially to accommodate the greater extent of local adaptation that the increased autonomy might create.

## Panasonic in the Next Round of Global Competition: From Spontaneous to Deliberate Coevolution

The lens of coevolution into the future of its global competition offers interesting insight into Panasonic's strategic moves. In 2009, it established the Lifestyle Research Center in Europe. Some of the know-how accumulated at China's research center was deployed at this European one. In 2010, a group with similar missions and functions of lifestyle research was created in India. Both of these represent the geographical dimension of coevolutionary expansion. Business domains represented another such dimension. In fact, China's center, in addition to home appliances, started working with other domain companies such as AVC Networks (TV, computers, DVD players) and Panasonic Electric Works (house/building interiors, personal care, health care). The center's most visible outcome has been in the area of home appliances, so-called white goods, because these products are more sensitive to differences in lifestyles. AVC products ("black goods") were largely standardized global products. But, since 2010, the center has also been conducting studies on possible local features of AVC products such as how TV sets are attached securely to the wall or a large piece of furniture in the living space.

These two dimensions of coevolutionary expansion, geography and business, are important for Panasonic's next round of global competition, but perhaps the scope of the expansion is most profoundly enriched by Panasonic's recent strategic move of *Marugoto* solutions. *Marugoto* in Japanese means "all-inclusive" or "wall-to-wall," and these solutions are integrated electric and electronic systems for the entire house or the entire building, from electric wiring to kitchen and bath systems to networked appliances and electronic products. *Marugoto* solutions create tremendous opportunities for significantly greater local adaptation, well beyond the possibilities that individual products can offer. Second, they also make it possible to exploit

the enormously greater complexity of global integration deep-
ened by the extensive needs for cross-business cooperation. A
complexity of this magnitude is a daunting management challenge for any MNC. However, it is also a strategic asset for a firm
that addresses the challenge and learns how to exploit it for
competitive advantage, because this advantage tends to deter
imitation due to the complexity engrained in the advantage.

Given these future prospects for leveraging the coevolution
dynamics for competitive advantage, a key question we address
is how well Panasonic is prepared to capitalize on this potential.
Panasonic's coevolution discourse certainly suggests its capabilities to coevolve the two themes of adaptation and integration.
But its coevolution has been a rather orderly step-by-step development where each step has been a natural consequence of or
a spontaneous response to another step. For instance, the shift
in authority distribution toward local operations (adaptation)
was a spontaneous response to the development of a cooperative,
trusting relationship between Kusatsu and China (integration),
which in turn was a natural consequence of the local capability
development for gaining deeper lifestyle insights backed by
systematic field studies (adaptation). Throughout the evolutionary discourse, a comfortable balance was maintained between
local adaptation and global integration, and there was no "hurricane" to swing the balance to the overdevelopment of one of
the themes. In general, the coevolution can take place through
corrective efforts to recover from the "hurricane damage" to
the balance. Given this full dynamics of coevolution, our sense
is that Panasonic falls short in deliberately leveraging the full
range of options available for pursuing the two competitive
themes. In particular, the extent of local adaptation has been
fairly modest, and hence its ability to invite greater integration
has been correspondingly limited. The remainder of this section
discusses three possible options for the full-scale dynamics of
coevolution.

## Establishing Strategic Coevolution Outposts

At Home Appliances Company, the BUs, their subsidiaries, and members of the Lifestyle Research Center working with BUs were the primary contributors to the coevolution, and hence the coevolution was more or less contained within each BU. But the coevolution could take place outside BUs and directly under the top management of the Home Appliances Company.

At GE's Healthcare Division, for instance, a small local organization, called the local growth team (LGT), was created in China outside the health care business units.[9] The mission of the LGT, which reported directly to the head of the division, was to develop and distribute drastically low-cost ultrasound medical imaging systems. These systems were originally developed for advanced markets, and their prices ranged from $100,000 to $350,000. It was not possible to reduce the cost sufficiently for emerging markets by stripping various features and functions from the models for developed economies. Rather, the models for emerging economies had to be designed and developed from scratch. The effort to develop such models was not placed within a business unit of the Healthcare Division, because business units tended to focus on mainstream customers in developed markets and were unlikely to understand the emerging markets. Hence the LGT was locally created in China directly under the Healthcare Division. The division's top management ensured LGT access to the GE's global R&D. Only with the cutting-edge R&D resources made available to the local team was the LGT able to develop a model for emerging markets with a completely new architecture and at a drastically lower cost of around $15,000.

The autonomy of the LGT was critical for its success. In contrast to Panasonic, the autonomy was developed not gradually but deliberately, instituted from the top down. Note also that the LGT was well integrated into GE's global R&D network, again through a deliberate decision from the top. The autonomy for undisturbed local adaptation and the cooperation for integration of cutting-edge technologies were simultaneously instituted top down. This creation of local outposts for top-down deliberate coevolution may well complement the BU-contained gradual coevolution Panasonic seems to excel in.

## Jump-Starting the Coevolution Through Adaptation-Intended Acquisition

Although Panasonic entered China mostly through joint ventures, many of them later became subsidiaries. The expansion of their presence in China was largely driven by organic growth through the gradual transfer of resources and capabilities. Although this expansion strategy was aligned well with the step-by-step, well-balanced coevolution dynamics, Panasonic was still a minor player in many of its businesses in China. The Home Appliances Company in China, in particular, still falls far behind domestic players. Even with its washing machines, for which it had established a relatively stronger presence, it had only a 9 percent market share in 2010, ranking third after domestic makers Haier (27 percent) and Little Swan (15 percent). For other categories, the presence of Panasonic was far weaker. For the refrigerator, Panasonic's market share was 2 percent in 2010, ranking tenth and falling behind dominant domestic players such as Haier (22 percent), Midea (12 percent), and Meiling (11 percent). Similarly, for air conditioners, its share was 2 percent in 2010, ranking eighth, again markedly behind domestic players such as Gree (26 percent), Midea (22 percent), and Haier (11 percent).

Here recall the case of Walmart China that we introduced earlier. Despite its overwhelming leadership in global retail industry, Walmart still ranked twentieth in China in terms of sales in 2004. After nearly ten years of struggle characterized by its single-minded focus on integration, as opposed to a more balanced adaptation-integration engagement, Walmart finally shifted its China strategy and made a series of concerted strategic moves for deeper localization. One of them was acquisition. In 2007, Walmart acquired Trust-Mart for $1.32 billion. Trust-Mart was ranked thirteenth in sales in 2004, significantly above Walmart in China. With the acquisition, Walmart surpassed Carrefour, which was ranked fifth in China in 2004.

The combined scale was critical for its competition in China, but more significant, Trust-Mart, being Taiwan based and without the Walmart legacy that was often incompatible with local conditions and constraints in China, was far more deeply localized in China than Walmart was. Given Walmart's legacy business model, developed in a vastly different environment, the Trust-Mart acquisition was the cornerstone for Walmart's accelerated local adaptation in China. Unlike Panasonic's self-contained gradual coevolution, Walmart created a strong swing toward local adaptation through the acquisition, which opened up a blank space to fill in with strategic moves to promote global integration. Again, this acquisition-driven coevolution may well be a powerful complement to the self-contained gradual coevolution Panasonic has been pursuing in China.

## Cultivating the Coevolution Mind-Set

Recall the dynamic nature of the tension-embracing structure that we illustrated through the series of activities undertaken by the Lifestyle Research Center in Shanghai and the BUs in Kusatsu. Here the tension-embracing structure was constantly created and recreated through mindful activities, as witnessed in the director's leadership at the China Lifestyle Research Center and the staff interpreting the data in terms of lifestyle, technology, and cost implications. This is an excellent example of the dynamics of a tension-embracing structure that unfolds positively. However, tension-embracing structures can also constrain and even discourage tension-embracing activities. A good example is the organizational matrix structure. A typical matrix structure for MNCs has two dimensions: one representing the geography, mainly for local adaptation, and the other embodying the business, primarily for global integration. Many corporations adopted the matrix scheme, only to abandon it after some years of unsuccessful attempts to make it functional. The key reason behind this near universal failure was the rigidity of the formal matrix structure, which constrains and often discourages tension-embracing activities instead of facilitating and enabling them. As one executive correctly observed, "The challenge is not so much to build a matrix structure as it is to create a matrix in the minds of our managers."[10]

"A matrix in the minds of our managers" is essentially what we mean by the coevolution mind-set. To give a more precise definition, we first elaborate on the meaning of *mind-set*. "Mind-set," in the context of the coevolution perspective, is the interface between tension-embracing activities and tension-embracing structure. It refers to a cognitive scheme shaped by two primary dimensions of mental engagement: differentiation and integration. In the discussion of human cognitive capacity in general, differentiation refers to the extent to which the human mind can embrace distinctive elements in the given domain of mental operation, while integration measures the mental ability to exercise synthetic views on dissimilar elements in the given cognitive domain. When one can deal with a larger (smaller) number of more (less) distinct elements, the person is said to have a mind-set with high differentiation (low differentiation). Similarly, when a person can hold a more (less) profound and more (less) extensive synthetic view over diverse elements, his or her mind-set is of a high-integration (low-integration) nature.[11] In the context of the coevolution perspective, differentiation refers to the capacity for accommodating the variation that results from or can result from local adaptation, while integration corresponds to the synthetic outlook associated with the extent of global integration. The coevolution mind-set is the high-differentiation/high-integration mind-set in the context of pursuing both local adaptation and global integration.

Given the definition, the question now is how a firm can cultivate the coevolution mind-set so that its tension-embracing structure can facilitate, rather than constrain, tension-embracing activities. Again, a good example is Panasonic's Lifestyle Research Center in Shanghai, more specifically what the center's director has done since its launch. The essential nature of the director's contributions was structuring the workplace environment so that people at the center and its vicinity (the BUs and their subsidiaries in China that the center works with) could pursue local adaptation and global integration. In other words, he was driving the coevolution process, and through participation in the process, other people were acquiring the coevolution mind-set. We call managers in charge of driving the coevolution process *coevolution drivers*. Thus, one effective way of nurturing the coevolution mind-set in organization is to place coevolution drivers in key positions for local adaptation or global integration.

Note as well that the full-scale dynamics of coevolution is likely to require top-down leadership engagement. In today's global competition, top management simply cannot afford to be mere observers for spontaneous coevolution. They should serve as critical coevolution drivers and create the tension-embracing structure in order to lead more deliberate coevolution strategies.

## Conclusion

In today's global competition, an effective strategic framework for MNCs is to create and harness complexity so that the competitive advantage they derive is less likely to be copied by their competitors. A source of such complexity is often a pair of competing strategic themes, with each representing a critical dimension of global competition. The tension intrinsic to such a pair, when addressed properly, can be a great source of competitive advantage, as we have discussed through the case of local adaptation versus global integration. The adaptation-integration tension in global competition is increasingly intensified as the locus of growth shifts from developed to emerging economies. MNCs from developed or emerging economies must cope with vast differences between the two economies, a source of the intensified tension between the two themes. But again, the intensified tension means greater complexity available to the firm. It is tempting for the firm, however, to view the tension from the trade-off perspective, as the trade-off is an immediate issue in many specific situations. But from a larger strategic standpoint, the coevolution perspective, coupled with the notion of dynamic tension-embracing structure, is more appropriate in framing and exploiting the complexity and leveraging the intensified tension for global competitive advantage.

Thus, a good strategy for a developed economy MNC to outperform its local rivals in an emerging market is to create an effective tension-embracing structure that accommodates global resources unavailable to the local rivals. Similarly, a good strategy for a developed economy MNC to outperform its global competitors is to cultivate a superior tension-embracing structure, again of an increasingly complex kind, that is capable of deeper localization and correspondingly profound global integration while its global rivals are grappling with the trade-off perspective for the two competing themes.

# 4

# HOW SOME JAPANESE FIRMS HAVE SUCCEEDED AGAINST LOW-COST COMPETITORS IN EMERGING MARKETS

Junjiro Shintaku, Tomofumi Amano

Emerging countries such as China, India, and Brazil are continuing to mature into giant markets. However, Japanese firms have found it difficult to count themselves among the successful participants in these markets. The competitive edge of Japanese firms, driven by high product quality, has ironically been one of the major sources of failure where these made-in-Japan products are too expensive for the average emerging market consumer. This predicament is similar to the so-called innovator's dilemma. The lack of accurate understanding of local markets causes a mismatch between Japanese products and market needs. Economic and social situations in emerging countries are quite different from those of developed countries, yet Japanese companies have allocated most of their business resources in Japan.

In response to this problem, Japanese firms should first understand the root causes of the dilemma and reshape their products with reasonable quality that more closely meets the needs of emerging markets. Japanese firms should also reorganize their pattern of resource allocation and develop organizational capabilities for penetrating the huge middle-class market. They should strategically allocate their resources such as human resources, capital, and knowledge to the emerging market if they believe these markets are a source of their future growth. Based on cases and data collected from original field studies, we suggest in this chapter some directions that Japanese firms can take for rebuilding their strategies in emerging markets.[1]

## Tapping Emerging Markets

Emerging economies hold tremendous opportunities for Japanese firms, especially in the middle of the pyramid. However, it is essential for them to make strategic adjustments and develop new business models for the emerging markets.

### Middle of the Pyramid in Emerging Markets

Amid the economic slowdown in the United States, Europe, and other developed countries as a result of the financial crisis, emerging markets in developing countries continue to draw a great deal of public attention. Even before this crisis, the importance of BRIC countries (Brazil, Russia, India, and China) and other emerging countries was well recognized. One might say that the financial shock was the call that sharply accelerated the shift in focus from developed to emerging countries.

Recent work has addressed penetration strategies in developing country markets including the base of the pyramid (BOP).[2] However, when we consider the main market segments of Japanese firms in developing countries, it is usually one up from BOP, that is, the middle of the pyramid (MOP), and there seem to be few empirical studies of Japanese firms in these markets compared with Western firms.[3] According to the "2009 Manufacturing White Paper" by Japan's Ministry of Economy Trade and Industry, middle-class markets in BRICs grew from 250 million people in 2002 to 630 million in 2007 (China, 270 million; India, 140 million; Russia, 100 million; Brazil, 120 million). So the interesting question is, when Japanese firms attempt to

## Figure 4.1 The Growth Process of Japanese Firms

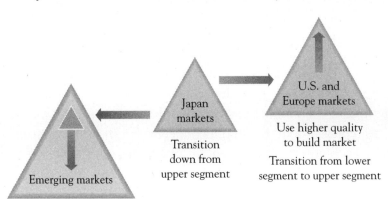

enter such rapidly growing markets, what kinds of problems do they encounter, and how do they address them?

Figure 4.1 summarizes the relationship between market levels and the growth process of Japanese firms. After World War II, Japanese manufacturing industries first grew based on their home market. Soon they began exporting to the United States and other developed countries, though their product quality was poor. Japanese automakers entered at the low end of the market, targeting their cars to used-car buyers. Honda, for example, was even forced to recall the first motorcycles it exported to the United States. Japanese firms that manufactured photocopiers entered the market with machines that were small and quite slow, and in fact they struggled to improve their quality and upgrade their products toward the middle and upper ends of markets in developed countries. Therefore, it is not surprising that for most Japanese firms, quality improvement has always been a priority.

Although high quality has often been central to strategies for developed markets, that is not the case for emerging markets. In these markets Japanese firms must face the challenge of down-grading their products instead. In that sense, what they are now encountering is in sharp contrast from what they have experienced in the past.

Three problems arise from this discontinuity. First, Japanese firms are providing products with excess quality or performance and with prices that are too high for these markets. Second, local customers who are unfamiliar with the products do not grasp or appreciate the product excellence. Third, the product specifications typically do not match local needs. For most Japanese firms, these problems present a new set of hurdles to clear.

When we examine the products of Japanese firms that repeatedly fail in emerging markets, we find that in many cases, the product itself is not of poor quality. Japanese firms have strong technical and manufacturing competencies. It seems instead that their unsuccessful results point to a lack of business models that use their technical and manufacturing competencies and marketing to convert their manufacturing competencies to customer values in new markets. In fact we have seen some cases of Japanese firms in emerging markets that can indeed be understood from this perspective. In addition, many Japanese firms trying to enter emerging markets keep most of their product and business development in Japan. If Japanese businesses want to be successful in these markets, they might have to restructure or reallocate their resources in research and development, production, and sales activities in global manufacturing value chains.

## The Innovator's Dilemma

The problems that Japanese firms are facing in emerging markets are similar to the innovator's dilemma, articulated by C. Christensen in his book *The Innovator's Dilemma*. In this work, Christensen asks several key questions: Why do excellent leading firms fail in innovation? What are the characteristics of innovation in which leading firms fail? Previous research on innovation held that the causes were technical novelty or difficulty. Christensen, however, explains the failures from market perspectives.[4]

Christensen bases his arguments on research conducted in the hard disk drive (HDD) industry. He asserts that leading firms fail because they persistently work to meet the needs of their mainstream customers and overlook the emergent needs of new customers. The commitment to existing customers has been a success factor in the past, but it cannot secure the ability to adapt to different type of customers in new markets. In the 1970s, HDDs were mainly used in mainframe computers, and mainframe customers wanted HDDs with a large storage capacity, a high processing speed, and high reliability. Thus, leading HDD manufacturers vigorously invested in basic technologies and products to increase storage capacity, processing speed, and reliability. But since small HDDs appeared with small disk sizes for the PC market, which was created as the low end of the market relative to mainframes, the performance that customers demanded of HDDs became very different from those in the past. Important factors for the PC markets were "small" and "low cost," and, in the case of notebook PCs, "energy efficient." The manufacturers of small HDDs accelerated product development and innovation to satisfy these new demands. But traditional HDD manufacturers did not because their main customers did not see any value in smaller size or reduced price if they had to sacrifice durability, processing speed, and reliability.

Issues challenging Japanese firms in emerging country markets are quite similar to this phenomenon, which we call the "emerging market dilemma." To illustrate this, we introduce the case of a Japanese printer firm, Epson, in Asian markets.[5] In the 1980s, Epson's printer business in Japan invented the technology of dot matrix printers (we will refer to these as SIDM printers, for "serial impact dot matrix printers"). However, because of the low speed and the small potential for color printing, the industry and market moved from SIDMs to ink-jet printers and laser printers in the 1990s with the basic technologies of SIDM printers, including head processing technologies, transferred to and renewed in the development of ink-jet printers.[6] Engineers of the firm also shifted from SIDMs to ink-jet printers. However, in the late 1990s, because price competition in the ink-jet printer market became so intense and product development cycles became so short, most of the firms in the industry struggled to make a sufficient profit from the hardware business. As a result, printer manufacturers created a new business model, the supply business model, in which profits are gained from supply products such as ink cartridges and ribbons rather than hardware products.

SIDM printers entered the market before the supply business model became popular. Thus, the hardware was relatively expensive and their supply products were relatively inexpensive. After SIDMs had matured in developed countries, replaced by ink-jet printers, they were mainly exported to or locally produced in developing countries such as Indonesia, China, India, and Brazil.[7] In these countries, the products were sold through sales representatives for business use such as printing receipts at shop registers. SIDM printers have few head troubles because of their simple structure, and in addition their ink ribbons are cheap. As a result, the printers sold well among business users in emerging countries where businesses used printers more frequently than home users did. Since business users required convenient after-sales services, Epson leveraged SIDMs to spread its sales and service network throughout these countries. These sales and after-sales service networks became a strong source of support when Epson introduced ink-jet printers later.

In Indonesia, Epson established a sales arm in 2001 to introduce ink-jet printers. Since these printers appeared after the supply business model became dominant, the printers themselves were much cheaper than SIDMs, though the ink cartridges were more costly. Epson brought this business model to Indonesia without making any changes. And it turned out that the higher cartridge price became a bottleneck for business users who closely watched the cost of running the printers. The outcome was that in Indonesia, many users turned to using Chinese-made ink cartridges rather than the genuine Epson ink cartridges. Moreover, new businesses popped up all over for modifying printers in a way that enabled the easy use of these low-priced cartridges.

Leading firms in developed countries always challenge cutting-edge technologies and innovations in order to differentiate themselves from other competitors in developed country markets. But these products are not necessarily well suited to emerging country markets, as the Epson story shows. Japanese firms that have succeeded mainly in developed country markets have done so through their competencies in technology and innovation. They have built organizational capabilities and leading business models and have succeeded in upgrading their brand values in these markets. These are extremely important assets, but in emerging markets, firms are under pressure to make a different type of strategic change for meeting market conditions and customer needs. We call this the "emerging market dilemma" for companies in the traditional markets.

## Analytical Perspectives of Emerging Market Strategy

When firms in developed countries approach middle-class markets in emerging countries, the more strengths they have in technological competencies, the more common it is for them to have mismatches with local markets. How can this dilemma be resolved? Here, we introduce two perspectives for market penetration: repositioning of products targeting specific market segments and resource allocation and local capability development.

### Repositioning of Products in Quality and Price

Products produced by Chinese firms are indeed low priced and have problems of quality. Conversely, Japanese products are too expensive for the Chinese market but are of high quality. This is a common problem called "excess quality": Japanese products provide a quality in excess of that sought in the local markets, which results in extremely high prices relative to local competitors.

A typical example is the recordable CD (CD-R) market for recording optical disks created in the early 1990s. Sony advocated this disk standard, and Taiyo Yuden developed the core materials and the manufacturing process technologies. Japanese firms held an almost 100 percent market share at the beginning, although this was limited to niche markets such as creating masters for music CDs. Although these markets were small, entering firms were able to maintain high prices and the markets were mostly stable and dominated by Japanese firms.

When PCs started to be installed with CD-R drives in 1997, the market grew, and global production volume increased rapidly. Now over 10 billion CD-R disks are sold annually. CD-R drives became an overwhelmingly large market compared to that of the old recording media such as magnetic tapes and floppy disks. However, even during that growth period, Japanese firms' production inched along as Taiwanese firms led production growth. Production also grew in India starting around 2001. Looking at price trends, after Taiwanese firms entered the CD-R market around 1997, prices plummeted by two-thirds in one year. As a consequence of such profound price drops, the profitability of many Japanese firms suffered. Forced to review their operations, many Japanese firms halted production, and some of them with strong brands (TDK, Hitachi Maxell, and Mitsubishi Chemical Verbatim) switched from internal production to original equipment manufacturer (OEM) purchasing from Taiwanese firms.[8]

Taiwanese firms with growing production did not have any strong brands themselves, so they instead supplied disks to Japanese firms through OEM contracts. In addition, Taiwanese firms did not usually have their own capabilities to develop basic materials for disk production (for example, dye and polycarbonate), manufacturing equipment (for example, molding machines), or the manufacturing formulas. Thus, Japanese firms sold dye and formulas to contracted Taiwanese firms and supervised production all the way through to quality control. In other words, Taiwanese firms produced CD-Rs and received guidance from Japanese firms. Taiwanese firms not only supplied CD-Rs to Japanese firms but to the U.S. company Imation and other U.S. and European firms as well. However, few U.S. and European firms invested in R&D on optical disks, so they made original design manufacturer (ODM) purchases from Taiwanese firms.[9] In short, instead of specifying materials and formulas like the Japanese firms did, they evaluated the prototypes proposed by Taiwanese firms, negotiated prices, and then purchased them. Thus, we can identify three business models for Taiwanese firms: OEM supply to Japanese firms based on their strict quality control, business under their own brand, and ODM supply to U.S. and European firms with much lower prices.

According to our interview survey of engineers at Taiwan's major disk firms, in OEM for Japanese firms, they complied 100 percent with the materials, formulas, and quality control items specified by the Japanese firm, but the level of quality control fell in ODM for U.S. and European firms. It is a rough impression, but if rating quality control items for Japan is at 100, the level is about 20 to 30 in their own brands and ODM products for the United States and Europe. Basically, they reduced prices by sacrificing quality.

Quality and price are generally in an upward sloping relationship as shown in Figure 4.2. Products from Japan are of good quality but also priced higher. However, the world's average customers seem to be saying that they generally do not seek such high quality, and even if quality is sacrificed a little, they are happy with the lower prices. Small and medium-sized Taiwanese firms and Chinese firms, however, lacking technical strength, produce inferior products. Both Japanese products with excess quality and Chinese products with low-grade quality can gain only in small niche markets, while products with medium-level quality and price that are of reasonable quality are likely to achieve the largest sales. This is how Taiwanese firms think of

## Figure 4.2 The Relationship of Reasonable Quality and Price

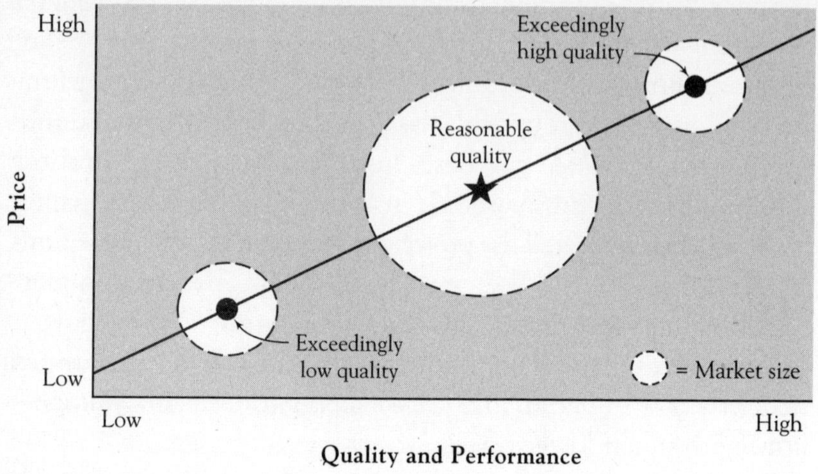

Figure showing a scatter plot with Price (High/Low) on the y-axis and Quality and Performance (Low/High) on the x-axis. Labels include "Exceedingly high quality," "Reasonable quality," "Exceedingly low quality," and a legend "= Market size."

quality. And this mind-set seems to be a rational view of quality and price.

However, there is not just one level of "reasonable quality." The appropriate level of quality and price depends on the market. Even for CD-Rs, Japanese brand products (so-called excess quality products) are still sold in the Japanese market. This means that high-quality, high-price products are considered "reasonable quality" in the Japanese market. Korea-based Samsung Electronics boasts a large market share overseas, but one reason that its products are not sold in Japan at all seems to be that its products do not represent the "reasonable quality" that the Japanese market demands.

## Finding Reasonable Quality for Emerging Markets

Even for the same product, sellers differ in different markets because of the different distributions of preferences in each market. For the same product, some consumers care about price and others about quality and performance. Consumers who care about price tend to focus less on quality and performance, so they choose products made by Taiwanese firms. In contrast, consumers who care about quality and performance choose products made by Japanese firms. The latter comprise a higher percentage in the Japanese market, and thus Japanese products sell well in Japan. However, such consumers seem to comprise a small percentage of the market in China, so Taiwanese products sell better in there. Similarly, even for the same LCD panels, Japanese products sell better in the large TV market that emphasizes performance, while Taiwanese products sell best in the PC market, which emphasizes price. In this way, even for the same type of products, the way a product sells best depends on the countries and regions or market segments. Here, we refer to the quality/performance and price combination of the best-selling products as "reasonable quality." So for emerging market strategy, what is first required is for the firm to consider how to choose the best combination of quality or performance and price that is most appropriate for the particular market. This requires that the firm design its product strategy accordingly.

## Allocating Resources and Developing Local Capability

Another viewpoint is that the low market share of Japanese firms in emerging markets is closely related to the international distribution of a firm's business resources. Japanese firms tend to create products with excess quality because the key activities of product planning and development design are highly centralized in Japan. Market unsuitability comes from the characteristics of resource allocation, so the problems will not be solved unless this is revised.

We will examine this in the same HDD industry as Christensen studied in his work. In this industry, along with the growth of small HDDs, specialized firms in the United States that led in small HDDs grew rapidly and those that developed drives for mainframes and minicomputers declined. Especially with the market expansion of small HDDs for PCs, the total HDD market size grew exponentially. As a result, firms were forced to produce a huge volume of drives, and mass production was shifted to Asia to gain production scale. Soon mass production in Asia became a prerequisite for the very survival of entrant firms.

Many firms that could not commit necessary investments for mass production withdrew from the market. Seagate and other specialized firms in the United States reigned at the top of the industry for a long time. They established mass production bases in Singapore as early as the 1980s, positioned them as their Asian hubs, and strengthened them. They cooperated with local governments, universities, engineers, managers, and suppliers. They positioned Singapore factories as the center of process technology development and transferred the new technology developed to other Asian countries. These U.S. firms were accepting product designs from the United States, developing the prototypes and the production processes in Singapore, and then transferring the knowledge and formulas for production processes to other production sites, including Thailand, Malaysia, and China. With these development efforts in Asia since around 2000, the U.S. sites have been putting much effort into basic research, product development, and development and manufacturing of core parts and components. This pattern of international division has built U.S. firms' overwhelming advantage in product development, manufacturing cost, and mass production volumes.[10]

Japanese firms were selling disk drives to existing customers at the upper end of the market for mainframes and the captive market for internal sales. Also, they did not commit to the development of technological capabilities in Asia. Rather, most of their development activities, including process development, remained in Japan. Their foreign production ratios were still low even in the late 1990s. Viewed from the perspective of a full-scale industrial concentration in Asia, looking at human resource development, and formation of development resources and their use in production strategy, it seems that Japanese firms were lagging far behind their U.S. counterparts even though these Japanese firms had superior technologies.[11]

In *The Innovator's Dilemma*, Christensen states that when disruptive technology exists, it is more important to form a project team within the market of disruptive technology separate from the market of mainstream technology. In similar manner, when a company faces the emerging market dilemma in entering markets in emerging countries, it could be more important to form knowledge development sites near the local markets or the local mass production sites, more or less separate from the existing mainstream routines in the home country. The local knowledge development sites will contribute to a flexible market response, quick mass production launching, and the development of local human resources.

The emerging market dilemma could arise not only from the market difference but also from the gap between resource allocations in developed countries and the ideal resource allocation in emerging markets. To overcome this, firms should review their multinational management strategy and organizational structure and work to reallocate business resources to the frontiers of sales and production activities in growing emerging markets to enable easier local organizational learning and build up the necessary human resources.

Also, among emerging markets, it might be relatively easy or difficult, depending on countries or regions, to build learning-oriented organizational capabilities. From the standpoint of resource allocation and location strategy, it is important to identify the potential abilities of the region's human resources and decide where to invest capital and resources. In other words, a firm should plan location selection and international division of labor among locations in the regional network from the perspective of the "comparative advantage of organizational capabilities."[12] This could also be suggested based on the case of the HDD industry.

## Honda's Success Against Low-Cost Competitors in the ASEAN Motorcycle Market

We raised the two perspectives of emerging market strategy: repositioning of the product and resource allocation and local capability development. In this section, we explain both perspectives using the case of Honda's motorcycle business in member countries of the Association of Southeast Nations (ASEAN). We start by introducing the first perspective with patterns of product strategy: decision making regarding market segments and related quality levels.

### Low-Priced Products with Reduced Excess Quality/Performance

We start by looking at Vietnam's motorcycle market.[13] In Vietnam, motorcycles are a popular mode of transport for ordinary people, and the roads in Hanoi and Ho Chi Minh are packed with motorcycles. In the late 1990s, the market was about 500,000 units; in 2000, the market size leaped to over 2 million; and in 2003, it dropped back to 1 million (Figure 4.3). The cause of these sudden market fluctuations can be attributed to the entrance of Chinese motorcycles to the market.

China entered the motorcycle market with models copied from Honda and came to dominate the market, leaving Honda with less than 5 percent of the market share in China. However, Chinese firms also suffered from domestic price competition and targeted the ASEAN market. The first target for Chinese firms was the Vietnamese market. Low-priced, low-quality made-in-China motorcycles entered Vietnam in 2000, with made-in-Vietnam Chinese models also flooding the market. For Honda, which had lost the vast market in China, the entry of Chinese-made motorcycles into Vietnam was a serious threat to its ASEAN market share.

Previously Honda had maintained a dominant position in the ASEAN market; in Vietnam alone, it boasted up to a 30 percent

### Figure 4.3 Vietnam's Motorcycle Market, 1998-2003

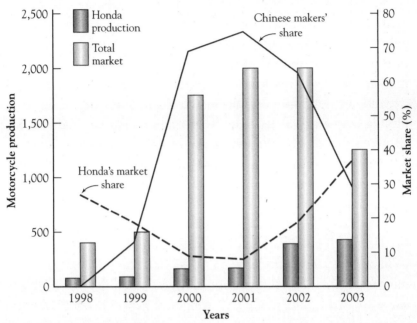

*Source:* Data from Honda Vietnam.

market share. Honda's main product in the ASEAN market was the Super Cub, a motorcycle designed by the founder of Honda, Soichiro Honda, about fifty years ago. (In fact, Honda was selling several types of smaller motorcycles generically referred to as "cubs," including the Super Cub, Dream, and the Honda Wave series models.) This long-selling product was priced at about 200,000 yen in Japan, and sold in Vietnam at an equivalent price of about $2,000, which was expensive for the average Vietnamese. Honda introduced the Dream in ASEAN countries including Vietnam, a localized model of the Super Cub developed by Japanese and Thai R&D teams in 1997. But its price was still about $1,500.

China-made motorcycles came roaring into the Vietnamese market with a price tag of only $500 to $700. At about only one-third to one-fourth that of the Super Cub, these motorcycles were well within the reach of many Vietnamese families. Although Vietnamese incomes did not grow so quickly, the market size for motorcycles leaped 200 to 300 percent up to 2 million units. However, for Honda, the news was not so rosy: its market share declined to 9 percent as Chinese motorcycles expanded the bottom end of the Vietnamese market. From this, Honda learned that the overall Vietnamese market had become sizable through the introduction of Chinese motorcycles. It became aware of the huge market for lower-end motorcycles and observed similar trends in other countries such as Indonesia. This understanding moved Honda in the direction of a full-scale introduction of low-priced models in ASEAN countries.

Honda then embarked on radical cost reduction and planned to introduce a new model at $1,000—half the price of the original Super Cub. To achieve this, it investigated the possibility of using low-cost parts made in China and ASEAN countries and revised the design to one with reasonable performance, thereby targeting at local middle-class users. However, Honda faced many problems with parts made locally and in China. Many of them could not be used since they did not meet the existing design requirements. Similar to other manufacturing industries, Honda's design requirements are authorized by Japan's headquarters. However, in this case, if Honda were to use parts only to comply with Japan's requirements, it would remain far from reaching the price goal of $1,000.

Thus, as part of product planning, Honda reviewed the performance requirements that Vietnamese users demanded. First, in Vietnam, motorcycle traffic is very heavy in urban areas and acceleration is difficult, so speeds over eighty kilometers per hour were not necessarily required. The maximum speed of the planned new model would differ from the Wave 100, a cub sold in Thailand, though the base unit would be the same.

Then Honda revised its design requirement standards and tried to procure more local parts and imported parts from China that could pass the revised requirements of local and Chinese markets. At the same time, Honda put time and resources in supporting local suppliers that could provide low-cost parts. It also used functional parts that were already developed and produced at reasonable cost. It thus reached the cost target in many ways.

Although design standards could usually be raised, they were rarely downgraded. Engineers want to design things that are better in some way from the past. Designs influence the entire firm's brand value, and such decisions are made by the headquarters president, not by a local subsidiary president. Although raising design standards can be achieved in a bottom-up process based on the ideas of engineers, lowering design standards is a different case because it can be achieved only through a top-down management process.

In January 2002, Honda introduced into the Vietnamese market a new cub called the Wave, which cost no more than $800. The average price difference between Honda's motorcycles (including the Super Cub and the Dream) and the lower-price Chinese bikes was about 2.3 times in 2000, but after the introduction of the Wave in 2002, it fell to 1.37. The cost performance of the Wave in consideration of the price for quality and performance was acknowledged by consumers, and in 2003, Honda's production units in Vietnam rose to 420,000: the growth recorded was approximately 4.7 times that of 1999. Furthermore, about 80 percent of Honda's motorcycles sold in Vietnam in 2003 were the Wave. The introduction of low-priced models expanded the market and drove Honda to raise its production capacity significantly.

The decline in the unit sales of Chinese motorcycles in the Vietnamese market from 2002 must also be noted. In addition to Honda's change in product strategy, several other factors can be considered. First, along with a tariff increase, total emission control was also imposed on import goods as of September 2002, and Chinese companies that violated this regulation were subject to stricter enforcement of this control. Second, due to the increasing problem of air pollution from emissions and the increasing number of traffic jams and accidents, the government began in 2003 to control the number of motorcycles that could be produced. Only one motorcycle could be registered per person, and new registrations were restricted in the Hanoi central district. The registration fee was also raised, and carrying a driver's license became mandatory. On the basis of such regulations, consumer logic dictated that if a person could own only one motorcycle it should be a better motorcycle. Moreover, news reports on Chinese motorcycle accidents and quality defects had also heightened consumer awareness of quality. In such market conditions where the Wave was competitive not only with regard to price but also with regard to the combined needs of the market including quality and design, Honda increased its market share.

Figure 4.4 shows the repositioning of Honda in the previous section's framework. Japanese firms usually reduce costs without reducing quality and performance when they cut prices. However, that alone cannot solve a huge price difference. Honda took the following process for its repositioning: it reviewed performance

## Figure 4.4 Product Repositioning

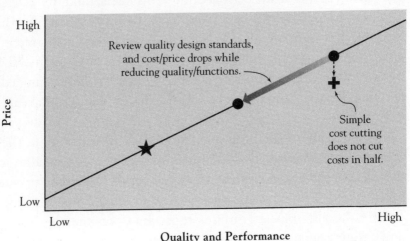

requirements, revised design requirement standards, used low-cost parts, and made a radical price cut while maintaining reasonable quality. The changes made a significant cost reduction possible, and Honda's products became competitive even against products made in China.

## Resource Reallocation and Capability Building for Market Penetration

Another issue is important when considering strategy for emerging markets: resource strategy. The resource conditions for business activities in developed markets and emerging markets are different. Firms entering emerging markets usually have initial resources insufficient for penetrating the middle-class market in developing countries. Local organizational capabilities must be newly developed through learning-by-doing activities in local markets. This aspect is not addressed often in the international business literature, which posits that a firm's technological and managerial resources are mainly developed in its home country and then transferred to host countries.

Almost all firms that have accomplished a transition to a strategy of low price and reasonable quality have also made major changes in resource allocation. This was true not only for the ASEAN strategy of Honda motorcycles but also for the foreign market strategy of Samsung Electronics and Nokia's recovery in the China mobile phone market. A change in market strategy requires a leap in local resource conditions that should be arranged with the company's strategic supports. In other words, whether a low price–positioning strategy like Honda's can be accomplished depends on local resource development.

Let us examine the case of Honda introduced in the previous section. In 2002, Honda launched the Wave in response to the quick growth of Chinese motorcycles in the Vietnamese market. This product launch enabled Honda to recover and transform itself to be competitive even in a market in which volume was important. In the same period, it introduced the Wave 100 in Thailand and the Super Fit in Indonesia. Honda also has low-price motorcycle models that share a similar platform as the Wave. For the Thai market, low-priced models were introduced to regain sales volume after the Asian financial crisis in 1997, whereas in the Indonesian market, there was also an influx of Chinese motorcycles around 2000 as in Vietnam, and Honda started selling low-price models in response. Therefore the Wave is interpreted as one product within a series of Honda's overall ASEAN market strategies. For Honda, these products changed its development and production system in the ASEAN market.

Like automobiles, motorcycles are sensitive to trends. Even within the ASEAN market, Thailand, Indonesia, and Vietnam each prefers different exterior designs. Moreover, regulations like emission controls also differ by country. Thus, depending on the country, the design of parts requires different specifications. Based on market research for each country, local market data are transferred to the Honda motorcycle R&D center in Thailand, and engineers at the center plan and design motorcycles for each country. After model specifications are determined, the design information moves to the production sites in each country, where die making, mass production, and procurement of parts and the assembly of the motorcycles are implemented.[14]

"Reasonable quality" was handled differently from the design stage. In order to guarantee reasonable quality in the motorcycle's drive system, Honda tried to standardize some engines and other core parts among different models and different countries in ASEAN. This can be called a platform strategy. It also located the design and development of these internally standardized parts in Thailand.[15] Data on motorcycle use in each country are gathered in Thailand, and the core drive parts of common platforms for ASEAN are also designed centrally there.[16] The design data are transferred to production sites in each country, where metal forming and mass production of parts are implemented mainly through in-house production.

## Figure 4.5 Honda's Division of Labor in ASEAN Motorcycle Development

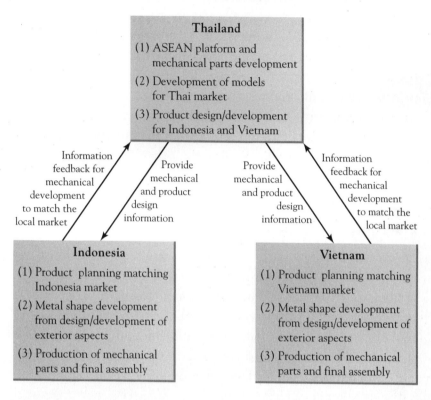

Figure 4.5 shows this division and network of development. In this network, the Thai R&D site develops standardized mechanical parts used in the ASEAN Cub platforms, models for the Thai market, and products for Indonesia and Vietnam. Near the Thai R&D center, Honda also has a motorcycle factory where parts are mass produced, the final assembly of motorcycles is implemented, and some parts are exported to other Asian countries. Vietnam and Indonesia perform market research and data reporting for product planning in each country's market, metal shape development and die-making, and mass production of parts and assembly of motorcycles in each country.

This R&D and production strategy enables mass production of products of reasonable quality. For instance, the local procurement ratio for parts in Vietnam was 53 percent in 2001 but rose to 76 percent in 2003. In Indonesia, in addition to final assembly, upstream processes are being developed in factories: aluminum casting, machining, engine assembly, pressing, welding, and painting. In addition, the number of suppliers has broadened to about 130 with Honda's technological assistance.[17] These numbers are evidence that Honda's cost-reduction activities have achieved reasonable quality.

## Managing High-Volume Production in Emerging Markets

In growing markets with market conditions different from the home country, so-called market experiments avoid the risk of home country bias and are an attempt to obtain on-site information for the development of local business. The same logic could be applied to production as well. The home country's production conditions are somewhat different from those in emerging market countries. So, businesses that are considering establishing full-scale mass production in emerging countries must take into account uncertainties and risks that are unimaginable in home country production. For example, there can be problems with a vast production scale and fluctuations; large-scale labor and organizational management as a prerequisite for labor-intensive production activities; and a failure to meet quality, cost, and delivery requirements because of inadequate local capabilities. These risks are interrelated and tend to increase with scale. When a firm turns to a low-price strategy, it must take these issues into consideration.

A common perspective is that the home country's mother factory should supervise and control local mass production. However, the traditional mother factory system does not always work, for a number of reasons:

- Production in the home country is highly automated, and its systems are different from labor-intensive production in local countries.

- When product designs are localized, problems related to their production should also be solved locally.

- As the scale of local production becomes very large, production risks become much higher.

- Rapid launch of local production is needed, considering the product's life cycle.

- Mother factories lack enough qualified engineers with the requisite knowledge and skills to fix local production problems.

In such cases, it becomes useful to have problem-solving resources near the local production sites for supporting production process development, production launch, and daily operations. Honda Motorcycles' R&D center and factory in Thailand are truly local bases that provide technological support to other Asian factories. These technological and production bases could be called "the second mother factory." Based on product plans and design drawings created in the home countries, the second mother factory develops production processes based on local conditions. It can launch mass production lines, standardize production know-how and transfer it to other developing countries, and support mass production in those other countries. Building organizational capabilities locally is an effective production strategy for adapting to emerging markets.

Companies like Honda and Seagate tend to produce their products internally. However, many firms use outsourced production extensively. Even in these cases, the concept of a second mother factory is still effective. A firm develops production processes and launches production in the home country and also in other countries in Asia, creating know-how on mass production and transferring it to the outsourced firms as a turnkey system.

When an Asian production base is used as the second mother factory, local engineers establish production process and create English-language documentation with this know-how, which allows them to directly communicate with outsourced production sites.

Mitsubishi Chemical's optical media business is an instructive case. Japanese firms once had a large share of the optical media market of CD-ROMs and CD-Rs, but as the technology matured, Taiwanese firms and other late-entry countries boosted their market shares. Around 2000, new products such as recordable DVDs and rewritable DVDs were launched in the market. Facing a forecast that firms lagging in these fields would soon catch up, Mitsubishi Chemical took decisive action. Until this time, it had been developing products and production processes in Japan and moving them into mass production in Japan and Singapore. However, its production bases in Japan and Singapore had limited production capacities, making it difficult to boost its market share. Moreover, the company lacked the capital for investing in large-scale mass production.

Then, along with the introduction of DVD-Rs and DVD-RWs, Mitsubishi Chemical switched to a new model for international production. It now develops technologies and products in Japan and then establishes production, gains production know-how, and standardizes it mainly in Singapore. Singaporean engineers transfer these standardized formulas to contracted firms in India, Taiwan, and other countries.

The Indian and Taiwanese outsourced firms are electronics manufacturing services (EMS) firms with vast production scales and very large capital investments. They are producing Mitsubishi's media with Mitsubishi's technical support. They are also consuming Mitsubishi's core materials and using their equipment in producing the media. Therefore, Mitsubishi realizes profits from multiple sources—license fees for intellectual property, sales of optical media products, and supply of raw materials and equipment to contracted EMSs—at the same time that it substantially reduces the financial risks of high-volume production. As the second mother factory, Singapore is playing a vital role in this turnkey business model.

## Market Evolution Following Low-Priced Products

In the motorcycle industry, up to about the mid-2000s, low-priced models were playing a critical role in Honda's motorcycle business recovery and industry growth in the ASEAN markets. However, in the latter half of the 2000s, companies, including Honda, were facing a relatively different situation. Economic growth in the 2000s had boosted the average income of people living in large cities, and more people could afford better-quality durable goods.

In the case of the motorcycle industry, even though traditional Cubs like the Wave 100 are still popular in ASEAN countries, a new market segment has emerged for motorcycles: scooters.[18] Scooters are easy to drive even for beginners because drivers do not need to shift gears when changing speed. However, scooters are not as powerful as Cubs, so they are not as popular in rural areas, where there are many changes in terrain on dirt roads, making gear shifting necessary. Therefore, customers in the countryside prefer Cubs and those in towns and cities prefer scooters.

In the latter half of the 2000s, purchase of motorcycles has been rapidly changing, especially in urban areas of ASEAN countries. Scooters have become more popular, even though their costs range from 20 to 50 percent above that of most cubs, because incomes have risen in urban areas. But we think other reasons are important too. Most of these new customers are younger, and, more important, half of them are middle-class women. For these customers, the "easy-drive" and "fashionable" values tend to become more important than price. In other words, since many younger customers are entry users of motorcycles, they are not accustomed to driving them and are willing to pay more for functions and technologies that realize their "easy-drive" and "fashionable-drive" values within their budget. Scooters technology can realize it. As a result, motorcycle companies, including Honda, are vigorously introducing new models of scooters into the ASEAN markets.

Due to this recent market change, the ASEAN markets are now divided into two large segments: one segment is the traditional volume market for Cubs, which is common in all ASEAN member countries, including the countryside, and the other is the new market for scooters, which are used mainly in cities and towns. Since there are large populations in both cities and rural areas, there seems to be a strong demand for both products in both areas for the foreseeable future. When the market segments of scooters emerged, local business resources developed and inherited in the period of Cubs, such as strong brands, sales networks, R&D centers, and production facilities, were all applied to the business of scooters. This is upward adaptation to gradual market changes, different from the case of the Wave series. It could be depicted within the scope of Christensen's sustaining technology.

## Conclusion

This chapter has raised important issues for emerging market strategy from the perspectives of marketing and resource strategies. Following the economic crisis, some scholars believed that radical innovation would break the stagnation that industries and economies had been experiencing. But it would be ill advised to lean on revolutionary innovation alone as a means to end this stagnation. In other words, it is not enough to rely solely on technology and innovation as a strategy for competing successfully in emerging markets.

Another important issue for emerging market economies is the danger of thinking that since income levels are low in emerging markets, cutting prices regardless of other considerations makes good sense. Certainly price reduction is important as one of the steps toward developing the market, but price reduction in and of itself is not important. Aiming to reduce prices without trying to understand the market is unlikely to lead to long-term success. In the long-term evolution of local markets, customers gradually learn about products, and their buying behaviors then follow not only their budgets but also their levels of product knowledge. Entrant firms must understand this market dynamic.

On the resource side, firms approaching the middle class of emerging markets will face a discontinuous situation of resources and realize that local resources may be limited. Since the target markets have a certain scale and need newly developed internal and external resources, building organizational capabilities in local contexts is critical for success. If a resource strategy is not systematically implemented, the overall strategy will falter. It is important to understand how to obtain local resources and develop them in the implementation of overall strategy.

While Japanese firms have manufacturing competencies as their foundation, if they recognize that emerging markets will be the next battleground of global competition and the next potential pool of business gains, now is the time for them to rebuild these competencies from the perspectives of a strategy for emerging markets.

# 5

# TRANSFERRING HOME-GROWN MANAGEMENT PRACTICES

## The Case of Toyota in China

### Akira Tanaka, Yue Wang

In less than two decades, China has transformed itself from a country known for its bicycles to the world's largest market of car consumers and the world's largest car producers as well. After replacing Japan as the world's second largest car market in 2006, China soon took the lead as the world's largest auto market, surpassing the United States in 2009. Today, virtually all of the top global automakers have positioned themselves in joint ventures (JV) with domestic Chinese firms to take advantage of this boom. At the same time, a large number of Chinese carmakers are growing rapidly in both size and quality. Yet global carmakers know little about the management practices adopted by their emerging Chinese counterparts. Since China does not allow wholly foreign owned subsidiaries in the automobile industry, the lack of knowledge on indigenous Chinese management practices has impeded global automakers' ability to work well with their Chinese JV partners and gain an important foothold in China's rapidly growing yet highly competitive market. The lack of knowledge on (and confidence in) Chinese management practices has also compelled foreign carmakers to transfer their home-grown practices to local JV operations, but how best to cooperate with local Chinese partners in the transfer of home-grown management practices remains a fundamental challenge to global carmakers.

This chapter aims to provide foreign executives based in China with managerially relevant insights into these issues through a longitudinal case study of the JV between Toyota Motor Company (TMC) and Tianjin Automotive Group (TAG) in China, with a particular focus on how Toyota transferred its supply chain practices to TAG. We compare TAG's parts supply management with the established practices of its JV partner, Toyota, to shed light on Chinese practices. In addition, we look at Toyota's efforts at transferring its parts supply practices to TAG and then analyze the problems Toyota faced during the process and the strategies it adopted while addressing them. Through this case study, we demonstrate that China's macroinstitutional environment provides important insights into the differences between the Chinese and Japanese parts supply practices and the problems Japanese firms faced during the transfer of their supplier management practices to China. We also assess the Toyota way of resolving these difficulties in China's unique institutional environment and offer general advice to multinationals on how to manage the successful transfer of their home-grown management practices to their China operations.

## China's Automobile Industry

China embarked on a market-oriented economic reform in 1978, and from about the early 1980s the automobile industry really started to take off. Before the 1990s, however, its scale remained quite small. By 1990, China produced a mere 0.5 million units of vehicles, while in the same year Japan and the United States produced 13 million and 9.8 million, respectively. Most of China's vehicles were not passenger cars but commercial vehicles (trucks and buses) produced by the hundreds of state-owned automakers all over the country under the direct control of central or local governments.[1]

Since the 1990s, the Chinese automobile industry has grown rapidly, particularly in the passenger car segment, as the Chinese government has encouraged private car consumption. In its 1994 Automotive Industry Policy, the government abolished the restriction on private car purchase and encouraged consolidation in the domestic automobile industry.[2] The policy particularly targeted to support so-called Big Three, Small Three passenger car projects based on foreign technology, which included the three large Sino-foreign JVs of First Automotive Works (FAW)-VW, Dongfeng-Citroen Motor Company, and Shanghai-VW and the three smaller JVs of Beijing Jeep (with Chrysler), Tianjin Daihatsu, and Guangzhou Peugeot.

The Chinese government realized that the domestic automobile industry could not become modernized and competitive without foreign capital, but it was also wary about possible foreign automaker domination in the industry as a result of the liberalization of foreign direct investment (FDI). In order to manage this dilemma, the Chinese government placed regulatory restrictions on foreign capital. For example, foreign equity participation of 50 percent or more was not allowed in finished passenger cars and engine manufacturing. In addition, FDI in automobile distribution and retailing was generally prohibited. Furthermore, to protect the Big Three, Small Three, new passenger car projects were prohibited. These policy restrictions were in place until the early 2000s when China entered the World Trade Organization.

## Toyota's Strategy Toward China

In 1990, Toyota was the world's third largest automaker, with 4.7 million units of production, following General Motors (7.2 million) and Ford Motor (5.6 million). But Toyota's overseas production ratio (only 9.8 percent) was much lower than the other two automakers (41.0 percent and 50.3 percent, respectively). To transform itself into a truly multinational company based on FDI, Toyota started full-scale overseas production in Kentucky in the United States in 1988 and the United Kingdom in 1992, and then it aimed at opening another plant in China.

During the process of globalizing its production bases, one of the biggest issues Toyota faced was whether its competitive advantages in operations generated at home could be transferred overseas. There were several aspects of the "Toyota way" that were considered difficult to transfer, and one of the most widely cited was its supplier management system.

In Japan, Toyota purchases auto parts and components from about 150 tier 1 suppliers directly, and at the same time it operates a huge supplier network consisting of almost ten thousand companies organized hierarchically. Furthermore, Toyota has a vast franchise dealer network. Most of those companies constituting the supply chain are neither Toyota's subsidiaries nor affiliates, but they exchange information frequently and coordinate their operations flexibly according to market conditions through two mechanisms. First, in the short term, the supplier network facilitates the quick allocation of a large quantity of models and product specifications according to daily orders from downstream in the supply chain. Second, in the long term, the network facilitates the faster development of a new model through tighter collaborations among the various functions, including the most efficient and specialized auto parts suppliers along the supply chain. This supplier network serves as an effective substitute for both hierarchical and arm's-length organization for buyer-supplier interface, and it has brought Toyota remarkable competitive advantages. On the one hand, by cooperating closely with independent but dedicated suppliers, Toyota reduced the costs of running and coordinating a large number of in-house suppliers. This kept it lean and flexible.[3] On the other hand, it avoided the costs of negotiating, monitoring, and enforcing supply contracts in the market, which could result in the delay of new model development and slow responses to fluctuations in demand.[4] This kind of informal but institutionalized interfirm relationship made cost sharing between carmakers and suppliers possible and provided endless cost-cutting opportunities.[5] Essentially a large number of legally independent yet organizationally closely affiliated supplier companies are working as a single network under Toyota's leadership in market competition.

Until recently, this Toyota network has been seen as embedded in a long Japan-specific history of domestic competition and hence has been difficult to transfer.[6] But since the 1990s, Toyota has pursued transferring its home-grown parts supply practices to its overseas plants with as few modifications as possible. Although Toyota often needed a certain number of Japanese suppliers to build transplants overseas together with its finished car assembly plants, overall the transfer of Toyota supplier management practices was relatively smooth. Previous studies have shown, for example, that the transfer of Japanese parts supply practices to the United States and the United Kingdom has been generally successful.[7]

China, however, was a different case. In response to the 1994 Automobile Industry Policy announcement, Toyota began serious negotiations in China. Toyota Group visited China in September of that year and made a proposal to the Chinese government for a JV to produce a midsize sedan, the Corona, with Tianjin Automobile Group (TAG), a leading national automaker in China during the 1980s and 1990s. Its main model, the Xiali, was a small car licensed in 1986 by Toyota's affiliate automaker, Daihatsu Motor; it was second by sales units in China's passenger car sector for a number of years. At the height of its popularity, it commanded a little over 20 percent of the market share. (Figure 5.1 shows performance records for the Xiali.) However, for a number of reasons, China rejected Toyota's JV proposal. First, in order to protect the Big Three and Small Three, the Auto Industry Policy clearly specified that no new JVs in finished car manufacturing be approved. Second, TAG was cautious about launching any new model until the annual production of Xiali reached the projected capacity of 150,000. Third, until about the early 2000s the Tianjin Municipal Government had full control over TAG, and it was often said that Toyota had not accepted the Chinese government's offer to establish a JV in the past, and

## Figure 5.1 Sales Performance of Major Car Models in China: Xiali Versus Others

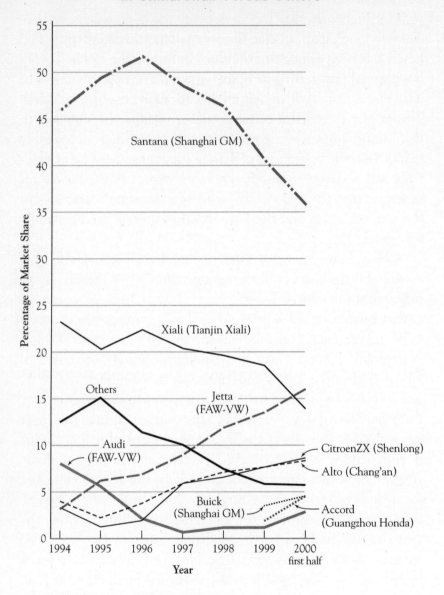

hence, had not won enough trust from the Chinese government and state-owned enterprises (SOEs) administered by the Chinese government. Fourth, at that time, TAG preferred licensing over JVs for passenger car manufacturing. For the time being, Toyota had no choice but to pursue cooperation with TAG in parts manufacturing for TAG's existing model, Xiali, while waiting for a future JV opportunity in finished-car assembly.

For the first step toward local production, Toyota and some of its major suppliers (in short, the Toyota Group, which we use to refer to Toyota and its suppliers involved in Toyota's operations in China) had to join the existing Tianjin Xiali's supply chain in parts and components manufacturing. To appreciate the difficulties Toyota faced, one has to understand how the old supply chain at TAG worked.

According to a TAG brochure describing the company in 2000, the group consisted of nineteen state-owned companies, nine collectively owned companies, twenty-three international JVs, and one holding company administered by the Chinese government, for a total of fifty-two companies with sixty thousand employees under the direct control of the holding company Tianjin Automobile Industry (Group) Corporation, the so-called General Corporation (GC), or *Zong-Gongsi*.

GC, as the core firm, had twelve offices and departments, including a general office, a production planning department, and a department of contractual and equity jv. Its main function was to unify and administer the group across functions in the areas of production planning, materials purchasing, importing and exporting, and personnel.

In addition, at the core level of the business group, there were four other branch companies and business centers with various functions: a sales company, a supply company, a workers' training center, and an import and export company. There were also manufacturers assembling finished cars and tier 1 suppliers producing functional parts and components of automobiles. The main assembler was the Tianjin Xiali Automobile Co. Ltd. (in short,

Tianjin Xiali), which before 1997 was known as the Tianjin Mini-Auto Works.[8] The second biggest assembler was Tianjin Huali Automobile Ltd., which produced the Huali minivan. Assemblers in TAG were either consignment production companies or branch factories. By comparison, in Japan, the automakers assembling finished cars are the core firms; they take responsibility for the maintenance of brand and oversee the company network. However, the core firm in TAG was the holding company, GC.

At TAG, there was almost no difference in function between companies and factories. Most companies in TAG were JV companies with foreign capital, and they used to be factories before entering into JV agreements.[9] To facilitate JV agreements, parts factories, which had been part of the internal organization of TAG, were created. In recent trends, an increasing number of factories are being converted to limited liability companies in which the state has a 100 percent holding. The Tianjin Automobile Industry Sales Co. Ltd. (Sales Company), a subsidiary under the direct control of GC, carried out the sale of TAG's products. The Sales Company organized 35 outlets under its direct management, 206 service centers, and more than 100 dealers (in 1997). Most of the dealers were not exclusive and often sold both Xiali and Santana, the most popular model of passenger car, made by Xiali's main rival, Shanghai VW.

The production plan for Xiali was made on both yearly and monthly projections. At the end of every year, the dealers and the Sales Company's outlets held a meeting during which they made a yearly demand estimate on the basis of the previous year's sales records and the macroprojections for the following year. GC's production planning section then made a yearly production plan on the basis of this demand estimate. This production planning was conducted at the same stage in the planning process as the corresponding production estimate plan conducted by automakers in Japan. Once yearly production estimates had been made, seasonal variations in sales were considered, and the yearly production plan was divided into monthly production plans. In general, there were no seasonal or daily planning adjustments of the kind that were often conducted in the Japanese car industry. While the production planning for Xiali may not be quite the same as the supply chain management seen in Japan, it was still a significant development considering the prevailing management practices in China's planned economy of the previous decades.[10] We might characterize it as "make-to-stock production with market forecasts," different from "make-to-order production" in Japan. However, two unstable factors remained. First, dealers tended to supply inaccurate information with inflated sales figures. Second, the production plan was often amended by "administrative guidance" from the Tianjin Municipal Government. As a result, more often than not, the company ended up with an excessive stock of finished cars.

Let us take a closer look at the case of an engine part as an example. First, a meeting about auto parts orders in Tianjin was held once a year during November and December. At this meeting, the yearly production plan for mass-produced parts and the yearly contract with GC were finalized. The yearly production plan was then broken down into four terms (beginning in January, April, July, and October), taking market trends into account. Then, following a meeting held on the twenty-fifth of each month by managers from the core-level companies, GC's production planning section established the monthly plan. In this way, each assembler and supplier in TAG received a set production level for each product or part from GC.

The new finished car plant for Xiali was built in 1996 at a cost of about 20 billion Chinese yuan (about 2.5 billion U.S. dollars). Maximum production capacity was about 150,000 units per year when two shifts were working. The production method was basically a mass production system for a single car model similar to the Ford system of the early twentieth century. TAG had only a single assembly line in the plant, which carried out lot production for two models of Xiali, a sedan and a hatchback.

That was very different from the standard method in Japan, which is to produce small quantities of many models and designs in the same line. Considering the fact that at that time in China final design options such as body color and accessories were not as varied as in Japan, lot production seemed a reasonable choice for a single model and design. The variety of parts and materials could also be correspondingly limited, and there was no need for fine daily coordination of supply chain as Toyota needed in Japan.

In fact, TAG's degree of synchronization of parts supply was closer to the old Ford system than the Toyota Production System. The Xiali parts and materials supply cycle for major suppliers was as follows. At the end of every month, GC sent the confirmed production order for the following month. In most cases, suppliers produced and delivered their monthly scheduled quota before the end of the month. Depending on parts and materials, the delivery cycle varied from five or six times a day to twice a month. The Japanese *kanban* system, which involves tier 3 suppliers, was not implemented in TAG's parts supply arrangements.

The differences in the cycles for various suppliers were determined by the size of the parts to be delivered, the percentage of local content from tier 2 suppliers, and the lead time for the product. For example, since interior parts are large and bulky and it is undesirable to accumulate large stockpiles on either the supplier's site or at the finished car plant (Tianjin Mini-Auto Works), a daily delivery schedule was given every month. In this case, a relatively high synchronization of deliveries was established.

It has been alleged that the parts stockpiles at the Mini-Auto Works are sufficient for only one or two days. The lower the frequency of delivery is, the greater the stockpiles that suppliers must hold. The level of synchronization in TAG's production activity may be characterized as "$n$-day batch synchronization," meaning synchronization mediated by a fixed amount of intermediate stock.[11]

Whereas in Japan companies have achieved online synchronization based on the *kanban* system, which is equivalent to leveled one-piece flow production, the synchronization of parts delivery at TAG remains at the level of $n$-day batch synchronization. The *kanban* system was not adopted at TAG, where coordination of production was administered centrally by the production planning section of GC. That was not inappropriate in the context of local market conditions at that time, as the Chinese car market demanded mass production of a limited number of models with limited design options. But there were serious weakness in Xiali's supply chain and TAG's interfirm, system, as we will discuss.

How, then, did TAG as a company synchronize the supply of parts and materials? The next section examines the operation of TAG's interfirm system in 1996 and 1997 when JV projects on parts and components with the Toyota Group were beginning.

## Settlement of Payment

The settlement of TAG's parts payment did not correspond to each transaction. Instead, income from finished car sales was distributed among the group. The income from finished car sales at directly managed stores and at dealers was first sent to TAG's Sales Company. On the last Wednesday of each month, a payment distribution meeting was held between the Sales Company's accounting center and core-level companies, including finished car plants and several tier 1 suppliers, and payments to each company were decided. Distribution was basically made to each core-level company according to the cost of sold parts. Then payment was made from the core-level companies to each supplier to cover their costs of producing parts and components.

Although monthly settlement is also a feature commonly observed in Japan, at TAG, the payment did not necessarily correspond to the quantity of parts supplied. If there was a lag between business results and the estimation of demand or the production plan, stocks of finished cars increased accordingly. If the costs of finished cars were not recovered, payment was not made for parts and component costs. Hence the relationship between creditors and debtors resulted in the so-called triangle debts, which expanded in an upstream chain reaction.[12]

## Renewal Negotiations for Parts Prices

In Japan, with price reductions as the intended outcome, renewal negotiations on parts unit prices are customarily held every six months. The reduction in unit price is usually less than any cost reduction realized by suppliers' improvements in production. That is, in order to give suppliers an incentive to reduce costs, the savings from the cost reduction are distributed prudently between automaker and suppliers. If the price cut is too large, suppliers will not have the capacity to invest in further rationalization. And if it is too small, they will have less incentive to invest in rationalization.[13]

In the case of TAG, GC held the right to set the parts prices and conducted negotiations for price changes with suppliers at the end of every year. According to reports from Sino-Japanese JV parts suppliers (hereafter, we refer to them as Japanese suppliers), GC's demand for price cuts at these negotiations completely siphoned off the fruits of any cost reduction. In some cases, the prices set for parts were lower than the production costs. Consequently, negotiations on parts costs with several Japanese suppliers were extended for prolonged periods during which parts had been supplied in the absence of any fixed prices.

## Exclusiveness in Parts Transactions

In the Toyota Group in Japan, suppliers whose intragroup (*keiretsu*) sales ratio was less than 70 percent increased to more than one-third by the mid-1980s. More recently, the *keiretsu* sales ratio has declined even further. This diversification of customer base reflects the high degree of competitiveness among companies within the group and is indicative of the strength, rather than the weakness, of the group.

In contrast, there was a high degree of exclusiveness in parts transactions in TAG. Each supplier sold almost 100 percent within TAG, demonstrating an extremely high level of exclusiveness. This is due in part to the historical fact that most suppliers in the group are spin-offs from Tianjin Auto's branch factories and in part to Tianjin Municipal Government policies known as "the priority of dealing within the group" (*xian nei, hou wai*) and "the priority of dealing within the city" (*xian benshi, hou waibu*).

Among these suppliers, one decided on a policy of actively seeking to increase its sales outside the group. It began supplying parts to Chang'an-Suzuki Auto Co., which produced the Alto, a rival to the Xiali in the small car segment. Its target was to reduce sales within the group from 93 percent in 1997 to 70 or 80 percent in 1998. Gradually other Japanese suppliers also adopted the strategy of customer diversification to reduce the reliance on within-group sales.

## The Interfirm System in TAG

So far we have examined four aspects of buyer-supplier relationships in TAG, and in all four, there is a significant gap between practices adopted by TAG versus those of the Toyota Group.

First, whereas in Japan, payment for parts is settled on monthly terms according to the quantity supplied, in TAG, gross income from finished car sales was distributed roughly among the group. Furthermore, as the Sales Company's unsold finished car accumulated, "triangle debts" grew among the parts suppliers. Second, in parts pricing, Japanese practices allow suppliers to benefit from cuts in production costs so that they have an incentive for continuous improvement. In TAG, negotiation of parts prices was frequently fierce and opportunistic. Third, in Japan, Toyota encourages its suppliers to deal with customers outside the Toyota Group, and diversifying the customer base is widely practiced. In TAG, dealings within the group remained exclusive.

Because of GC's lack of recognition that suppliers are independent profit centers, parts supply practices were ineffective. Historically, parts suppliers in TAG evolved from Tianjin Auto's branch factories, which in reality remained part of TAG's internal organization. As the virtual headquarters of a single entity, GC tended to redistribute the profits from well-managed units to poorly performing units, all of which gain only a nominal legal status as separate companies from GC under the Chinese government's so-called business group policy. Consequently it was rather difficult for Chinese managers to distinguish internal organizations from external organizations, and they had a strong sense of integration. Even when auto parts were delivered to the Tianjin Mini-Auto Works, the party responsible for procurement was not the Mini-Auto Works but GC. From such an integrated viewpoint, the business relationship between assemblers and suppliers was naturally considered as business within the group instead of between truly independent companies, or even simply as a form of profit (re)distribution.

Although Japanese suppliers understood the Chinese reality and TAG's historical background, they could not accept such practices in managing an interfirm system and thus attempted to minimize the negative impact of such practices on their businesses through the introduction of home-grown Japanese supply management practices into their JVs with TAG.

## The Transfer of Supplier Management in TAG: Phase I (1990s)

The Toyota Group's effort to transfer management practices and systems to its JV partner met with limited success.

## Piecemeal Transfer Within Parts and Components JVs

In the JVs between TAG's supplier and Toyota's suppliers, TAG usually provided land use rights, factory building, machine facilities, and labor instead of cash.[14] Then according to their equity share in the investment, Chinese and Japanese managers would share the positions of chairman and president in the JV company; in many cases, a Chinese national would assume the position of president and a Japanese national (located in China) the vice president, and another Japanese national would assume the position of chairman (based in Japan). However, this arrangement made it difficult for Japanese managers to carry out any improvements without the Chinese president's agreement. In general, the Chinese side was mostly interested in technology transfer from the Toyota Group, especially of advanced machinery and equipment. However, the Toyota Group wanted to transfer its management practices as much as its technologies.

TAG and the Toyota Group established ten JV companies in 1995, four in 1996, and two in 1997, and they were in operation by 1998. Among them, the Toyota Group invested in only four companies for manufacturing parts and material, including Tianjin Toyota Motor Engine Co., whose plant was newly built to produce the 8A engine for new model of Xiali.

In 1995, Toyota also established the Toyota Motor Technical Center (China) to promote improvements for the Xiali supply chain in TAG. The Technical Center, incorporated in 1998, also conducts and coordinates improvement activities for a number of Japanese suppliers in China. Each JV company had experienced numerous problems in China arising from differences in management practices and systems, Chinese companies' inertia to adhere to their established practices, and innate national characteristics. In order to systematically address these problems, a society for Japanese managers, the Tianjin Kyoho Society, was formed in 1998, with the Toyota Technical Center playing a leading role.[15] The society engaged in discussing and seeking solutions to these problems.

At its inauguration, seven companies, comprising JV subsidiaries of Araco, Aisan, Denso, Toyoda Gosei, Asmo, the branch of Toyota Tsusho Corporation, and Toyota Technical Center, participated. By October 1997 twelve local subsidiaries and two branches were participating. In April 2004, its membership expanded to include Japanese managers and technicians working for twenty-one local subsidiaries and three branches.

The first priority for the Tianjin Kyoho Society was to conduct research into various management issues facing companies involved in the JVs. Once every two months (in the odd-numbered months), Japanese management from member companies and other Japanese people in decision-making positions met to discuss such themes as wage structure, production plans, price renewal, and debt collection. Information from each company was exchanged, and opinions and ideas were collated. This feedback was passed on to TAG's GC through the Toyota Technical Center. As a result of these activities, in January 1998, initial informal discussions among the Tianjin Kyoho Society, TAG's GC, and the Tianjin Municipal Government began.

A second priority for the Tianjin Kyoho Society was self-improvement activities, called *Jishu Ken*, held in Japan. The Toyota Technical Center conducted these activities during even-numbered months. Senior management staff and factory managers (both Japanese and Chinese) came together, and member companies made presentations about improvements in the workplace and on-the-job training. Currently the Technical Center also invites senior management staff from Chinese group companies such as GC. Particular attention in each company was given to the introduction of the 5S (a series of virtues for factory management), security measures, "enhancing the quality of production," and the introduction of the performance factor in the wage system.[16]

A secondary but still significant aim of the Tianjin Kyoho Society was to "pave the way for Toyota to make inroads into Tianjin." For Toyota, with its strong ambitions to open a finished car plant in Tianjin, the fact that experienced Japanese suppliers were steadily introducing the Toyota Production System and adapting it to Chinese conditions through a proper exchange of information was excellent preparation for a smooth entrance into local production.

## Problems in Phase I

Change, however, was extremely slow. Three factors hindered efforts for improvement: the institutional barriers and local policies for state-owned enterprises, including the strict regulation of fifty-fifty JVs; problems in the distribution channels of finished cars; and problems in parts supply management practices in TAG.

First, although efforts for improvement showed some gains in efficiency, local government continued to block moves to cut excessive labor. Japanese suppliers had inherited much overemployment from Chinese JV counterparts, and because they were not allowed to fire anyone, they had to increase the scale of their business to absorb the excess capacity of these laborers.

Second, TAG had difficulties increasing the sale of its finished cars because of structural problems in the distribution channel. In China, "shipment" of a finished car did not mean "sales." Dealers did not have to pay cash on delivery, and in reality, payment by dealers to the Sales Company was made on a "when you have it" basis. In addition, many older dealers were not dedicated to TAG but were selling multiple brands of car models, including those made by TAG's rivals. With this system, dealers tended to place excessive orders so that they could hold as much stock as possible, and they tended not to devote their resources and efforts to selling a particular make of finished car. This was another serious weakness in Xiali's supply chain.

Third, TAG could hardly increase production volume on its own. GC decided how much the Tianjin Mini-Auto Works should order; suppliers had no voice in the decision-making process. Furthermore, suppliers were restricted from dealings outside the TAG group. In addition, GC tended to demand a greater return from group companies with better performance, which severely distorted the incentive structure along TAG's supply chain. To make matters worse, the Tianjin Municipal Government often gave "administrative guidance" to increase production, and the production plan developed by GC's production planning section could be suddenly modified. Such administrative interference further disturbed the leveling of production and created an obstacle to the introduction of the *kanban* system.

For these reasons, Toyota Group's attempts to transfer its supplier management practices to China were limited to within each JV company for the first several years. This problem was not serious until 1999 because TAG's main model, Xiali, enjoyed robust sales. Change would remain slow as long as Xiali sales figures were in good shape.

## The Transfer of Supplier Management in TAG: Phase II (2000s)

As market competition in China intensified, slumps in Xiali sales encouraged deeper cooperation with Toyota.

### Changes in Market Conditions

From 1999 to 2000, market conditions changed dramatically and became unfavorable for TAG. First, the market did not expand according to the Central Government's estimate, and yet market competition intensified. A five-year plan (the ninth of its kind), drawn up in 1996, anticipated car sales of 1.4 million in 2000, and on the basis of this estimate, new manufacturers with foreign capital and refurbished facilities were allowed access to the market one after another, and new models and designs continually appeared. However, car sales in 1999 remained at 570,000, and for the first half of 2000, only 270,000 units were sold.[17] A price war affecting mainly older models broke out when Xiali cut its price in January 2000, and it continued to intensify as time passed. Moreover, demand, driven mainly by wealthy buyers from the private sector, increased; in 1999, private buyers accounted for more than half the market. High-end cars such as Audi, Buick, and Honda Accord and small cars such as VW Jetta, Citroen ZX, and Suzuki Alto attracted these private buyers, boosting sales significantly. Santana and Xiali, with their ten-year-old models, drastically lost ground with this daunting new competition. Finally, registration regulations based on displacement and exhaust emissions, which were introduced beginning in 1997 in big cities such as Beijing and Shanghai, further created an unfavorable climate for Xiali sales. Consequently, there was an obvious slump in Xiali sales. In the latter half of 1999, Xiali's monthly sales ranking dropped to third in the small car sector, and its market share fell at an increasing rate. This sales slump clearly highlighted latent weaknesses in the supply chain management. Sales information showing the true state of the market was not appropriately relayed back to the production plan, and distribution stock, which did not show up in the statistics, was accumulated.

## Restructuring in Tianjin Xiali

This slump in Xiali sales, which normally accounted for two-thirds of TAG's sales volume, created a management crisis. TAG, moreover, did not have the technology to develop a new product on its own account. GC, in desperation, decided to take cooperation with Toyota a step further and began joint production of a new model. This landmark decision was made at the Tianjin Xiali Automobile Co. Ltd. general shareholders meeting in November 1999. At the same time, the Chinese government and

GC undertook a restructuring of the company. First, the Chinese government began to deregulate state-owned enterprise regulations to challenge market competition better. In 2000 the Chinese government reduced the retirement age for all employees by five years. Second, to reform the distribution channel, GC set up a new subsidiary sales company, the Tianjin Xiali Sales Co. Ltd., which sold Xiali exclusively, and it began preparing the ground for an exclusive dealers' network. Third, for TAG suppliers, dealings outside the group were liberalized in 1998 and 1999. In turn, in January 2000, it was announced that after 2001, dealings with companies without ISO 9000 recognition would be terminated. Given the changes in both the external and internal environments, what happened then to TAG's interfirm system involving Japanese suppliers?

First, the settlement of payments for parts had not been fundamentally improved. The increased stockpiling of finished cars led directly to a lack of cash flow in the Sales Company, which in turn led to an increase in triangle debts among suppliers. This became a sticking point at joint negotiations with Toyota, and GC had no choice but to promise to cancel the trade debts of suppliers affiliated with Toyota. Second, concerning the setting of unit prices for parts, price renewal negotiations are now held every six months rather than once a year, a reflection of the crisis in management. The demands for price cuts from GC have become even stronger. Third, suppliers' exclusive sales relationships within the group are generally lessening. This trend was triggered by Xiali's sales slump, but we can expect it to continue as long as the market remains competitive.

## The New Finished Car JV

Negotiations between Toyota and GC on a new project were concluded with the following outcomes. First, with new licensing, full cooperation, and technical support from Toyota, Tianjin Xiali started producing two models of a small car, Platz and Vitz, under the Xiali brand name. Second, a new joint venture company, the Tianjin Toyota Motor Corporation, was established with Toyota and Tianjin Xiali Automobile contributing equally and plans to begin production of a newly developed model of small car (later renamed Vios) in 2002. Despite the fact that it is a fifty-fifty JV, the Japanese side was allowed a stronger presence in the top management team of Tianjin Toyota, and the car has been sold under the Toyota brand name as Toyota Vios.

Plans for these new projects were made on the shared interests of Toyota, which had been aiming to produce cars in Tianjin for many years, and TAG, which was facing the serious challenge of restructuring its management. With this JV agreement, Toyota finally got the whole supply chain, from auto parts to finished car and dealer network, under its control. TAG in the 2000s thus had two supply chains for passenger cars, Xiali's and Toyota's, and they shared JV suppliers, but Toyota's supply chain is not under TAG's GC control.

For its dealer channel, Toyota first selected one hundred candidate shops that met its dealer standards, and then the Chinese side selected dealers from among them. The standard adopted here was Toyota's common worldwide standard, and the sales customs peculiar to China were abolished. As for suppliers, many companies affiliated with Toyota stepped forward. Certainly the conditions were right for establishing a supply chain unique to Tianjin Toyota.

In August 2002, China FAW Group Corporation, the national flagship automaker in China, amalgamated with TAG and Sichuan Automobile Group and entered into a strategic cooperation agreement with Toyota.[18] As a result, Toyota's sole joint partner in its existing Chinese business became the FAW Group. Tianjin Toyota was renamed Tianjin FAW Toyota Motor Co., Ltd. in October 2002. This change in partners allows Toyota to operate in China more freely. First, FAW Group had already set up JV projects for passenger cars with Volkswagen Group and

Mazda; it tends to give foreign partners a free hand in the passenger car business, for which it has less knowledge. Second, the central government has prohibited foreign JVs from distributing finished cars. But after joining the World Trade Organization, China's central government made an exception for the Big Three (including FAW) to allow them to set up additional JVs in finished car manufacturing. In 2003, then, FAW Toyota Motor Sales Co., Ltd. opened in Beijing to manage the distribution of Toyota-brand cars. The Japanese-style interfirm system advanced dramatically within TAG as Tianjin Toyota was empowered to coordinate market research, estimation and supply of parts, and production and sales across the production chain.

## Conclusion

This chapter provides a historical account of Toyota's entry into China with a focus on its efforts to transfer Japanese supplier management practices to its JV partner, Tianjin Automobile Group. At the beginning, Toyota sought to develop its China business in the same way as in the United States, but it was problematic at best due to the unique institutional conditions in China during the 1990s. Normally, when manufacturing companies try to develop foreign businesses, they start with downstream operations. That was not the case for Toyota's beginning of operations in China. Toyota was required to start with only parts and components manufacturing with no finished cars or dealer network due to the Chinese regulatory regime. This was extremely outside the bounds of the Toyota way of overseas expansion. Unfortunately, Toyota has had to spend a great deal of time and money in the finished car market since it entered much later than rivals such as Shanghai GM and Guangzhou Honda.

Toyota was aiming for a 15 percent share of the Chinese market by 2010, but it still has a way to go for realizing this goal. Toyota selected the small car Vios to be the first model it manufactured in China and promoted it to become a strategic model throughout Asia. Toyota believed its competitiveness in high quality and low price derived from efficient intra- and interfirm collaboration and coordination along the supply chain. But that viewpoint may be shaky because Toyota's interfirm system might prove to be too costly to offer small cars for the Asian middle class in direct competition with a large number of low-end models never seen in developed countries.

In China, Toyota is still a long way from recovering its competitiveness from the first misstep in Tianjin. During the 1990s, China emerged through the transition from planned economy to market economy. But there were severe institutional barriers for global automakers. Toyota at that time aimed to establish the local manufacturing transplant in Tianjin as the first step of its local production in China. But there were strict capital restriction, and the local government would not approve Toyota's FDI in final assembly, so Toyota had to support local state-owned automaker TAG mainly in auto parts manufacturing in order to gain entry to the country. This required adopting an internationalization process totally different from its usual overseas expansion strategy, starting with manufacturing auto parts and then followed by final assembly and local distribution.

Most noteworthy from this case is Toyota's experience in transferring its home-grown management practices known as the Toyota Production System to its JV partner, TAG. The case reveals several key insights for executives and managers responsible for transferring management know-how such as the Toyota Production System into China. First, the system works well as an integrated system for establishing supply chain from parts manufacturing to finished car distribution, which requires the complete control over the production chain in China. Any piecemeal transfer only in parts operations will not work well enough, as we showed with Toyota in its cooperation with TAG's suppliers in the 1990s. Second, companies that are not facing direct pressures of market competition will not seriously accept foreign management know-how, especially in emerging or transition economies such as China. It is crucial for foreign companies considering transferring their home-grown management practices to emerging market firms to identify whether their local partner is subject to market competition. In fact, our research shows that the difference in ownership structure (for example, between state-owned enterprises and private companies) does not really matter. As long as the local partner is subject to market competition, it is likely it will have incentives to adopt advanced foreign management practices and hence smooth the knowledge transfer process.

# Part Three

# ACQUISITION-DRIVEN GLOBALIZATION FROM EMERGING ASIA

# 6

# DUBIOUS VALUE OF INTERNATIONAL ACQUISITIONS BY EMERGING ECONOMY FIRMS

## The Case of Indian Firms

### Aneel Karnani

Companies originating from emerging economies have been increasingly pursuing international acquisitions. This is to be expected and has been predicted for a long time. Companies need certain ownership-specific advantages to compete successfully outside their home markets. Such advantages are likely to increase as emerging economies reach higher levels of development. This internationalization trend by firms has been driven by a number of factors—for example, liberalization of their domestic economies, globalization of their industries, intensity of competition, managerial capabilities, and access to capital markets. The share of emerging economies in global cross-border acquisitions rose from 4 percent in 1987 to 13 percent in 2005 to 20 percent in 2008.[1] Furthermore, over the past decade, the scale of these foreign acquisitions has increased significantly: Tata Steel from India acquired Corus Steel for $13 billion, Hindalco Industries purchased Novelis for $5.7 billion, Chinese oil company CNPC acquired PetroKazakhastan for $4.2 billion, Lenovo Group bought IBM's personal computer business for $1.8 billion, Mexican building materials company CEMEX acquired the British RMC Group for $5.8 billion and the Australian

I thank Harsh Chheda for excellent research assistance with this chapter.

Rinker Group for $14.2 billion, and the Brazilian mining company Vale acquired Inco for $18.9 billion.

These megadeals involving acquisitions by emerging economy firms have attracted much attention from the business press. In developed countries, some welcome this as a positive trend: a new source of capital and knowledge; this is globalization at its best and benefits everybody. Others regard these acquisitions as threatening: as the world becomes flat, new competition is coming from unexpected places. Some have even called for protectionist intervention. Not surprisingly, in the emerging economies, the business press has been unequivocally positive, even euphoric, about these foreign acquisitions. There is much talk about emerging giants and new powerhouses. Some see this as the revenge of former colonies against the imperialist powers. The Indian newspaper *Economic Times* exclaimed, "Corus, the erstwhile British Steel and one of the icons of Her Majesty's Empire will now fly the [Indian] Tricolour."[2] But what often is underemphasized or assumed away in this discussion by the popular press is to what extent the acquiring firms create value for their shareholders. This issue might be less critical if the acquisition is carried out by a state-owned enterprise or a sovereign wealth fund pursuing a national interest. But many of the acquiring firms are private, publicly listed firms that have a fiduciary responsibility to their shareholders. This chapter addresses whether such publicly listed companies from emerging economies create shareholder value through foreign acquisitions, and, in particular, through large acquisitions.

The popular business press usually views foreign acquisitions by emerging economy firms very positively, whereas stock markets have often reacted negatively to the acquisitions. Management always claims that the acquisition is in the long-term strategic interests of the firm. This chapter attempts to shed light on these conflicting positions: short term versus long term and financial versus strategic logic. A story will illustrate the tensions.

On January 31, 2007, Tata Steel increased its offer price to acquire Corus Steel to 608 pence a share, topping the 603 pence offer from its rival bidder, the Brazilian company CSN, thus clinching the deal. The managing director of Tata Steel, B. Muthuraman, cast his firm's victory in broad light as a milestone for Indian business and the country's economy. This upbeat mood was echoed by India's finance minister, Palaniappan Chidambaram, who said the successful bid reflected the newly found confidence of Indian industry.[3] But the shareholders of Tata Steel were not nearly so enthused and penalized the stock by 11 percent the next day. Ratan Tata, the chairman of the Tata Group, responded, "Quite frankly I do feel [the stock market] is taking a short-term and harsh view. In the future somebody will look back and say we did the right thing." Analysts argued that Tata was overpaying for the acquisition, citing, for example, that the price was nine times Corus's earnings before interest, taxes, depreciation, and amortization (EBITDA), which that dwarfed the six times that Mittal Steel recently paid to acquire Arcelor. Muthuraman accepted that the deal "may look expensive" but was in fact in the strategic interests of both companies, allowing Tata Steel access to Corus's markets and Corus the access to cheap raw materials and lowered costs of steelmaking.

I outline the conceptual arguments for and against international acquisitions, especially by emerging economy firms. I then empirically examine the stock market performance of all large foreign acquisitions by Indian companies from 2000 to 2009. I supplement this small sample study by examining in depth the three largest acquisitions using a case study approach and conclude that the foreign acquisitions from India have not created shareholder value. The causes of this underperformance are too little integration, agency problems, and easy capital. Finally, I use a case study to illustrate a successful approach to foreign acquisitions, which led to significant synergies, reasonable price, and deep integration.

## Stock Market Returns

Acquisitions create value due to synergy between the acquiring and target firms. However, most of this value created is captured by the target firms. Much research has confirmed that acquiring firms on the average do not gain value; somewhere between half to three-fourths of acquiring firms actually lose shareholder value.[4] Given this well-accepted result, other explanations are needed for why so many acquisitions take place. There might be an agency problem: managers do acquisitions to maximize their own utility at the expense of the shareholders. Another possibility is that hubristic managers overestimate their competence with respect to identifying and exploiting synergies.[5]

The argument for synergies in the case of cross-border acquisitions is stronger than in the case of domestic acquisitions because of greater market frictions. Firms might extract higher profits from foreign direct investment by exploiting host country market imperfections. But there are also increased challenges with postacquisition integration stemming from cultural and institutional barriers. A survey-based study conducted by the consulting firm KPMG concluded that 83 percent of seven hundred cross-border deals from 1996 to 1998 had not delivered shareholder value. But, interestingly, in the same survey, 82 percent of the respondents believed that the deal they had been involved in had been a success.[6]

International acquisitions by firms from developed countries are often motivated by a desire to exploit some firm-specific specialized resource. In contrast, international acquisitions by emerging economy firms might be motivated more by the potential to acquire specialized strategic resources. There are inherent problems in transacting intangible resources and capabilities through market mechanisms. Foreign acquisitions might be the best way for emerging economy firms to gain these strategic capabilities quickly. This reverse flow of specialized resources and capabilities from the target to the emerging economy acquirer is often mentioned in both the academic literature and the popular press as the major benefit of such acquisitions. The driving logic for these acquisitions is to exploit or acquire specialized firm-specific resources that result in competitive advantage and higher profitability.

There has been little empirical research on international acquisitions by emerging economy firms. However, the popular business press is very positive on foreign acquisitions by emerging economy firms. A good example of this genre is the recent book, *India's Global Powerhouses: How They Are Taking On the World*, which concludes that Indian companies "have become self-assured and savvy investors, financing large deals and paying global prices."[7] The empirical evidence I present in this chapter does not support such positive assertions.

My research shows that the number of large foreign acquisitions by Indian firms exhibiting positive and negative stock market performance is about equal (see Tables 6.1 and 6.2).[8] These results demonstrate that large foreign acquisitions by Indian firms have not created shareholder value, contrary to the view often presented in the popular business press.

## Financing Acquisitions

"Unlike most international M&A transactions that typically feature stock swaps in the financing arithmetic, Indian acquirers have for the most part paid cash for their targets, helped by a combination of internal resources and borrowings."[9] This is even truer for the large foreign acquisitions in my sample. All seventeen foreign acquisitions in the sample were paid for with cash; of the four domestic acquisitions, only two were paid with cash. The cash acquisitions involved an increase in debt leverage and thus increased the risk in the acquisitions. Easy access to inexpensive debt capital during the boom years 2006 to 2008 might also have contributed to a preference for cash acquisitions. Although this could not have been anticipated at the time of

**Table 6.1 Large Acquisitions by Indian Firms, 2000–2009**

| Acquiring Firm | Target Firm | Target Country | Industry | Announcement Date | Completion Date | Acquisition Value ($ million) |
|---|---|---|---|---|---|---|
| Tata Steel Ltd. | Corus Group Plc. | Great Britain | Iron and steel | October 17, 2006 | April 5, 2007 | 13,454.7 |
| Hindalco Industries Ltd. | Novelis Inc. | United States | Aluminum | February 11, 2007 | May 18, 2007 | 5,706.1 |
| Oil & Natural Gas Corp Ltd. | Imperial Energy Corp Plc. | Great Britain | Oil and gas | August 26, 2008 | February 1, 2009 | 2,607.2 |
| Tata Motors Ltd. | Jaguar Land Rover Operations | Great Britain/ United States | Automotive | March 26, 2008 | June 2, 2008 | 2,300.0 |
| Reliance Industries Ltd. | Indian Petrochemicals Corp. | India | Petrochemicals | March 10, 2007 | February 22, 2008 | 2,117.1 |
| HDFC Bank Ltd. | Centurion Bank of Punjab Ltd. | India | Banking | February 23, 2008 | July 16, 2008 | 1,652.6 |
| Tata Power Co. Ltd. | Kaltrim Prima Coal & Arutmin | Indonesia | Electricity/coal mines | March 31, 2007 | June 27, 2007 | 1,300.0 |
| United Spirits Ltd. | Whyte & Mackay | Great Britain | Beverages | May 16, 2007 | May 16, 2007 | 1,176.6 |
| GMR Infrastructure Ltd. | Intergen NV | Netherlands | Engineering and construction | June 24, 2008 | October 13, 2008 | 1,100.0 |
| Suzlon Energy | Repower Systems AG | Germany | Electrical equipment | February 9, 2007 | May 25, 2007 | 1,008.6 |

| Acquirer | Target | Country | Industry | Date | Date | Value (million) |
|---|---|---|---|---|---|---|
| Tata Chemicals Ltd. | General Chemical Industrial Products | United States | Chemicals | January 31, 2008 | March 27, 2008 | 1,005.0 |
| Oil & Natural Gas Corp Ltd. | Greater Nile Oil Project | Canada/Sudan | Oil and gas | October 30, 2002 | March 12, 2003 | 766.1 |
| Tata Group & Tata Tea | Energy Brands Inc. | United States | Beverages | August 23, 2006 | May 25, 2007 | 677.0 |
| Aban Offshore Ltd. | Sinvest ASA | Norway | Oil field services | January 9, 2007 | April 2, 2007 | 671.4 |
| HCL Technologies Ltd. | Axon Group Plc. | Great Britain | Software | September 26, 2008 | December 16, 2008 | 608.3 |
| Rain Calcining Ltd. | CII Carbon Llc. | United States | Chemicals | June 3, 2007 | August 20, 2007 | 595.0 |
| Dr. Reddy's Laboratories | Betapharm Arzneimittel Gmbh | Germany | Pharmaceuticals | February 16, 2006 | March 4, 2006 | 570.3 |
| Wipro Ltd. | Infocrossing Inc. | United States | Information tech. | August 6, 2007 | September 21, 2007 | 547.9 |
| Suzlon Energy Ltd. | Eve Holding NV–Allianz SE | Belgium | Electrical equipment | March 17, 2006 | May 10, 2006 | 525.8 |
| Tata Consultancy System Ltd. | Citigroup Global Services Ltd. | India | Information tech. | October 8, 2008 | December 5, 2008 | 512.0 |
| Idea Cellular Ltd. | Spice Communications Ltd. | India | Telecommunications | June 25, 2008 | July 7, 2008 | 509.2 |

*Note:* All acquisitions listed in this table are above $500 million.

**Table 6.2 Stock Market Returns from the Day Before Acquisition Announcement to One Year After**

| Acquiring Firm | Target Country | Relative returns |
|---|---|---|
| Aban Offshore Ltd. | Norway | 144.0% |
| Tata Power Co Ltd. | Indonesia | 110.4 |
| United Spirits Ltd. | Great Britain | 67.6 |
| Rain Calcining Ltd. | United States | 67.0 |
| Reliance Industries Ltd. | India | 48.8 |
| GMR Infrastructure Ltd. | Netherlands | 42.5 |
| HCL Technologies Ltd. | Great Britain | 26.8 |
| Tata Steel Ltd. | Great Britain | 25.2 |
| HDFC Bank Ltd. | India | 7.2 |
| Oil & Natural Gas Corp Ltd. | Great Britain | 6.8 |
| Suzlon Energy | Germany | 4.0 |
| Wipro Ltd. | United States | −3.1 |
| Tata Chemicals Ltd. | United States | −4.8 |
| Oil & Natural Gas Corp Ltd. | Canada/Sudan | −9.4 |
| Dr. Reddy's Laboratories | Germany | −16.5 |
| Idea Cellular Ltd. | India | −21.2 |
| Hindalco Industries Ltd. | United States | −26.1 |
| Tata Motors Ltd. | Great Britain/ United States | −36.3 |
| Suzlon Energy Ltd. | Belgium | −39.5 |
| Tata Group & Tata Tea | United States | −43.2 |
| Tata Consultancy System Ltd. | India | −44.0 |

the acquisitions, the increased leverage often turned out to be a problem during the financial crisis and credit squeeze. For example, Tata Motors had problems in 2009 as it sought to refinance the bridge loans it had incurred to acquire Jaguar Land Rover.

As a general proposition, target firms prefer stock swaps and receive equity when they are confident that the assets they are selling will create value for the buying firm. It is not a positive signal that all Indian foreign acquisitions were done for cash. One reason for the cash transactions could be that many Indian firms are owned or controlled by promoter shareholders, who also comprise the management. Foreign sellers are often hesitant to invest through stock swaps in firms they perceive may not always be run "professionally," according to some private fund insiders.[10]

Another explanation for the cash transactions could be that Indian promoters are wary of stock swaps because they might not want to dilute their equity share in the company. In general, acquiring firms prefer cash transactions if they believe their stocks are undervalued. With the benefit of hindsight, it is difficult to argue that the stocks of the Indian acquiring firms were systematically undervalued during the two and half years leading up to the financial crisis. It is true, however, that the Indian stock market has recovered dramatically since March 2009.

It is also notable that all the acquisitions in my sample were friendly deals. This by itself does not imply that the Indian acquirers overpaid for the acquisitions. It is, however, true that a generous price will tend to make the deal friendlier. Another reason for friendly deals is that the Indian acquirers have a strong preference to retain the current management of the target firms.[11]

## Case Studies

To understand what factors led to value creation or destruction, I next examine the three largest foreign acquisitions in greater depth: Tata Steel-Corus, Hindalco-Novelis, and Tata Motors-Jaguar and Land Rover.[12] These three acquisitions have garnered much public attention; it is not coincidental that Kumar, Mohapatra, and Chandrasekhar mention these three acquisitions in the introductory chapter of their book on India's emerging powerhouses.[13]

## Tata Steel and Corus

Tata Steel belongs to the Tata Group, the largest business group in India, with a presence in a wide variety of industries ranging from information technology to chemicals to hotels. After the initial announcement in October 2006, Tata Steel and the Brazilian firm CSN engaged in a bidding war to acquire Corus Steel, an Anglo-Dutch company previously known as British Steel. The stock market did not move much in reaction to the initial announcement. On January 31, 2007, Tata Steel increased the offer price and clinched the acquisition. Tata Steel's stock price immediately plunged by 11 percent. The top management of Tata Steel responded by saying that the stock market reaction was shortsighted and that the acquisition would create shareholder value in the long term. The stock price, which was 459 rupees the day before the increased offer, quickly recovered to 471 rupees on April 16. In apparent vindication of top management's position, the stock price zoomed up to 935 rupees on January 2, 2008, far exceeding the gains in the Sensex index.

Managing director Muthuraman said that Corus brought to Tata Steel a capacity of 19 million tons per year at a cost of about $710 per ton, which is little more than half the cost of greenfield capacity of $1,200 to $1,300 per ton. It gave Tata Steel access to the developed and mature markets in Europe, where product quality and service are important. Corus also brought high R&D capability. Muthuraman forecast up to $350 million in savings after about three years from synergies in procuring materials, marketing, and shared services. Steel prices would rise, driven by demand from explosive growth in the biggest markets in the developing world: India and China. Finally, Muthuraman believed there was tremendous cultural fit between Tata Steel and Corus. For the deal to work, Tata had to improve Corus's efficiency, whose profit margins at 7 percent were a quarter of those of Tata Steel. Ratan Tata stated, "I think our plan would be to try to make the UK operations more profitable."[14] Maybe the strategic logic of the acquisition was right after all, and it took the stock market about fifteen months to fully appreciate the complexities and subtleties involved in the acquisition. Or, as I argue, the strategic logic of the acquisition was flawed, and some other confounding event explains the rise in the stock price.

Tata Steel's cost of production at around $450 per ton is among the lowest in the world. Even in 2009 when the global average cost had reached about $700 to $750 per ton, Tata Steel managed to keep its costs to about $500 per ton. But this advantage is not transferable to Corus. Captive raw materials are the primary source of Tata Steel's competitive advantage. Tata Steel meets 100 percent of its iron ore requirements and 50 percent of its coking coal requirement through backward integration, whereas Corus is completely exposed to raw material price volatility due to lack of any significant backward integration. One important synergy stated at the time of the acquisition was the leveraging of low-cost slabs from India that Corus could use to produce various finished products. But in 2006, Tata Steel did not have spare slab capacity. Tata Steel also benefits from low labor costs and tight capacity in its primary market of India. Corus, in contrast, has high labor costs, strong unions, and excess capacity.

Tata Steel paid about $710 per ton of capacity, which is low compared to greenfield costs of $1,200 to $1,300 per ton. But this is a faulty comparison since Corus was one of the highest-cost producers in Europe, and there is excess steel capacity in the European markets. When Tata Steel acquired two smaller Asian steel companies, NatSteel and Millennium Steel, in 2004 and 2005, it paid $374 and $333 per ton, respectively. In 2010, Anand Rathi Financial Services valued Corus's capacity at around $360 to $400 ton, which implies that Corus is worth little more than half what Tata Steel paid for it three years earlier.[15] Anand Rathi projects that in 2011, Corus would comprise 65 percent of Tata Steel's consolidated revenues but only about 23 percent of EBITDA earnings. Even based on expectations for 2012, Anand Rathi does not expect Corus's return on capital employed to exceed 3 percent, clearly low even compared to global peers.

Tata Steel paid nine times EBITDA to acquire Corus. In comparison, Mittal Steel acquired Arcelor in 2006 for an EBITDA multiple of 6. This was in spite of the fact that Corus was less profitable and less efficient compared to Arcelor. Also, the entire amount was paid in cash by Tata Steel as opposed to a combination of cash and share swap in the case of the Arcelor deal. Tata Steel probably overpaid for Corus.

In 2009 Corus began decommissioning its Teesside Cast Products plant in the United Kingdom, confirming that its capacity was not that valuable. Angry unions threatened strike action against Tata Steel-Corus because this capacity reduction would lead to laying off sixteen hundred workers, with a possible eight thousand more job losses in the local supply chain. A company statement said the Teesside plant was a major drag on profitability, denting it with $177 million losses during the September 2009 quarter due to restructuring costs.

It can be argued that the acquisition involved minimal synergies and that Tata Steel overpaid for Corus. The rise in Tata Steel's stock price is driven more by the steel cycle than by the acquisition. Steel prices (represented by freight-on-board price of hot rolled steel) in the international market increased from an average of $564 a ton in 2007 to $714 a ton in 2008. However, as global steel demand cracked in the second half of 2008, steel prices in the international market started declining significantly, falling from the highs in 2008 to $380 in June 2009. Steel prices have recovered and in 2010 were hovering at $575 a ton.[16] In parallel to the steel cycle, the stock price of Tata Steel moved from 410 rupees on January 31, 2007 (the day the acquisition was agreed to), to a peak of 922 rupees on May 21, 2008, to a trough of 151 rupees on November 28, 2008, to its recent price of 629 rupees on March 22, 2010. Tata Steel's stock price has been extremely volatile, driven by the steel cycle and the economic cycle. The Corus acquisition is equivalent to the shareholders of Tata Steel placing a highly leveraged (of the $13 billon acquisition price, $9 billion came from increased debt) bet on steel prices. If that is what the shareholders wanted, they could easily have done it on their own in the stock and futures markets, without an expensive acquisition.

## Hindalco and Novelis

Hindalco is the flagship company belonging to the Birla group, one of the largest and most diversified family business houses in India. Hindalco, an industry leader in aluminum and copper, is one of the biggest producers of primary aluminum in Asia. In 2007 it acquired Novelis, a world leader in aluminum rolling and can recycling. After the acquisition, Hindalco as an integrated producer ranks among the global top five aluminum companies. Hindalco paid a price of $44.93 per share for acquiring Novelis, which represented a premium of 16.6 percent over the price before the announcement on February 11, 2007. However, this was a premium of 49.1 percent to the closing price on January 25, the day before speculation of a possible Hindalco bid surfaced.[17] On the day of the announcement, Hindalco shares fell 13.7 percent; by the end of the next day, Hindalco shares had underperformed the Sensex by nearly 15 percent in two days. Kumar Mangalam Birla, Hindalco's chairman, asked his shareholders to remain "patient" and wrote in the annual report, "However, if you look at the bigger picture, this is one of the most striking acquisitions and over the long-term will undeniably create enormous shareholder value." One year after the announcement, the stock of Hindalco had underperformed the Sensex by 26 percent.

Hindalco forward-integrated from smelting into rolling products by acquiring Novelis. Debu Bhattacharya, Hindalco's managing director, explained the strategy as follows: profitability in the upstream business is higher but more volatile because prices are set on the London Metal Exchange (LME); the profitability of the downstream business is lower but also less volatile. Hindalco acquired Novelis to "optimally balance" upstream and downstream operations as a natural hedge against volatility in the commodity prices of aluminum on the LME. This is weak strategic logic, and the aluminum industry structure is changing in exactly the opposite direction: toward deintegration.

The aluminum industry can be divided into two value chain stages. The upstream segment includes bauxite mining, alumina refining, and primary aluminum production. The downstream segment produces finished aluminum products and includes rolling mills, extrusion, and casting. This is a natural breaking point in the industry since aluminum ingot is a commodity, and transactions between the upstream and downstream segments can be done easily through markets. There is thus little reason to vertically integrate across these two stages in the aluminum industry.[18] The fully integrated aluminum company has become increasingly less common.[19]

According to Richard Evans, executive vice president of Alcan, the aluminum industry has correctly been deintegrating between the upstream producers of primary aluminum and downstream producers of finished products, "each with its own business imperatives and needs. . . . One of the best recent examples of this is of course Alcan's own spinoff of the new rolled product company Novelis."[20] This trend has been driven by two changes in the industry: in the late 1970s, LME began trading contracts for aluminum that rendered transparent the underlying price, and in the mid-1990s, downstream producers started charging their customers for conversion only and passing through the price of aluminum. Because of these changes, the integrated business model was "no longer the highest value alternative," according to Alcan top management.[21] Brian Sturgell, the first CEO of Novelis after the spin-off from Alcan, said, "From that point on, it was a question of when and how Alcan would optimize these upstream and downstream models."[22] In May 2004 Alcan decided to spin off its rolled products business as Novelis, so that the upstream and downstream businesses would be free to concentrate on their core competencies. Rio Tinto, a diversified mining company, forward-integrated by acquiring Alcan in November 2007 and increasingly has been divesting the downstream businesses such as packaging products.

Although most downstream producers passed on the aluminum price volatility to their customers by charging separately for conversion, Novelis signed fixed-price contracts with four major customers in the hope of increasing its profit margins. Unfortunately for Novelis, aluminum prices shot up a few months after the contracts. In the first nine months of 2006, Novelis reported a loss of $170 million, largely because of these fixed-price contracts, which ran up to 2011. Hindalco had to carry these contracts after the Novelis acquisition. In the third quarter of fiscal year 2008–2009, Novelis reported $472 million in unrealized losses on derivatives to hedge exposure to commodities and foreign currencies. These derivatives are used to hedge exposure to aluminum, primarily related to fixed-price contracts.

Hindalco financed the Novelis acquisition with debt, which caused its debt service coverage ratio to drop from fifteen times in 2006–2007 to only three times in 2007–2008, thus significantly increasing its risk profile. The Novelis profitability has not lived up to the expectations of Hindalco management. Novelis reported a net loss of $1.8 billion in the third quarter of fiscal year 2008–2009, including charges of $1.5 billion for asset impairment. Hindalco had the dubious distinction of being the first Indian company to take a charge for goodwill impairment. More recently, Novelis may have turned the corner toward profitability: it reported a net income of $68 million for the third quarter of fiscal year 2009–2010.[23]

## Tata Motors and Jaguar Land Rover

Tata Motors is the largest manufacturer of commercial and passenger vehicles in India. In 2008 it acquired from Ford Motor

Company the two luxury car brands Jaguar and Land Rover (JLR). The stock market's immediate reaction to the JLR acquisition was negative. In the few days following the announcement of the acquisition, the stock price of Tata Motors underperformed the Sensex index by about 5 percent. Balaji Jayaraman of Morgan Stanley said that buying Jaguar and Land Rover was "value-destructive given the lack of synergies and the high-cost operations involved." However, Tata Motors officials expressed confidence in the deal's long-term potential. Managing Director Ravi Kant said the company was "pretty confident that Jaguar and Land Rover will add positively to our consolidated balance sheet. . . . People are free to make their own opinions, but I think time will prove who is right."[24] Instead, the stock performance of Tata Motors worsened over the next year, and its shares underperformed the Sensex index by 36 percent. It is of course true that this period coincided with the recent economic turbulence in the world and a significant downturn in the global automotive market.

Ford had purchased Jaguar and Land Rover for $5 billon and sold them to Tata Motors for about half that price after several years of operating losses. It is difficult to see how Tata Motors would have greater synergies than Ford with JLR, and in fact, there are no significant synergies between Tata Motors and JLR. The two companies operate in different geographical markets, selling cars with different technology to very disparate customer segments. Around the same time, Tata Motors was launching its much-publicized Tata Nano, the world's cheapest car. Kant issued a clear directive: keep these vehicle lines separate and distinct. "Each is going to chart its own future and own course," he said. "The conflict would come if we were to try to put them together."[25] Tata has experience taking over global brands, and its strategy has been to let each business run its own entity, with modest input from the home office. This is consistent with the view that there are minimal synergies between the two companies.

Tata Motors financed the acquisition with debt, which significantly increased its risk profile. The company's ratio of

EBITDA earnings to interest paid, an inverse measure of the firm's debt risk, used to be in the range 9 to 11 during the years 2005 to 2007; after the acquisition, the coverage ratio dropped to 5.9 in 2008. By comparison, the coverage ratio for some successful auto companies in 2008 was 86 for Toyota, 45 for Nissan, and 31 for Audi. As mentioned earlier, Tata Motors had problems refinancing the bridge loan in 2009.

While discussing the disappointing performance of Corus and JLR, Ratan Tata conceded in an interview with the *Sunday Times* in 2009 that with hindsight, he might have gone too far too fast, but that nobody saw the crash coming: "If one had known there was going to be a meltdown then yes [Tata went too far] but nobody knew. Both the acquisitions were made, I would say, at an inopportune time in the sense that they were near the top of the market in terms of price."[26] Even if we accept the view that the timing of the JLR acquisition was unfortunate, there is still no positive rationale for the acquisition.

Lacking synergies, Tata Motors was behaving as a conglomerate in acquiring JLR. There is much evidence that such conglomerate diversification does not create shareholder value; in fact, conglomerates on the average trade at a discount to their breakup value. This situation is made worse if Tata Motors overpaid for the JLR acquisition, even if inadvertently. ICICI Securities valued JLR at only about $850 million in 2010, in contrast to the acquisition price of $2.3 billion.[27]

## Analysis

Based on the empirical evidence I have presented in both stock market performance and the case studies, I conclude that large foreign acquisitions by Indian firms have not created shareholder value for the acquiring firms and have probably destroyed shareholder value. The *Economist* comes to a similar conclusion that "several of corporate India's acquisitions now seem ill-advised."[28] The causes of this negative outcome are too little integration to achieve synergies, agency problems, and inadequate discipline due to easy capital.

## Too Little Integration

A strong economic or strategic rationale for synergies is the starting point for any successful acquisition. Virtually no acquiring company would dispute this statement. But many of the unsuccessful acquisitions involve weak logic dressed up with vacuous statements, such as "global footprint," "scale," and "optimal balance." The Tata Motors-JLR acquisition does not even try to make a strong case based on synergies. Hindalco attempts to justify the Novelis acquisition to achieve some vague balance to reduce risk. But there is no need for an acquisition to achieve an objective that shareholders can easily achieve on their own, such as diversify to reduce nonsystematic risk. A succinct but powerful way to state the logic of synergy is that an acquisition can create value when the company can exploit a (usually intangible) firm-specific resource that cannot be easily traded in a marketplace.

The Indian companies studied here approach integrating the acquisitions with a very light touch; Koushik Chatterjee, the CFO of Tata Steel, calls this the Oriental approach as opposed to the Western approach. He described the current Tata Steel-Corus conglomerate as two separate entities bridged by support functions like finance and human resources.[29] Citing examples from the Tata Group, Kale, Singh, and Raman urge companies not to "integrate your acquisitions, partner with them."[30] Using the example of Hindalco-Novelis, Kumar argues similarly that Indian acquirers not try to consolidate acquisitions.[31] I think that a light approach to integration does not, and will not, lead to value creation.

Foreign acquisitions by firms in emerging economies often seek firm-specific intangible capabilities in areas such as technology, innovation, marketing, and distribution. These capabilities cannot be glued on to an existing organization. Exploiting a firm-specific resource through an acquisition involves applying, transferring, or replicating the resource from one firm to another. This involves integrating the new resources into the existing organization, which requires significant organizational integration. Specialized capabilities are woven into the fabric of the organization; that is what makes them "firm specific." If that were not the case, then there would be a reasonably efficient market for that resource and no need for the acquisition in the first place.

But that does not imply going to the other extreme. Chatterjee equates the Western approach to conquering the acquisition; such a heavy-handed approach is likely to fail, of course. But this is a false straw man argument. Kumar too falls into the same trap when he states that in the "traditional approach" to acquisitions, "the buyer has clear short-term aims, but may not have thought through long-term goals."[32] The challenge is to find the appropriate degree of assimilation that preserves the strengths of the two companies but still achieves the synergies available through the acquisition. Too little integration will lead to no synergies; too much integration might destroy the specialized capabilities of the companies. The devil is in the details as usual; put differently, good execution is critical.

The three firms studied here do not achieve this balance, and their approach to integration is too light to achieve synergies. Sharing finance and HR, as Chatterjee describes the Tata Steel-Corus company, is surely too little. This is why shared corporate services is not enough to justify conglomerate diversification. Tata Steel and Corus are in the same business, and there is much greater potential for achieving cost reduction through economies of scale, but that would require significant organizational integration. That has been the approach clearly followed successfully by Mittal Steel over decades of international acquisitions in the steel industry.[33]

Kumar points out that "Hindalco believed that Novelis's steady earnings would help offset the fluctuations in its profits from year to year."[34] It is true that achieving this benefit would not require any integration. But it is also not value creating in the first place. Shareholders can easily achieve such reduction in volatility by diversifying their portfolio, and Hindalco did not need to make an acquisition for this reason.

Kumar states that Hindalco was happy to leave Novelis's senior managers in place; for six months Hindalco supplemented them with only two of its own managers. This sounds more like abdication of managerial responsibilities than appropriate integration given that Novelis had significant managerial problems at that time. The CEO, Brian Sturgell, had been fired in August 2006, after which the board appointed an interim CEO and then an acting CEO. It had yet to appoint a permanent CEO. Novelis had severe issues with financial reporting and had recently replaced both the CFO and the controller. Its inability to file quarterly results on time had led to a potential violation of debt covenants. Contrary to the industry norm, Novelis had entered into fixed-price contracts taking on unnecessary risk that subsequently turned out badly when aluminum prices rose. Novelis has not been a value-creating acquisition. Stronger managerial intervention earlier might have helped improve the situation.

## Agency Problems

The traditional view of the agency problem is that the self-interests of the managers (the agents) diverge from those of the shareholders (the principals). One solution is to align their interests by compensating the managers with stock in the company; thus, the managers will have skin in the game. This solution does not work in the context of Indian firms. Many Indian firms are managed and controlled by promoter shareholders, who already have much financial skin in the game. The problem is that these promoter-managers are far richer than the other shareholders, and their financial perspective might be very different. They might be more motivated by nonfinancial factors, such as public recognition, serving a national goal, leaving behind a legacy, and the pride of managing a large multinational company.

Foreign acquisitions by Indian firms have prompted much nationalistic chest thumping about "rising India" by the media and the corporate and political elite. Indian newspapers discussed the Tata-Corus deal under shrill headlines, such as "India Poised for Global Supremacy," "The Empire Strikes Back," and "Global Indian Takeover." Confederation of Indian Industry president R. Seshasayee said, "Tata Steel's successful bid for Corus Group Plc. is a statement on Indian Industry's coming of age and takes our Mergers and Acquisition levels to a different paradigm. This is a testimony of the confidence and competence of Indian Industry."[35] Finance Minister Chidambaram said, "Our industry is capable of raising resources to acquire enterprises abroad and manage them efficiently."[36]

All of this popular attention might lead top managers to believe they are primarily responsible for achieving some nationalistic goals, even misconceived goals. In surprisingly candid comments, Ratan Tata revealed about the Corus acquisition: "We all felt that to lose would go beyond the group and it would be an issue of great disappointment in the country. So, on the one hand you want to do the right thing by your shareholders and on the other hand you did not want to lose."[37] Managers, even promoter-shareholder-managers, have a primary fiduciary responsibility to their shareholders. The Indian media expressed much enthusiasm for an Indian takeover of two U.K. brands, Jaguar and Land Rover, whose roots date back to British colonial rule. But as Thiyaga Rajan, a fund manager who sold his shares in Tata Motors after the acquisition announcement, put it, "Patriotic ebullience doesn't rub off on the shares."[38]

The true measure of firm or managerial performance is the economic value created. However, much of the discussion in the popular press confuses firm size with an automatic measure of performance. Completing an acquisition is considered a sign of success. Winning a bidding war for a target company is seen as "winning." But it is easy to increase firm size while losing money. Similarly, it is easy to "win" a bidding war by paying too much for a target company—the winner's curse. The nationalistic euphoria that focuses on firm size and acquisitions can lead to corporate overreach. Kumar, Mohapatra, and Chandrasekhar suggest that "in India's closely knit business community, it is almost becoming a kind of fashion statement for companies to make foreign acquisitions."[39]

Another problem might be that corporate governance in India and other emerging economies does not function well. Promoter shareholders have entrenched power, and there is not enough legal protection for minority shareholders. For example, none of the acquisitions discussed in this chapter involved a shareholder vote, even though some of them radically transformed the company. The market for corporate control is also weak and does not serve as a disciplining force on managerial power. For example, there are almost no hostile takeovers in India.

## Easy Capital

Kumar, Mohapatra, and Chandrasekhar outline three unique traits of Indian firms that lead to success in acquisitions.[40] First, many Indian companies are part of a group of companies. Second, Indian companies have historically had very high debt-to-equity ratios. Finally, despite being public, Indian firms are often controlled by powerful families and individual promoters who have considerable management leeway. These are three important traits common to many emerging economy firms. However, rather than being strengths, I view these as weaknesses in the context of foreign acquisitions. The third point about managerial power exacerbates agency problems, and the first two points lead to access to capital that is too easy.

Capital markets, by controlling access to capital, play an important role in demanding good managerial decisions and penalizing bad choices. This disciplining force is weak with

Indian acquisitions abroad. Groups of companies, such as the Tata and Birla groups, can leverage group assets to complete deals that would be difficult for any individual company. Both Corus and JLR have been difficult to finance and have required significant capital infusion from the Tata Group. A group functions as an internal capital market, the same as a conglomerate might do in developed countries. There is much research in finance and strategy that demonstrates that conglomerate diversification does not create shareholder value; in fact, it destroys value—the so-called conglomerate discount. There is much controversy about whether conglomerates create shareholder value in the context of emerging economies. Khanna and Palepu argue that conglomerates add value in emerging economies because of weak institutions to support basic business operations.[41] Even if one grants this argument in the institutional context of emerging economies, it is unlikely to hold for companies making large foreign acquisitions in a global environment. The lack of managerial focus and lack of the disciplining force of an external capital market probably leads to a conglomerate discount and is part of the explanation for why these acquisitions do not create shareholder value.

Historically Indian firms borrowed from nationalized banks whose mandate was to support India's economic development. The Indian firms thus had access to artificially cheap or implicitly subsidized debt capital.[42] It is not surprising that they had high debt-to-equity ratios. This tendency was exacerbated in the boom years before the recent financial crisis, when global financial markets had underpriced risk. This combination led to Indian firms' taking on much debt to finance their foreign acquisitions for cash. With the increasing globalization of Indian capital markets and the repricing of risk everywhere, Indian acquirers and their shareholders have paid a price for their risky behavior.

Given modern capital markets, deep financial pockets are not a reliable source of competitive advantage. Those pockets often have big holes, and easy capital leads to wastage. Deep insights and managerial capabilities are a much better basis for competitive advantage and value creation.

## Formula for Success

The empirical evidence I have presented shows that many large foreign acquisitions from India have not created shareholder value. This phenomenon is not unique to India; large foreign acquisitions from China have probably not done any better.[43] Many of China's foreign acquisitions have been in the areas of energy and natural resources, dictated by national security policy. Leaving these aside, Chinese firms have not done well when they have pursued large foreign acquisitions seeking technology, brands, and distribution—firm-specific intangible capabilities. For example, TCL, China's large consumer electronics company, acquired assets from France's Alcatel and Thomson in an effort to acquire technology and expand to a global market. After less than three years and large financial losses, TCL has shut or sold most of its operations in Europe.

This does not mean that emerging economy firms should not make foreign acquisitions. The basic formula for successful acquisitions in general applies just as well in this context. First, there needs to be a sound strategic rationale for synergies. Second, the acquisition price has to be reasonable such that the target firm does not capture all the value created. Third, actually achieving synergies requires good execution, which usually implies deep managerial integration. Successful firms like CEMEX and Mittal Steel have created tremendous shareholder value through a series of foreign acquisitions. Both companies put much emphasis on the above three elements, especially postmerger integration.[44] United Spirits from India too has achieved success with this approach: significant synergies, reasonable price, and deep integration.

United Spirits Limited (USL) is the flagship company of the United Breweries Group, a conglomerate controlled by Vijay Mallya. It is the third-largest producer of spirits in the world after Diageo and Pernod Ricard. USL controlled 60 percent of the market for Indian-made foreign liquor, the oxymoronic term for Western-style hard liquors manufactured in India. It had a smaller share in the premium and superpremium segments. In May 2007 USL acquired Whyte & Mackay, a privately held company that was the fourth-largest distiller of Scotch whiskies, for $1.2 billon. Whyte & Mackay produces W&M blended Scotch whisky and several brands of single-malt Scotch; it also had a large stock of aged single-malt whisky. The stock market reacted positively to the acquisition, driving up the price of United Spirits by 36 percent, relative to the Sensex index, in six days. Its relative returns over one year were even more positive: 67 percent.

There was a strong rationale for synergies from the acquisition. "The company sees significant revenue growth from this acquisition of Whyte and Mackay," a joint statement from the companies said. "In particular, The UB Group will provide access to India and other large emerging markets, allowing an acceleration of Whyte and Mackay's growth plans."[45] At 70 million cases a year, India is the largest whisky market in the world. The upper end of the market is growing rapidly, especially the Scotch whisky segment, which is growing at 35 to 40 percent per year.[46] "The potential for premium Scotch whiskey in India is enormous and, with the acquisition of Whyte and Mackay, we now have a strong portfolio of internationally recognized brands that we will immediately introduce into the Indian market and use our strong distribution muscle fully to our advantage," Mallya said. Another source of synergy was that due to "the shortages and rapidly increasing prices of Scotch whisky, we needed a reliable supply source to secure our future considering we use Scotch in our Indian blends." By January 2009, USL had introduced nine brands of Scotch whisky into the Indian market. It had also initiated local bottling of Scotch whisky to attract lower duties and make the product available at a lower price.

USL first bid £400 million to acquire Whyte & Mackay and finally closed the deal by paying £595 million ($1.2 billion) a year later, an increase in bid price of nearly 50 percent. While some analysts felt that USL had overpaid for Whyte & Mackay, Mallya insisted, "I am satisfied that the price agreed is attractive." At least in hindsight, a significant part of the acquisition price was justified by the inventory of Scotch whisky. Preacquisition, Whyte & Mackay had 117 million liters of whisky, and the prevailing value was £3.12 per liter; in 2009 the value had risen to £4.65 (about $6.5) per liter, an appreciation of 49 percent.[47]

USL played a major role in restructuring the operations of Whyte & Mackay and turning around its fortunes in less than one year.[48] Preacquisition, Whyte & Mackay had incurred a loss of about £1.2 million, but in 2007–2008 it reported a profit of £13 million. Soon after the acquisition, USL appointed Ashwin Malik, one of its top managers, as the CEO of Whyte & Mackay. Earlier, the marketing team was being operated with the help of consultants, but now USL has put in place a fully functional and experienced team. At the customer interface level, service replies that used to take two weeks have now been reduced to two days. Preacquisition, Glasgow was the only operations center that ran all its international businesses. USL has since decentralized international operations; the Indian operations are handled from India. USL has also shifted Whyte & Mackay's focus from selling bulk Scotch to bottling the product.

## Conclusion

Emerging economy companies contemplating foreign acquisitions would do well to heed the advice of Malvinder Singh, the former CEO of the pharmaceutical firm Ranbaxy: "It's important for companies to look at the economic rationale, and not get taken to extremes by emotion and ego."[49] Following his own advice, Singh's family, the promoter shareholders, sold its entire 35 percent stake in the company in June 2008 to Daiichi Sankyo, a Japanese drug producer. Daiichi paid about $5 billion to acquire a controlling interest in Ranbaxy. The Indian press echoed sentiments expressed by Anand Mahindra, chairman of Mahindra & Mahindra (a large Indian automotive company): "I can't help feeling a twinge of regret about an Indian MNC becoming a Japanese subsidiary." By May 2009 Ranbaxy's share price tanked by 70 percent compared to the acquisition price, forcing Daiichi to write down its investment by $3.6 billion. Singh resigned from the company and is "ready to move on to other healthcare businesses." As for the billions he earned from the deal, he says, "Money was not important."[50] Managers, however, would do well to remember that it is all about money!

# 7

# ACQUISITION ADVANTAGE

## How Emerging Market Firms Use Acquisitions, and What Incumbents Can Do About It

U. Srinivasa Rangan, Sam Hariharan

Consider the following announcements:

- Tata Motors of India acquires Jaguar Land Rover in the United Kingdom: Tata wins the auction in 2007 to acquire the British auto group from Ford in the face of bids from other companies.
- Bharti of India zooms into Africa: Bharti Airtel realizes its ambitions to expand into Africa with its acquisition of Zain in 2010, making it the fifth largest mobile operator in the world.
- Geely, the China-based automaker, acquires Volvo from Ford for $1.5 billion, doubling its worldwide automotive output and expecting Volvo to be the basis for its growth in the premium segments in both China and overseas markets.
- Lenovo's acquisition of IBM's personal computer business has made it a major player in the PC industry: Its dropping of the IBM brand name in 2008, well ahead of schedule, may be indicative of the successful transition Lenovo has made by its integration of this acquisition.

- The battle for Maytag: The battle for the acquisition of Maytag in 2005 witnessed the bold bid by Haier of China to acquire a major foothold in the U.S. appliances market thwarted by Whirlpool, one of the two remaining major players in the United States along with GE.

All of these announcements have this in common: they represent a new thrust by emerging market companies to compete more effectively in the global arena through acquisitions. These moves often represent a strategic challenge to large, established firms in developed countries. At the same time, Whirlpool's thwarting of Haier's bid to expand in the U.S. market illustrates how incumbents need to think ahead in the emerging global arena.

This chapter first presents data that show how global cross-border acquisitions by Chinese and Indian firms have been rising. It then outlines the various conceptual frameworks that could explain why there has been a quantum jump in acquisitions recently by Chinese and Indian firms. Using aggregate and anecdotal data, we show that the growth in acquisitions abroad marks a significant departure in the behavior of Chinese and Indian firms. Building on that conclusion and using a series of case studies, the chapter looks at the issue of how Chinese and Indian firms' global acquisitions pose a strategic challenge to established developed country multinationals. It ends with some suggestions on how multinationals from Europe, Japan, and the United States need to address the strategic challenge posed by Chinese and Indian firms.

## The Rise of Global Cross-Border Acquisitions by Emerging Economy Firms

Cross-border commerce often results in flows of cross-border foreign direct investment (FDI). Indeed, FDI from developed countries (DCs) to countries like China and India has been cited as showing how countries benefit from the investment of multi-national corporations (MNCs).[1] FDI also flows in the opposite direction from less developed countries (LDCs) to other countries, developed and less developed. Until recently, these small flows were generally ignored. True, in the early 1980s, some researchers looked into flows of such capital from less developed countries to other less developed countries, but that was an exception.[2]

Of late, observers have begun to notice that the flow of capital from LDCs has been rising fast. Recently, looking at Chinese FDI, the *Economist* argued that since China's share of global stock of FDI (which includes both acquisitions and green-field investments) is no more than 6 percent compared to 22 percent for the United States and 10 percent for Britain, it is not something policymakers should lose sleep over.[3] We believe, however, that managers involved in global competition cannot ignore the rising tide of FDI from LDCs. For managers, two factors are worthy of attention: the flow rate of FDI from LDCs affects the level of global competition, and global acquisitions by firms from China and India pose significant threats. Why? In the first place, while the stocks of FDI are historically determined, changes in the flow rates of FDI are more consequential because they may change the competitive landscape quickly. Second, FDI by acquisition allows firms to more easily overcome the traditional barriers to mobility across borders, as well as across segments and industries. So using cross-border acquisitions as a new conceptual lens to understand the changing landscape of global competition is useful.

In the post–World War II years, cross-border acquisitions rose rapidly, with firms from the United States and Europe dominating the market for acquisitions.[4] Given our focus on acquisitions by LDC firms, we begin in the 1980s. Table 7.1 shows that firms from the United States, Europe, and Japan dominated the world of acquisitions from 1983 to 2010. But Asian acquisitions are on the rise. The number of Asian acquisitions and the amount

**Table 7.1  Cross-Border Acquisitions from Various Regions**

| Country/ Region | 1983–1987 | | 1988–1992 | | 1993–1997 | | 1998–2002 | | 2003–2007 | | 2008–2010 | |
|---|---|---|---|---|---|---|---|---|---|---|---|---|
| | Number | Dollars (in millions) | Number | Dollars (in millions) | Number | Dollars (in millions) | Number | Dollars (in millions) | Number | Dollars (in millions) | Number | Dollars (in millions) |
| Americas[a] | 1,612 | $126,791 | 10,270 | $456,786 | 15,182 | $671,459 | 25,556 | $2,920,137 | 24,232 | $3,132,370 | 11,871 | $1,151,074 |
| Europe | 1,487 | 116,255 | 5,692 | 248,083 | 12,037 | 460,044 | 16,287 | 1,124,007 | 16,458 | 1,668,249 | 7,879 | 523,452 |
| Asia | 268 | 26,355 | 1,477 | 75,674 | 4,207 | 131,755 | 5,795 | 239,936 | 10,589 | 784,690 | 5,573 | 397,390 |
| Japan | 184 | 11,321 | 1,359 | 70,449 | 786 | 17,711 | 1,219 | 82,104 | 1,545 | 261,245 | 1,043 | 146,303 |
| Africa[b] | 33 | 1,606 | 202 | 9,737 | 632 | 27,425 | 1,109 | 44,625 | 1,278 | 77,307 | 749 | 83,043 |
| Total | 3,584 | 282,329 | 19,000 | 860,728 | 32,844 | 1,308,394 | 49,966 | 4,410,808 | 54,102 | 5,923,861 | 27,115 | 2,301,261 |

*Note:*  All transactions until April 30, 2010, are covered.

[a]The United States, Canada, and Latin America.

[b]Africa and Middle East.

*Source:*  Thomson One Banker Database.

involved in recent years (2003 to 2010) are several-fold what they were over 1983 to 1987. Indeed, recently, Asian firms have outpaced American and European firms. The number of Asian acquisitions between 2003 and 2007 was almost double, and the value of such acquisitions was more than double those for the previous five years. In that period, the acquisitions from the Americas declined slightly in number though not in total value.

Table 7.2 suggests that Chinese and Indian firms accounted for most of the growth in Asian acquisitions. Chinese acquisitions rose several-fold in recent years in terms of both number of acquisitions and amount spent on acquisitions. So did the Indian acquisitions during that period.

In the past, cross-border acquisitions were largely due to the global expansion and ownership strategies of MNCs in global industries.[5] Table 7.3 assesses whether this pattern still holds. Note how the list of key industry categories for acquisitions remained stable from 1982 to 2007. The salience of industries such as financial services, energy, telecommunications, pharmaceuticals (as part of health care), industrials, and media and entertainment indicates that global acquisitions still occur in industries where MNCs are dominant. Why are Chinese and Indian firms making acquisitions at a rapid pace in global industries? We turn to this issue next.

## Why Do Emerging Economy Companies Make Cross-Border Acquisitions?

As Chinese and Indian (C&I) firms acquire firms abroad, they are expanding internationally. Traditionally, international expansion has been explained by two major approaches, both deriving from the insight that multinationals come into being when a firm with an oligopolistic advantage seeks to exploit that advantage in other countries.[6] For global expansion of firms from developed countries, the application was straightforward because they possessed advantages in such areas as technology, manufacturing

## Table 7.2 Cross-Border Acquisitions by Firms from Asian Countries (Excluding Japan)

| Country | 1983–1987 | | 1988–1992 | | 1993–1997 | | 1998–2002 | | 2003–2007 | | 2008–2010 | |
|---|---|---|---|---|---|---|---|---|---|---|---|---|
| | Number | Dollars (in millions) | Number | Dollars (in millions) | Number | Dollars (in millions) | Number | Dollars (in millions) | Number | Dollars (in millions) | Number | Dollars (in millions) |
| Hong Kong | 51 | $3,116 | 231 | $7,976 | 501 | $24,453 | 699 | $33,244 | 1,057 | $47,066 | 458 | $60,439 |
| China | 6 | 173 | 25 | 619 | 120 | 1,797 | 162 | 3,822 | 470 | 45,069 | 370 | 58,535 |
| Singapore | 5 | 20 | 118 | 2,378 | 492 | 10,369 | 624 | 37,095 | 1,066 | 74,417 | 456 | 41,017 |
| Taiwan | 4 | 37 | 36 | 1,909 | 52 | 679 | 113 | 4,084 | 116 | 4,488 | 95 | 2,533 |
| India | 2 | 12 | 17 | 33 | 60 | 1,795 | 212 | 4,526 | 629 | 23,174 | 338 | 16,207 |
| Philippines | 2 | - | 6 | 14 | 56 | 837 | 40 | 960 | 53 | 3,028 | 30 | 1,554 |
| South Korea | 2 | 13 | 23 | 555 | 106 | 6,249 | 98 | 4,598 | 198 | 13,624 | 172 | 19,034 |
| Malaysia | 1 | 6 | 51 | 630 | 333 | 13,426 | 214 | 6,449 | 610 | 15,592 | 290 | 15,938 |
| Total | 73 | 3,377 | 511 | 14,920 | 1,722 | 59,998 | 2,164 | 95,137 | 4,201 | 226,567 | 2,213 | 219,057 |

Note: All transactions until April 30, 2010, are covered.

Source: Thomson One Banker Database.

**Table 7.3 Global Cross-Border Acquisitions by Industry**

| Industry | 1982–1991 | | 1992–2001 | | 2002–2007 | |
|---|---|---|---|---|---|---|
| | *Number* | *Dollars (in millions)* | *Number* | *Dollars (in millions)* | *Number* | *Dollars (in millions)* |
| Financials | 10,115 | $522,812 | 28,314 | $3,173,619 | 13,180 | $1,632,494 |
| Energy and Power | 3,887 | 393,421 | 13,279 | 1,847,742 | 6,734 | 1,131,135 |
| Telecommunications | 1,281 | 100,682 | 7,168 | 2,366,044 | 3,162 | 881,577 |
| Industrials | 9,124 | 407,809 | 29,893 | 1,320,598 | 13,036 | 750,753 |
| Real estate | 1,484 | 63,160 | 8,617 | 518,335 | 4,887 | 745,257 |
| Health care | 2,801 | 150,619 | 10,887 | 881,750 | 5,776 | 732,623 |
| Materials | 7,290 | 393,868 | 21,597 | 1,270,427 | 9,296 | 693,340 |
| Media and entertainment | 5,065 | 286,219 | 18,699 | 1,507,977 | 8,015 | 670,243 |
| High technology | 4,138 | 109,374 | 27,372 | 1,107,161 | 14,423 | 572,411 |
| Retail | 2,725 | 177,733 | 9,740 | 488,450 | 4,744 | 388,670 |
| Consumer Staples | 5,075 | 331,029 | 15,627 | 729,524 | 6,633 | 359,361 |
| Consumer products and services | 4,565 | 140,365 | 21,788 | 508,275 | 10,267 | 331,020 |
| Government and agencies | 67 | 2,820 | 363 | 18,708 | 154 | 18,847 |

*Source:* Thomson One Banker Database.

expertise, marketing knowledge, and brands that were far superior to what other countries possessed.[7] In the absence of such superior capabilities, for developing countries' firms going abroad, the theoretical explanation switched to such factors as low-cost Third World products, ethnic connections, and appropriate technology.[8]

Our analysis suggests that recent Chinese and Indian acquisitions abroad do not fit well under the rubric of Third World multinationals and are more consistent with explanations advanced for mainstream multinationals.[9] Chinese and Indian firms have shifted from a localized developing world focus to a more global, developed world focus.[10] North America and Europe account for most foreign acquisitions of Indian firms since 1995. Similarly, Chinese firms have shifted their acquisition focus from developing regions to developed ones such as Europe and the Americas. Between 2002 and 2007, these two markets accounted for a large part (39 percent in terms of numbers and 59 percent in terms of value) of the foreign acquisitions by Chinese firms. The average deal value for Chinese acquisitions in Europe and the Americas is getting bigger too.[11] It seems that Chinese firms are maturing, becoming more sophisticated, and are more willing and also better able to take bigger risks. The pattern of Chinese and Indian acquisitions abroad resembles closely that of traditional MNCs. Clearly, then, the recent geographic pattern of the international expansion of Chinese and Indian firms cannot be explained by low-end products, low-end technology, or ethnic ties.

## Globalization Thesis

If Third World advantages in low-end products, low-end technology, and ethnic ties do not explain emerging economy firms' acquisitions, could the reason be lack of domestic opportunities? If so, we should see acquisitions in industries where domestic growth in China and India is lagging. This is not so. In industries where C&I acquisitions have taken place—industrial manufacturing, financial services, health care including pharmaceuticals, and consumer goods—the domestic growth is high. Economic growth in C&I has been broad based, with most industries benefiting from liberalization and as evidenced by Western MNCs rushing in to exploit the growth. Thus, lack of domestic opportunities cannot explain C&I acquisitions abroad. However, there are other facets of globalization that may explain such acquisitions. We turn to them next.

In the first place, the industries in which C&I firms have made overseas acquisitions are largely global industries rather than multidomestic industries.[12] In global industries, economies of scale, brands, and global strategies rather than country-segmented strategies play a major role. As Table 7.4 shows, MNCs dominate such sectors. Why would acquisitions of C&I firms focus on global industries? There are at least three reasons and all of them appear to have played a role.

One reason is that global industries call for global strategies in which achieving global scale and learning through global presence become a competitive necessity. Failure to make acquisitions abroad could be detrimental to competitive strategies in global industries.[13] For example, between 2003 and 2007, all major (greater than $100 million) overseas acquisitions by Indian firms occurred in global industries such as high technology, industrials, and pharmaceuticals.[14] In other words, these firms seem to have recognized the strategic imperative to compete globally in these industries. As latecomers, they are using the acquisition route to catch up with their established global rivals. Also, as we argued earlier, most of these major acquisitions took place in developed regions such as Europe and North America. A similar pattern holds for Chinese private sector firms.[15]

Second, in global industries, when domestic firms are locked in a fairly tight oligopoly, firms tend to imitate each other's competitive moves. In international business, such oligopolistic imitation has been shown to be true in many industries.[16] Table 7.5 illustrates this trend in Indian acquisitions. In industries

**Table 7.4 Global Players in Industries Where Chinese and Indian Acquisitions Have Occurred**

| Industry | *Major Global Players* | | | |
|---|---|---|---|---|
| Energy and power | Exxon Mobil | Royal Dutch Shell | BP | Chevron |
| Health care | McKesson | Cardinal Health | AmerisourceBergen | WellPoint |
| High technology | HP | IBM | Hitachi | Samsung |
| Materials | Arcelor Mittal | Dow Chemical | Nippon Steel | Anglo American |
| Financials | Citigroup | Bank of America | HSBC Holding | JPMorgan Chase |
| Industrials | General Motors | Daimler Chrysler | Toyota Motor | General Electric |
| Telecommunications | Vodafone | Nippon Telegraph and Telephone | Verizon | Deutsche Telecom |
| Consumer staples | Altria | BASF | Unilever | Tyco |
| Consumer products and services | Procter & Gamble | TESCO | Kroger | Metro AG |

*Source:* "The Global 2000," Forbes.com. Mar. 29, 2007, http://www.forbes.com/lists/2007/18/biz_07forbes2000_The-Global-2000_IndName _14.html.

**Table 7.5 Global Industries in Which Indian Acquisitions Have Occurred in Tandem**

| Industry | Country of Acquisition | First Acquirer | Acquisition Date | Second Acquirer | Acquisition Date |
|---|---|---|---|---|---|
| Consumer staples | Italy | Fibres & Fabrics International | August 5, 2004 | Malwa Industries Ltd. | May 10, 2006 |
| Financials | Indonesia | SBI | December 16, 2006 | Bank of India | February 14, 2007 |
| Health care | Belgium | Jubilant Organosys Ltd. | June 2, 2004 | Matrix Laboratories Ltd. | June 20, 2005 |
| | China | Aurobindo Datong Bio-Pharma Co. | April 29, 2003 | Matrix Laboratories Ltd. | October 3, 2005 |
| | Germany | Wockhardt Ltd. | May 16, 2004 | Dr. Reddys Laboratories Ltd. | March 4, 2006 |
| | United Kingdom | Dr Reddys Laboratories Ltd. | April 1, 2002 | Wockhardt Ltd. | July 8, 2003 |
| | United States | Dr Reddys Laboratories Ltd. | May 6, 2004 | Jubilant Organosys Ltd. | July 1, 2005 |

*(continued)*

**Table 7.5 Global Industries in Which Indian Acquisitions Have Occurred in Tandem** *(continued)*

| Industry | Country of Acquisition | First Acquirer | Acquisition Date | Second Acquirer | Acquisition Date |
|---|---|---|---|---|---|
| High technology | Germany | Polaris Software Lab Ltd. | February 16, 2001 | Aftek Infosys Ltd. | March 13, 2003 |
| | United States | BFL Software Ltd. | August 23, 2000 | Silverline Technologies Ltd. | January 15, 2004 |
| | United States | Patni Computer Systems Ltd. | November 4, 2004 | Mahindra-British Telecom | November 28, 2005 |
| | United States | Wipro Ltd. | April 3, 2006 | ICICI Infotech Services Ltd. | November 5, 2001 |
| Industrials | United Kingdom | Sundram Fasteners Ltd. | December 22, 2003 | Amtek Auto Ltd. | December 31, 2003 |
| | United States | UCAL Fuel Systems Ltd. | June 23, 2005 | RSB Group | November 30, 2006 |
| Materials | Australia | Sterlite Industries India Ltd. | December 31, 2001 | Hindalco Industries Ltd. | March 7, 2003 |
| | United Kingdom | Tata Chemicals Ltd. | March 7, 2006 | Gujarat Heavy Chemicals Ltd. | February 9, 2007 |
| Telecommunications | Bermuda | Reliance Gateway Net Pvt Ltd. | January 23, 2004 | Videsh Sanchar Nigam Ltd. | February 13, 2006 |

*Source:* Thomson One Banker Database.

ranging from consumer staples to health care (pharmaceuticals) to high technology (mainly information systems), a foreign acquisition by one Indian firm seems to trigger a similar acquisition, often in the same foreign country, by another Indian firm that is a rival to the first in India. In other words, oligopolistic reaction appears to be a reasonable explanation for the recent flurry of acquisitions by Indian firms. One suspects that a similar pattern of oligopolistic reaction holds good for Chinese overseas acquisitions.

Third, under globalization, a version of such oligopolistic imitation also occurs when the domestic industry is invaded by foreign players. Again, in the case of Indian and Chinese firms, many of their formerly protected domestic markets have seen entry by foreign companies since the early 1990s. Other things being equal, one would expect that Chinese and Indian firms, suddenly faced with intense competition from foreign firms, would seek to level the playing field, so to speak, by moving abroad. Since overseas acquisition is the fastest route to gaining a toehold in other countries, we could expect to see such international acquisitions by Chinese and Indian firms, especially in industries in which foreign firms have entered domestic markets. Anecdotal evidence seems to bear this out.

Consider some of the industries in which Indian firms have made acquisitions since 1991: steel, pharmaceuticals, automotive components, and information technology. In each, foreign firms have made significant forays into India. In steel, POSCO of Korea is building a major plant in India. In pharmaceuticals, Novartis, Pfizer, and Eli Lilly have increased their investments in India.[17] In the auto sector, following the arrival of Ford, Honda, and Hyundai in India, several foreign auto component suppliers entered India. Finally, in information technology (IT), IBM has returned in a big way.[18] HP, Dell, Accenture, and EDS have also built up their presence in India. It appears that in response, Indian firms such as Tata Steel (in steel industry), Ranbaxy (in pharmaceuticals), Sundram Fasteners (in auto components), and Infosys (in information technology) sought to become larger global players themselves. Similarly, Chinese firms in the automotive industry (Geely and SAIC), high technology (Lenovo), domestic appliances (Haier), and consumer electronics (TCL) have gone out to make acquisitions abroad even as they face increased competition in China due to the entry of MNCs from abroad in these very sectors.

If the evidence so far suggests that Chinese and Indian firms have recognized the need to become global, it would also imply that C&I firms would seek to gain competitive advantages through their acquisitions. We turn to that topic next.

## Value Chain Leverage Thesis

At its core, this argument suggests that a firm acquires a company abroad when it recognizes the opportunity to take advantage of the value chain strengths of the other firm domestically or globally. Using acquisitions to leverage their own strengths in one part of the value chain by combining it with another firm's strength in another part of the value chain is well recognized.[19] Such leveraging of another firm's value chain competences can take place in three principal ways, and all three seem to have been at work in C&I overseas acquisitions.

First, when a foreign firm acquires another firm, it gains access to the latter's investments in the value chain. For example, when a local firm has a strong distribution system, acquisition helps a foreign firm gain control of distribution. It speeds entry by saving on creating a distribution system afresh. When Coca-Cola entered India, it acquired the local soft drink firm Parle for this reason. Second, such leveraging can occur in multiple parts of the value chain. Coke's acquisition of Parle also gave it the locally valuable Thums Up brand of Parle. Third, the acquisition may permit a firm to restructure the combined firm for greater global efficiency and effectiveness. When Daimler acquired Chrysler, it could potentially exploit economies of scale and scope globally in several parts of the value chain.

In the case of Indian acquisitions abroad, value chain leverage was often at work. For example, Tata Tea's acquisition of Tetley of the United Kingdom and Eight O'Clock Coffee in the United States gave them access to both brands and their distribution systems. Ranbaxy gained manufacturing plants and economies of scale through acquisitions. In industries as varied as consumer products, information systems, automotive manufacturing, and chemicals, Indian firms have recognized the need to augment and leverage their value chain advantages globally. This pattern also holds across firms since both large, established firms such as the Tatas and Reliance, as well as newer firms such as Spentex and Silverline, have used similar strategic logics to justify their forays abroad. Lenovo and Geely of China also pointed to such leverage across brands, technology, and distribution access while justifying their overseas acquisitions.

If globalization has such obvious benefits for C&I firms, why did we see such a flurry of foreign acquisitions starting only in the 1990s? To explain that, we need to look at two additional factors: regulatory changes in China and India and the changes in global capital markets.

## Regulatory Changes Thesis

Until the early 1990s, India had a highly restrictive foreign exchange regime. It did not allow free flow of capital even on the trade account side, let alone the capital account side. To reduce the need for Indian capital, the government required Indian firms to form joint ventures when they went abroad. It even asked firms to limit their capital contribution to joint ventures to export of Indian machinery. Indeed, the Third World multinationals phenomenon mentioned earlier may have been due to such stringent restrictions since expansion into Third World nations could easily be done through low-cost and technologically low-end machinery from India.[20] After the reform process started in the early 1990s, restrictive foreign investment rules were relaxed. As capital constraints loosened, Indian firms took to acquisitions. By 2006, the Indian government allowed firms to make investments abroad automatically so long as the total overseas investments were less than twice the net worth of the Indian firm making the investment.[21]

A related development in Indian regulations since 1992 was the wider latitude granted to Indian firms to raise capital overseas. It came at a propitious time for Indian firms seeking to expand abroad as the global capital markets were especially receptive to Indian firms' capital needs after 1992.

As in India, in China too, policy changes in the past two decades have encouraged overseas acquisitions and investments by Chinese firms. Beginning in the mid-1980s, China began to make policy changes and consistently simplified the processes required for direct investment by Chinese firms. Meanwhile, it also facilitated Chinese companies' access to capital required for such acquisition activities by providing cheap financing through many state-owned banks. For the first time, all economic entities could apply to invest and establish foreign ventures. In 2001, China announced the "going abroad" (*zou chuqu*) strategy in China's tenth five-year plan (2001–2005) when the government pledged to establish favorable policies and coordinated schedules for Chinese enterprises to invest beyond Chinese borders. In 2002, at the Sixteenth National Congress of the Chinese Communist Party, FDI investment by Chinese companies was emphasized as one of the two general strategies for economic growth along with attracting foreign direct investment into China. In 2004, Chinese premier Wen Jiabao advocated that all Chinese firms should increase their international competitiveness through direct investment into foreign markets. In 2007, the government encouraged leading domestic firms to acquire key technologies, brands, and access to natural resources abroad. By 2010, the "Going Abroad" slogan formalized the government's support for cross-border investments. It allowed governmental agencies to implement and coordinate this strategy, enabling Chinese firms to gain support at both the national level and regional levels.[22]

## Global Capital Markets Thesis

Capital markets do not create demand for acquisitions, but they serve as an accelerator for acquisition activity.[23] Peak periods of acquisition activity are associated with low interest rates, a robust debt market, and a strong equity market, which create a market awash with liquidity that facilitates acquisitions. Two macroeconomic factors helped this process from the early 1990s to 2008: for much of this period, the U.S. Federal Reserve kept a rather loose monetary policy, and as China and other Asian economies continued to focus on export-led development, these countries accumulated vast foreign exchange reserves that were available to global capital markets. These factors led to a highly liquid global capital market.

The liquidity in the market resulted in an increased demand for investment alternatives by investors. As the economic growth prospects of Asia rose, pension funds and other capital market players began to allocate more of their investment dollars to Asian countries. Between 1990 and 2006, cross-border capital flows rose at an annual rate of 14.6 percent, according to an October 2008 report by McKinsey Global Institute.[24] As the Indian economy continued to grow fast, global capital markets revised their views on the investment prospects of Indian firms. This allowed Indian firms to raise capital more easily at home and abroad. As for Chinese firms, China's burgeoning foreign exchange reserves meant easy access to capital from state-owned banks eager to support the government's "going abroad" strategy for China's aspiring multinationals.

## Implications of Growing Cross-Border Acquisitions by Emerging Economy Companies

An important question that confronts managers and researchers, then, is this: If Chinese and Indian firms are beginning to behave like Western multinationals, what are the implications of this development for managers? We discern three broad approaches:

1. Treat the development as a revolutionary break in the history of global business and hail the acquiring firms as bringing unheralded changes to the world of commerce. This perspective views the overseas acquisitions by emerging market firms as a natural trajectory of their internationalization. Researchers writing in this vein carefully document and celebrate the growth of MNCs from emerging markets but leave unexplored the implications of the phenomenon.

2. Acknowledge that acquisitions by C&I firms are indeed rising but question whether they are indeed value creating. Taking the cue from traditional finance and strategy literature, this approach asks questions such as these: Have the buyers from newly industrializing countries overpaid for these acquisitions? Do such buyers have the wherewithal to add to or extract value from their overseas acquisitions? If the answer to these questions are in the negative, then incumbents in global industries have little to fear from or worry about such acquisitions.

3. This final approach, which we adopt, is to acknowledge that acquisitions by firms from China and India are indeed rising. But we then ask a different set of questions, primarily from a competitive perspective. Taking the cue from strategy literature, this approach asks questions such as: How do these overseas acquisitions by firms from newly industrializing countries change the competitive landscape in global industries? How do they influence the strategic options open to incumbents in these industries? In what ways do different responses to the questions influence how incumbents react, or should react, to these overseas acquisitions by Chinese and Indian companies in their industries?

The first approach is exemplified by writers who praise the growth of multinationals from China and India but stop there.[25]

A recent book on emerging Indian multinationals cites a number of Indian firms, such as Tata Motors, Tata Steel, Godrej, Suzlon, Bharat Forge, and Hindalco, that have made acquisitions abroad and indicates that it is part of the companies' strategy to globalize. The authors do not, however, ask why it should matter to their global rivals. Witness their description of Suzlon's acquisitions: "Suzlon acquired Hansen Transmissions of Belgium in 2006 . . . [which] cemented Suzlon's position . . . as a top-tier global manufacturer."[26] The authors then go on to describe how Suzlon is trying to overcome challenges associated with globalization such as managing cultural diversity, maintaining financial performance, and growth. There is no discussion about what challenges Suzlon's rise poses for its global rivals and how they could and should respond to them. Many commentators in newly industrializing countries have taken to writing paeans of praise for globalizing firms. For our purpose, though, such pronouncements of greatness of globalizing firms from India or China are not of much help.

The second approach acknowledges the rising trend in overseas acquisitions by Chinese and Indian firms but then goes on to question the value of such acquisitions. This approach takes a firmly financial perspective. The literature suggests that a large proportion of acquisitions does not, in general, create value for the acquiring firm. Some researchers have concluded that between half and three-fourths of acquiring firms have actually cost their shareholders by destroying shareholder value.[27] One researcher has used this value creation perspective to question the usefulness of Indian firms' overseas acquisitions.[28] He argues that Indian firms' recent overseas acquisitions have not been value creating but value destroying. Using detailed case studies of acquisitions in the steel industry (Tata Steel's acquisition of Corus), aluminum industry (Hindalco's acquisition of Novelis), and automotive industry (Tata Motors' acquisition of Jaguar and Land Rover), he argues that these acquisitions fail the test of value creation. He hypothesizes that management hubris and nationalistic cheerleading have led to poor strategic assessments, followed by overpayment and poorly conceived integration efforts. These have combined to make these acquisitions poor strategic moves. His conclusion is that Indian firms' acquisitions have destroyed shareholder value and are more of an albatross around the necks of Indian companies rather than opportunities for enhancing long-term advantage. Presumably similar arguments can be made of Chinese acquisitions abroad.

This criticism of Indian firms' acquisitions has to be tempered by some considerations. One is that the acquisitions considered in the three case studies—Tata-Corus, Tata-Jaguar, and Hindalco-Novelis—are large ones. Large acquisitions tend to be more complex to execute, and so the stock market tends to react more negatively to them. It may be unfair to infer from these that all Indian acquisitions are value destroying. Second, it is generally believed that firms that do large one-off acquisitions do worse than firms that tend to do a series of small to medium acquisitions since the latter allow firms to develop expertise in pre- and post-acquisitions capabilities over time to make the acquisitions pay off. A good example is the Mexican cement firm, CEMEX, which has concluded several acquisitions over two decades working from a disciplined acquisitions playbook. Indeed, in India, there are a number of companies, such as Bharat Forge, that have adopted this approach. It will be interesting to see what their track record has been with respect to value creation through overseas acquisitions.

Thus, we have a paradox. While some writers' unbridled praise for overseas acquisitions by C&I firms with its attendant nationalistic triumphalism is not illuminating, others who take the opposite position focus narrowly on value creation or destruction. Neither addresses the question as to whether and how the competitive landscape is being changed by such acquisitions. It is possible that many of the overseas acquisitions by C&I firms may turn out to be poorly thought out and may not help the firms to be successful globally over the long run, but it does not mean they have no consequences for businesses competing against these firms. Even if one concedes that these acquisitions by C&I firms may destroy value for shareholders, they pose challenges for their rivals. In other words, it is possible that these acquisitions may significantly affect the fortunes of their global rivals in the short to medium run.

Our preference is to focus on the question: What are the implications of overseas acquisitions by Chinese and Indian firms for other firms? To answer, we need to go back to why firms choose to acquire rather than expand abroad through greenfield investments. Companies acquire for three reasons: (1) quicker entry into other markets by gaining access to distribution networks, brands, and customers, (2) access to specialized resources such as unique or valuable technology that may take a long time to develop in-house, and (3) economies of scale and scope for existing assets located domestically or overseas. In sum, overseas acquisitions help a firm either to vault over entry or mobility barriers or help it to compete with a different business model by leveraging its existing assets in a new locale. Since most of today's multinationals from Europe, Japan, and the United States have painstakingly accumulated assets and advantages over the years, the sudden influx of new rivals from emerging markets such as China and India may upset their well-laid plans to dominate their industries. Established multinationals must recognize the impact of overseas acquisitions by emerging market firms on changes in the competitive landscape and respond effectively.

## Emerging Economy Acquirers: Four Case Studies

To examine how overseas acquisitions by emerging market firms have played out in the pre- and postacquisition periods within the acquiring firms and how they have affected the competitive landscape, we have taken a closer look at a number of emerging market firms in different industries. To the extent possible, we also look at how incumbent firms have reacted to the competitive moves of emerging market firms. We examine two case studies each from India and China to illustrate our analysis.

## Bharat Forge

Bharat Forge Limited (BFL) of the Kalyani Group of companies in India is a manufacturer of forged and machined components for automotive and nonautomotive sectors. Until the late 1990s, BFL was largely a domestic firm with a reputation for quality engineering and manufacturing. Since then, it has become a global player mainly through acquisitions. Over ten years, BFL has acquired six midsized firms in England, Germany, Sweden, and the United States.

How did BFL succeed in becoming a global competitor using acquisitions? What challenges does it pose for its rivals?

BFL followed a disciplined script with respect to its acquisitions. It rarely overpaid. Its first acquisition in England, for example, cost the firm only about 3 million British pounds (against the original asking price of 10 million British pounds). It achieved this by structuring a deal in which it lined up other buyers for things it did not want, such as the land, buildings, and plant, while at the same time picking up things it wanted, such as tools and dies as well as long-term contracts worth 10 million British pounds for the next seven years.[29] It also integrated its acquisitions effectively in a short period of time to make them productive parts of its global operations. For example, BFL completed the integration of its German acquisition within three years while increasing its sales and profitability. In addition, BFL developed an acquisition and integration methodology that allowed it to make a series of well-timed and well-thought-out acquisitions and to integrate them effectively.

BFL executed these acquisitions within the context of a well-planned globalization strategy. It developed a strategic positioning that combined some differentiation based on speed to market and technology with low-cost production. For instance, it produced a new part for its German and U.S. customers with excellent quality within three weeks of being requested to do so.[30] Then it exploited the complementary competences located in the different parts of global operations with skillful distribution of roles and responsibilities. Its German operation, for example, works closely with customers using its strong design and engineering capabilities, whereas its Indian operation is leveraged as a low-cost manufacturing base. Finally, over time, BFL has evolved what it calls the dual-shore capability to serve its global customers better. Under this approach, BFL has a design, forging, and manufacturing capability, "one close to the customer and one in a low cost but technologically competitive destination," such as India (and perhaps, in the future, China).[31] Backed by a full-service capability and dual-shore model, BFL has become a provider of end-to-end solutions from product conceptualization to designing and finally manufacturing, testing, and validation to customers that now include the top five passenger and commercial vehicle manufacturers in the world and a large number of automotive original equipment manufacturers and tier 1 auto components firms.

For BFL's global rivals, the most interesting question posed by BFL's globalization is this: How does it change the competitive landscape? Through its well-executed acquisitions, it has overcome the mobility barriers in the global auto components industry. Historically, these barriers have been access to critical customers such as top-tier vehicle manufacturers and top-tier auto components firms that often serve as system integrators for large end-product makers, design and process capabilities, and high-quality production capability. BFL's acquisitions in Europe and the United States have provided them to the company. BFL's imaginative combination of its low-cost manufacturing base and newly acquired technological capabilities has also allowed it to change the rules of the game in the industry. Its rivals now have to find ways to match its value proposition that combine speed to market, low cost, superior design, and customer intimacy. Witness how firms from countries like India and China may also be able to take this approach a step further by exploiting what has come to be called "frugal engineering": the ability of firms in emerging markets to take a clean-slate approach to designing products that could deliver significant improvements in both cost and new features simultaneously.[32] Finally, BFL's development of dual-shore capability has given it the option to selectively cut prices to put a crimp on its global rivals. If that happens, especially in a business cycle downturn, rivals will be in the unenviable position of having to choose between holding prices and losing market share or cutting prices and suffering margin erosion threatening their long-term viability.

## Bharti Airtel

A similar story may be unfolding in the global telecommunications industry with the entry of Bharti Airtel (BA) from India through cross-border acquisitions in South Asia and Africa. BA's cross-border acquisitions have allowed it to change the rules of the game in the telecommunications sector in the countries it has entered. Like BFL, BA honed its initial strategy in India, where it got its start in the mobile telephony sector in the early 1990s as India liberalized the economy. In the early 2000s, BA decided to try a radical strategic approach. Seeking faster growth in the highly competitive domestic cellular phone market, it decided to outsource the management of much of its technology network, including its information technology backbone infrastructure management, to IBM, Nokia, and Ericsson. Freed of the need for huge capital investment in technology and IT infrastructure, the company began to focus on "understanding customer preferences, regulatory barriers, and emerging markets, ranging from Blackberry service to digital television."[33] It was a revolutionary business model that had never been tried by any major telecom service provider.[34] It allowed BA to increase its revenue tenfold (from 25 billion rupees in 2003 to 250 billion rupees in 2008) while increasing the number of employees only fivefold (from five thousand in 2003 to twenty-five thousand in 2008).

In the early 2000s, BA entered neighboring nations such as Seychelles and Sri Lanka on its own. Then it acquired a mobile telephone service operator in Bangladesh. In 2010, it decided to move aggressively into Africa. It acquired the mobile operations of Zain in fifteen African nations, thereby becoming the fifth largest mobile operator in the world. What is interesting is that BA has brought its business model to Africa, Sri Lanka, and Bangladesh. In Africa, it has concluded an outsourcing agreement with IBM, Tech Mahindra, and Spanco to manage the IT and telecommunications network infrastructure. In Bangladesh. it has outsourced the management of its technology operations to IBM.[35]

The story of BA is similar to BFL. First, its acquisitions have allowed the emerging market firm to leapfrog over the entry and mobility barriers of customer base, local presence, and local brand recognition. Second, by replicating its new business model, honed in India, BA has fundamentally changed the competitive landscape in Africa. It has already signaled its readiness to combine its low-cost strategy with a big push for market growth and market share growth. Yet another emerging market player has changed the rules of the game to which its rivals have to respond. Third, it has forced its rivals to respond because they otherwise risked losing market position in the marketplace. Witness what Mickael Ghossein, chief executive officer of Orange Telkom Kenya, which is 51 percent held by France Telecom SA, has to say: "We have to review our business model and make it leaner and compete on price and have more quality in our network and to have more data. . . . We have to enhance our quality of networks."[36]

## Lenovo

Lenovo, the Chinese manufacturer of personal computers (PCs), started in 1984 with the blessings and financial support of the

Chinese government through the Chinese Academy of Sciences. Twenty-five years later, it is one of the top three PC makers in the world, with a globally recognized brand, products known for innovative features, and a global organization. In 2011, it surpassed Dell to become the second largest seller of PCs globally.[37] Lenovo's transformation too is a story of global ambitions and a well-planned acquisition strategy.

By early 2001, Lenovo's 30 percent domestic market share far outdistanced its rivals. Its leaders recognized, however, that it would soon face competition from abroad and decided to become a more global company. It recognized that it needed to develop a globally recognized brand supported by innovation and low-cost production capabilities.[38] In 2004, it signed up to become an Olympic Partner, becoming the exclusive provider of computing equipment and services for the winter Olympics in 2006 and summer Olympics in 2008.

In early 2005, it moved to acquire for $1.75 billion IBM's personal computer business, which included the Thinkpad line of laptops, using a mix of cash and stock. It was helped in the move partly by funding from government sources that left the Chinese Academy of Sciences as the largest single shareholder, with 27 percent equity but with no board seats. Lenovo received the right to use the IBM brand name for five years. Lenovo's stated intent was that "this is just the start. We have big plans to grow."[39] As the chairman of Lenovo, Yang Yuanqing, proclaimed, "We are proud of our Chinese roots," but "we no longer want to be positioned as a Chinese company. We want to be a truly global company."[40]

In order to become a more global firm, Lenovo had to overcome its lack of deep managerial expertise. It did this by hiring a number of international executives with experience at IBM, Dell, and other firms. As part of this global transformation, Lenovo has an organizational structure with no headquarters, choosing to rotate meetings of senior managers across several bases worldwide. In addition to creating virtual development teams, major efforts are directed to integrating the different cultures within the firm. Using IBM's reputation, Lenovo has been able to penetrate the large enterprise and midmarket, especially in laptops. Simultaneously, it has shored up its profitability by moving to strengthen its position in the still-growing China domestic market. The growth comes in part due to Chinese government stimulus under which subsidies are provided for the purchase of computers in rural markets.

The most critical thing that Lenovo did was to focus on developing a global brand. It settled on an approach that built up Lenovo as a strong master brand while retaining and strengthening the Thinkpad product brand.[41] It launched advertising campaigns that stressed how Lenovo was making the Thinkpad better and how the Lenovo master brand stood for innovation. Lenovo's marketing head argued, "We have very efficient base in China, along with a 5 percent after-tax profit and global infrastructure. Unlike the competition, we feel we have the ability to combine efficiency *and* innovation. That is what Lenovo is all about and it's what we've set down in our mission statement: *We put more innovation in the hands of more people so that they can do more amazing things.*"[42] Lenovo also formed joint marketing alliances with leading firms like NEC in Japan. Its growth in China gives it economies of scale, while its nearness and close relationships with component makers give it lower costs and a shorter supply chain.

Lenovo has arrived at the global arena through its imaginative use of a major acquisition to overcome the barriers of brand recognition and access to key customer groups. By combining brand name, innovative features, channel proliferation, and low-cost production, Lenovo has created a strong and defensible strategic position against rivals. Nothing illustrates its global success and its confidence in the future more than its decision to drop the IBM name from its advertisements two years ahead of schedule. It is clear that Lenovo has changed the competitive landscape for its rivals.

## Geely

While Lenovo's global strategy development based partly on its acquisition of IBM's PC business has already shown some impressive results, Geely's efforts in that direction are just beginning. Nevertheless, we can see here the same elements that drove Lenovo's globalization efforts. Geely also seems to be intent on changing the competitive landscape in the global automotive industry through its acquisition of Volvo.

Geely was established in 1998 as a privately owned automobile manufacturing firm with financing from state-owned banks and governments in China, including governments of provinces. By 2009, it was manufacturing 330,000 vehicles, most of them largely in the small, inexpensive segment. As its profitability rose, the company developed global ambitions. In 2008, it exported vehicles to Brazil. Exports to Russia and Algeria followed. Meanwhile, it expanded its product line to include pickup trucks.

In March 2010, Geely made a big move when it purchased Volvo for $1.8 billion from Ford. In 1999, Ford had paid $6.45 billion to acquire Volvo, a Swedish automaker with a strong reputation for cutting-edge technologies especially related to safety features and durability. Although Volvo was profitable when it was acquired, Ford never managed to turn a profit on it. In 2009, Volvo's annual sales had fallen to 330,000 vehicles from its peak of 450,000 in 2007, mostly as a result of stronger competition from other luxury carmakers such as Mercedes Benz and Audi, which introduced models competing directly with Volvo's lineup. In addition, as more carmakers began to focus on safety, Volvo's distinctive image in this dimension was blunted.

Not only would the Volvo acquisition allow Geely to double its production in one stroke, it would provide a launching pad to develop Geely's presence in the luxury car segment in China. China is one of the fastest-growing car markets in the world (from 330,000 units in the 1990s to more than 7 million units in 2009), and growth in sales of brands such as Daimler and

BMW suggests that the luxury market is probably poised for high growth. The luxury market is also very attractive for automakers since it yields high profit margins. However, Volvo sold only around 22,000 cars in China in 2009.

Geely's acquisition was financed by the government of China and the two provinces in which Geely promised to build Volvo plants. Geely has also pledged to retain Volvo's Swedish plants and Volvo's positioning as a luxury brand. Geely's plans for Volvo seem ambitious. It hopes to double in five years Volvo's global volume to 660,000 cars, referring to Volvo as a "tiger" in a zoo that would be liberated to pursue new opportunities. This acquisition gives Geely access to Volvo's outstanding research and development capabilities. Geely now has the potential to expand Volvo sales in China and an opportunity to sell its own vehicles through Volvo's worldwide dealer network.

In broad terms, Geely's strategy seems to be to build on its low-cost manufacturing base in China where parts and sub-systems may be manufactured for assembly in Sweden and elsewhere. It will leverage Volvo's technology to improve its own line of cars. It will also use Volvo's dealer network to sell Geely's cars in overseas markets. In other words, like Lenovo, Geely will try to change the rules of the game in the global automobile market to create a strong and sustainable position for itself.

The case studies of both Lenovo and Geely illustrate the growing global ambitions of players from China and how they have used acquisitions to establish a major foothold in developed country markets as they seek to realize their global ambitions. In both cases, the acquisition almost doubled their unit volumes and made them significant players. Their relatively easy access to capital from the national and provincial governments of China gives them a leg up in targeting overseas acquisitions. These acquisitions, in addition to providing access to attractive positions in mature and developed markets, also provide access to advanced technologies that allows these companies to upgrade their technological capabilities to compete more effectively against established players. Finally, these acquisitions provide in some cases ammunition for the acquirers to expand their domestic market positions, which translate into benefits of scale economies that when leveraged appropriately may strengthen their global competitive positions.

## Implications for Developed Country Multinational Companies

Let us summarize the competitive threat posed by emerging market multinationals that are invading markets abroad through acquisitions:

- Acquisitions allow emerging market players to leapfrog over entry and mobility barriers in other more mature markets.
- Acquisitions allow emerging market players to change the rules of the game in new markets by letting them combine low cost and some differentiation in new ways.
- Acquisitions allow emerging market players to leverage their competences such as frugal engineering in a novel way to compete in other markets.
- Given that many of these emerging market players are dominant players in their large home markets such as China and India, they already enjoy economies of scale in addition to absolute cost advantages relative to their rivals in developed markets.
- With creative configurations of their global value chains after acquisition, these market players are emerging in some cases as formidable competitors, threatening the competitive positions of their established rivals.
- Acquisitions may enable emerging market players to force established rivals to make unpleasant choices when responding to their competitive moves.

An interesting question that immediately arises is this: How can incumbents respond to these competitive moves by emerging market firms? From our observations, we identify a few.

Incumbent multinationals in developed countries need to develop responses to these newer developments. Here a few key points are salient.

- Incumbent multinationals must be careful not to underestimate the capabilities of these emerging market multinationals. The latter often have relatively good cost positions, product development and engineering skills, and competitive back-office operations. Also, their business models have been honed to be successful in demanding and challenging circumstances, often calling for innovations to succeed in a climate of frugality. These often make them do a lot more with a lot less than their better-endowed competitors abroad.

- Incumbents need to move beyond a regional mind-set that tends to insist on seeing the world as a congeries of independent regional markets and develop a more integrated global mind-set that recognizes trade-offs among different regional and country markets.

- Incumbents need to come up with creative responses based on a number of game-theoretic ideas such as: (1) deny advantageous entry opportunities through preemption, as Whirlpool did in the United States against Haier from China; (2) invade the home countries of emerging rivals, as IBM Global Services and Accenture have by moving into India and China in a big way to counter the threat of firms like TCS and Infosys; and (3) level the playing field by gaining low-cost production and innovation capabilities in emerging markets through innovative partnerships in those markets, as pharmaceutical firms have done in India and China.

# Part Four

## INNOVATION OPPORTUNITIES AND CHALLENGES IN EMERGING ASIA

# 8

# INNOVATING IN THE VORTEX

## New Perspectives from Radically Different Business Experiences in India

### Srikanth Kannapan, Kuruvilla Lukose

There is a populous and emerging global superpower where access to clean and safe drinking water is still a daily struggle across much of its expanse. Reliable electricity is still to arrive across most of its villages. Living is frugal.

This is the market into which an indigenously designed portable, electric-free, environment-sensitive domestic water filtration device has recently arrived. The Swach requires neither running water nor electricity to function and retails at less than twenty U.S. dollars. Resulting from several years of research, the filtration uses abundantly available husk, a by-product from milling rice, along with fine particles of nano-silver, to achieve affordable and reliable water purification. The market is vast—several million households. The inventor is Tata.[1] The country is India.

### Shifting Perspective

Conventional thinking views India as an information technology (IT) outsourcing destination. It misses something more profound: the beehive of market, talent, sociocultural, and business infrastructural context below the surface that, if understood, offers a new opportunity space. Companies are only beginning to appreciate this space: the opportunity to innovate, and innovate to create global value.

Recognizing such potential, however, requires shifting perspective below the surface, where one can understand the underlying factors of the India context. Such understanding enables companies and their leaders to play with these factors to drive business outcome in ways that leave others bewildered, in much the same way that remarkable green revolutions can result in less-than-perfect environments by a clever play of soil, seed, and irrigation.

Companies able to comprehend such factors peculiar to emerging economies stand to gain substantially today compared with the pre-2000 era, just as those who fail to do so will lose disproportionately. Accenture, for example, has about half its worldwide workforce operating from India, yet in the rapidly growing India market itself, it faces challenges in catching up with leaders like IBM in its core business areas of outsourcing and consulting.[2]

Taking advantage of such opportunities is challenging even for well-established local players. Consider the contrasting experiences of Mindtree and Sasken, both mid-tier Bangalore-based IT companies. Both made forays into the growing mobile communication handset market. Mindtree invested heavily in developing an Android phone for over a year but had to rapidly wind down due to expense overruns that were eating into profitability.[3] Sasken, building on its telecom industry specialization, developed an Inmarsat satellite phone handset, integrating both internal and acquired technology to great advantage. First-year sales to high-end worldwide markets are expected to exceed a respectable eighty thousand units.[4]

How can companies tap into this new opportunity space and succeed?

## A Pattern for Innovation

Addressing this question must start with a basic question: What draws business to India in the first place? At a simple level, it is the charm of a market with a billion wallets and the talent of a billion heads. In fact, it is less. The working population is about 64 percent of the total,[5] while the IT industry, for example, directly employs roughly 2.5 million workers, a mere 0.4 percent of the working population.[6] And with more specialization of skill, the winnowing continues. Neither is it really a billion wallets. Frugality abounds across wide swathes of the population pyramid, especially at the bottom of the pyramid (BOP).

Things are not what they seem at first, and this merely begins the complexity. Entering India for business or getting into business in India is like being drawn into a vortex of new experiences that are radically different from those in mature economies and distinctive even from other emerging economies.

Yet there seem to be patterns of successful innovation emerging from this complexity. We offer one such pattern of enterprise innovation that we have uncovered. The pattern is preliminary; it has been induced from a variety of empirical sources and serves as a basis for further validation and refinement.[7]

Here are the key elements of the pattern.

Enterprises drawn into India by the attractions of market and talent have to deal first with the complexities within these factors themselves. Soon they have to grapple with the additional factor of business infrastructure covering all components of soft and hard facilities and services that are the lifeblood of enterprises. While market and talent are factors that enterprises can do something to grasp and influence, business infrastructure is usually something that comes with the territory and is not under the influence of the enterprise.

Finally, and perhaps most important, there is the underlying factor of the sociocultural character of the country. In a country as large and multifaceted as India, this is hard enough to understand, let alone influence. The sociocultural base for India is extremely diverse and complex. It is also dynamic, considering that the estimated median age of the population is about twenty-five years.

The sociocultural factor characterizes the nature, behavior, and aspirations of people. And people are the base of any industry, as a market to sell to, a source of skill for the enterprise, and as the key interface to business infrastructure. Hence, this factor directly and indirectly is responsible for the radically new business experience in India.

For business leaders, these new business experiences lead to dilemmas on whether to comply with the local practices or impose their own, disappointments from mismatched skills, confusion from unpredictable demand for their products, and disorientation with respect to the sociocultural environment.

Leaders are subject to pressures of performance, caught between high expectations of success and growth that are supposed to accrue from participation in an emerging economy and the challenges arising out of practical realities. Although this situation can be a source of frustration, leaders are also aware that such situations can be fertile ground for creative solutions.

There are two guiding forces that leaders can employ to turn such frustration to creative flow. The first is to provide the guidance for agility in the enterprise. This is the business imperative of quickly responding to clearly visible opportunities. Agility guides the organization to "harvest the ripe fruit" before it spoils or is taken away by others. The second is for leaders to provide the guidance for patience—the business wisdom of gaining a deeper understanding of the environment, investing in the development of resources, and creating an environment of contextualized experimentation that ultimately results in creating differentiated value for newly discovered needs. This is the wisdom of "nurturing the tree" before the ripe fruit can be expected, which should provide a potentially bigger harvest. Encouraging innovation in this vortex of business experience requires agility and patience.

There are several important implications for practicing leadership when enterprises are drawn into the business experience in an emerging economy like India. The guiding forces of agility and patience must be unbalanced if any type of innovation is to be encouraged. We mean "unbalanced" in the sense that organizations must see one of these guiding forces as clearly dominating the other, and with some rationale and justification.

Over time, different types of innovation seem to result from leadership actions that unbalance the enterprise (or some part of it) more toward agility or more toward patience. Conversely, this may imply that depending on the leadership's unbalanced positions between agility and patience, their organization could be steered toward different types of innovation.

The next important issue about such innovations is what value they create for the enterprise. Is it a local and temporary blip of a sales chart or development of a minor variation of an existing product? Or is it something that opens up a new growth market, creates a new category of product that has global utility, or a business model that revitalizes the entire global enterprise? Examples of companies operating in India show that some innovations have revitalized their global enterprise when impact is suitably calibrated to the size of the enterprise: MNC, SME, or early stage.

We explore this pattern in more detail, beginning with a deeper assessment of the underlying factors of business experience.

## Underlying Factors of Business Experience

Our focus here is on the dimensions and variations embedded in the four factors underlying business experience since they can have a huge impact on business success in India: the market, talent, the business infrastructure, and the socioculture.

### Market Factors

Every market has dimensions of segmentation—consumer versus enterprise, domestic versus global—and distinct industry sectors spanning finance, telecom, retail, and others. Every cross-combination produces segments with potentially unique characteristics and trends. For example, most market watchers would not fail to notice the rapid growth in wireless telecom markets in India, while curiously observing the patchy growth in organized retail despite a rapidly growing consumer economy.

What is less known is revealed at the next levels of granularity. Let us take the telecom consumer market for illustration. India's telecom consumer market, while growing fast, has one of the lowest average revenue-per-customer yields in the world. Indian consumers are largely frugal. Whereas high-end lifestyles and business practices consume high bandwidth and services, the majority of the socioeconomic classes execute creative leaps in frugal behavior. A "missed call" is made by calling someone and hanging up before a connection. It is a preagreed message to indicate any number of things. And it is free to both caller and receiver.

Frugality is also revealed in the use of inexpensive dual-subscriber identity module (SIM) handsets. One SIM is allocated for incoming calls (free) and purchased only once, giving the owner a consistent and perpetual number on which to be reached. The other SIM, for outgoing calls (which are not free), is acquired and recharged opportunistically by choosing the lowest-cost service provider at a particular time. And the costs are indeed low; India has one of the lowest per-minute and even per-second rates in the world.

Another characteristic is the amazingly low number of postpaid consumers. Only 5 percent of users are postpaid customers who, unlike prepaid customers, pay their bills after services are rendered.[8] Since only postpaid customers are required to provide valid personal information during subscription paperwork, it is extremely hard to collect demographic use information and reliably analyze it for marketing, product development, and pricing. What do target marketing, customer retention, churn management, and customer lifetime value mean in the context of a large, emerging market with such challenges?

Tried-and-tested market strategies, tactics, and execution models developed with mature economy business experiences have little meaning in the face of this complexity. They have to be reinvented based on actual business experience in an emerging economy like India.

Similar complexities abound in other markets, cross-combining the dimensions of segmentation. Does this make the 1 billion wallet market less attractive? Not to the creative entrants who are learning to untangle the complexity and play them to an advantage. The 1 billion wallet market exists, but it is highly segmented and displays skews and extreme variation.

## Talent Factors

India has 1 billion heads of talent, and the story is similar to the 1 billion wallets, though with some important distinctions. As with the market factor, there are dimensions of segmentation and variation for talent: urban and rural; regional, cultural, and language variations; levels of concentrations of educational institutions; degrees of economic development; histories of local government initiative and investment. As with markets, every cross-combination of each dimension results in a talent pool with unique characteristics and a wide spectrum of capability.

Talent is hard to find, lead, manage, and transform for productivity and innovation anywhere in the world, but complexities in the India context require deeper understanding. A common mistake is to look for talent described in frames of reference of mature economies. Without local adaptation, one may find only a trickle of candidates or none at all for senior or specialized positions. But with some sampling of available talent and locally adapted job descriptor refactoring, one may discover a clutch of qualified candidates or even a flood of raw talent to pick from.

Here is an interesting example. A South India–based print and media production firm has worldwide educational, academic, and professional organizations among its clients. Its workforce, engaged in document layout and formatting tasks, is composed primarily of enthusiastic and effectively retrained grocery store sales staff. This was possible through task deskilling and localization, resulting in a team of highly productive, stable, content, and cost-effective workers.

Universal motivators such as money are one part of attraction and retention of talent. These are less tangible yet powerful talent attractors. In crowded and poorly connected metropolitan cities, as simple a thing as travel time from home to work could be the clincher. Another peculiarity is the strong influence wielded by the job seeker's family in the decision to join. Shrewd employers target family and friend circles through informal social interactions during the hiring process and beyond.

Organizations that manage to attract sufficient job applicants still need to ascertain their true credentials. An employer may discover, for example, that the true credentials of a candidate fall significantly short of his or her stated claims. Some surveys estimate that 30 percent of all résumés in the IT industry have discrepancies, compelling firms, including major ones like TCS, Infosys, IBM, and Wipro, to undertake periodic validation of employee credentials.[9]

The variation in quality of educational institutes is also far wider than in mature economies, ranging from institutes that do not even exist, to truly world-class colleges graduating the best and brightest in India.

These factors, combined with regional and economic variations, provide a glimpse of the dilemmas in building a competent workforce in an emerging economy like India.

## Business Infrastructure Factors

The need to align with even unusual local practices applies to everything, starting with setting up an office. Maintenance and security are appreciable tasks. Backups for crucial telecommunication and civic infrastructures are mandatory.

There is significant complexity in dealings with government and regulation at all levels. Specialized local knowledge in financial, legal, statutory, and other areas can be procured as a service, but the quality may be less than expected unless providers are carefully chosen.

Astute decisions on location, setup, and partnering are vital and cannot be left to chance. Contracts influenced by verbal or implied understanding may prove difficult to enforce. Excessive influence of brand image or references in partner selection can be dangerous. For example, 2G wireless telecom spectrum scams in India are revealing multiple situations where global brands have been drawn into investigations due to their local partner's questionable practices.

Despite these criticisms, India boasts some immensely impressive successes in this area. It successfully runs the world's most scalable and free multiparty elections across regional and national levels. This requires coordinating the bureaucracy, police, and scores of volunteers and using electronic voting machines with ballot validation in the presence of representatives of all contending parties. It also runs an online reservation system for a nationwide railway service that millions use daily.

## Sociocultural Factors

There are distinct dimensions and variability in the sociocultural context in India as well:

- *Diverse:* Diversity reigns in language, food preferences, education, religion, and economic class, leading to overlapping and contradictory definitions of individual and group identity. An otherwise illiterate housemaid may be found educating an urban grandmother on the economics of cell phone subscription plans.
- *Extremes:* India overlays the multiplicity of gatherer, agrarian, industrial, and knowledge economies across

geographical population distributions, resulting in juxtapositions of extremes: Mercedes, Nanos, and bullock carts all vying for space on the same dusty road of a booming mining town.

- *Ancient:* The layering of society over generations has led to complexities in beliefs, behaviors, and aspirations. Generalizations within groups of common identity may not stand. Conversely, similarities may exist across apparently distinct groups. Food habits, for example, are hard to predict from any one ethnological factor such as region or religion.

- *Undefined:* There are insufficient reliable data for any finely grained analysis of demographic or psychographic patterns in the population. Macrolevel data, when available, become the basis for decision making that may lead one astray or miss opportunities. For example, the discovery of a large and profitable bottom-of-pyramid market for personal care consumables packaged in a one-time-use format was entirely fortuitous.

- *Dynamic:* The dynamics of a youthful society on the move leads to unlikely disruptions. MNC cell phone manufacturers patiently built the Indian market for basic handsets, only to see these segments snatched away by nimble and later-arriving local assemblers of low-cost smart phones.

These dimensions of variation constitute the sociocultural foundation for business experience that enterprises entering India face.

## Corporate Leadership Guidance

Complexities inherent in each of the four factors compound to produce the overall business experience in India. Some of this is well known and has been written about.[10] But what is still needed is a framework for leadership with an awareness of its expected impact on organizations.

Returning to our analogy of the green revolution, large land tracts and abundant water are available, the seeds are entirely up to us to plant, and the climate seems receptive though unpredictable. But getting to the expected rich harvest seems challenging.

Let us revisit the two seemingly contradictory guiding forces that leaders can employ to turn such challenge to creative flow:

1. *Leadership guidance for agility:* This is the imperative of quickly responding to clearly visible opportunities and winning. Agility guides the organization to harvest ripe fruit.

2. *Leadership guidance for patience:* This is the wisdom of developing opportunities that few have recognized, tapping into them, and scaling them to breakthrough levels. Patience guides the organization to nurture the trees for a big harvest.

Such contradictions are akin to those originally explored by James March in the context of organizational learning, design, and adaptation where it is characterized as a trade-off between exploration of new possibilities and exploitation of old certainties.[11] A wider variety of research contributions in this area is assimilated by Gupta, Smith, and Shalley to show the interplay between exploration and exploitation through organizational implementations of "ambidexterity" or "punctuated equilibrium" where such dualities are rationalized through either synchronous activities or cyclic temporal activities.[12]

Our intent here is to deepen the understanding of such age-old dualities in the context of emerging economies such as India where such challenges reach new levels of complexity and dynamics.

## Leadership Psychology

Now consider the situation of leaders: dilemmas bubbling up from radically new business experiences, pressures to perform to the high expectations of emerging economy opportunities, and seemingly contradictory options to guide the organization to seize the moment and act with agility or work with diligence but practicing patience.

Leaders have the option of providing different guidance to different parts of the organization that is within their scope, whether it is a complete enterprise, a business division, or a department. Different guidance can also be given to managing the complexity of the different factors of the business experience: when entering a market, building a talent base, coping with business infrastructure, or grasping the nature of the sociocultural base. Even at the level of an activity, leaders can guide the work toward agility or patience. The question is how much to guide what in which direction.

This context and situation pose some common pitfalls that leaders must avoid. The simplest one is in not matching the guidance to the goal or the expected outcome. For example, creating a specialized training facility or a nationwide distribution network will most likely compromise on its goals with a strong guidance for agility. And a strong guidance for patience is most likely inappropriate when addressing a major social-media-driven consumer complaint or a short-fuse sales opportunity.

Here is the most insidious pitfall. It is natural for the dilemmas and disorientation resulting from the radically new business experience to diffuse into the psychological state of the leadership. Leadership in such a state may end up hedging excessively, overloading agendas, giving inconsistent or even conflicting messages of agility and patience to the organization, or leaving the forces guiding agility and patience more or less equally balanced.

Unfortunately, most of these leadership positions pass the dilemmas down to the subordinate organization with the ambiguous guidance of "harvesting the ripe fruit" while still "nurturing the tree," preventing either from occurring. It might be argued that such ambiguity generates the creative tension that can throw up new ideas and leaders, but there are two counterpoints to this argument. The first is that even such ambiguity passed downward would have to be resolved and acted on at some level, and that would be the level at which leadership can be seen to be exercised. The second is that emerging economies are unlikely contexts to provide the luxury for ambiguous leadership positions.

## Unbalancing Agility and Patience

If the pitfalls are avoided, and leaders become deeply aware of the situation, they intuitively recognize that they need appropriate use of the guiding forces of both agility and patience. More important, they need to see the value of taking a clear and considered position strongly toward agility or strongly toward patience, depending on the situation and the goal.

This unbalancing comes with some consequences. First, the asymmetry forces a choice. Notice that the celebrated cases of reverse innovation at GE in India were driven by such choices. It did require an early realization that top-skimming the market with existing products built for mature economies or stripping down products to meet lower price points were not the approaches to pursue to reach their business goals. After this realization, the leadership strongly aligned and drove the organization toward a patient approach of developing an India market–driven product, led by a local-growth team with both R&D funding and profit-and-loss responsibility.[13]

The second consequence of unbalancing is that expected outcomes can be matched correctly to the guidance. For example, a guidance for patience may mean allowing two prototyping cycles of a product to reach customer quality expectations, whereas a guidance for agility may shoot for a beta release faster. Hence, performance expectations of the execution team can be correctly calibrated to the guidance without killing them with unrealistic goals. Referring to GE again, it is clear that leadership guidance allowed a decentralized and local market focus to take hold in the team that was targeting the needs of the India market. Expectations were correctly calibrated to reach the target feature set at the breakthrough price of a thousand dollars for a handheld electrocardiogram.

The third consequence is that limited resources can be aligned with the dominant guidance. For example, a leader can mandate that a strategic R&D unit be created patiently, combining carefully selected expertise from within the organization with diligent local hiring. In contrast, the same leader may guide toward agility in market access by engaging a higher-cost national distributor as a means of rapidly gaining market share.

Fourth, the downstream effects of unbalancing must be addressed. A rapidly expanding customer base created through agile actions must be backed up with adequate customer service to avoid customer complaints.

Finally, the most important consequence is that unbalancing guidance enables innovation through an unambiguous charter. It unlocks confidence through the ranks and engenders responsible risk taking in full awareness of the goal. Such leadership, with the clarity of a charter, an environment of experimentation, and empowerment in execution seems to be the crux in turning goals and constraints in a radically new business experience into creative flow. Notice the pride and ownership demonstrated by the GE team that led to an energetic and intelligent product development and marketing exercise for portable medical equipment.

## Playing with the Potential of Innovation

An understanding of the four underlying factors, combined with a mind-set of unbalancing guidance for either patience or agility appears to release creativity within controlled experimentation.

Over time, if done mostly right, this can create and maintain a special kind of environment—a field with the potential for innovation. This is an environment where preparedness meets opportunity when opportunity presents itself. The powder is dry to spark innovation.

The opportunities include individual and team initiatives and improbable but fortunate catalyzing events. Some of them may fizzle out due to lack of continued initiative, lack of merit in the ideas themselves, or lack of continued support from the environment. But some yield practicable results through individual and team initiative. Leadership support can establish an environment where ideas are able to draw investments and resources and make a distinctive impact on the company or its ecology of markets, industry, and society.

## The Setting: Establishing the Potential Field of Innovation

Leadership guidance encourages different settings for the potential field of innovation at different organizational scales. These actions, implemented over a period of time, also interact in a time sequence with different time lags.

We present the following examples for illustration based on executive interviews conducted at IBM, Sasken, and Strand Lifesciences, together with media and reference literature.[14]

### IBM: Global on Demand

IBM, a globally dominant IT transnational corporation, has over 100,000 employees in India according to media estimates. Figure 8.1 illustrates how we believe that IBM's actions over time have set up a potential field of innovation and the ensuing decisions that have resulted in innovative outcomes. Many of these actions are unbalanced toward patience or agility.

# Figure 8.1 The Setting: IBM's Potential Field of Innovation in India

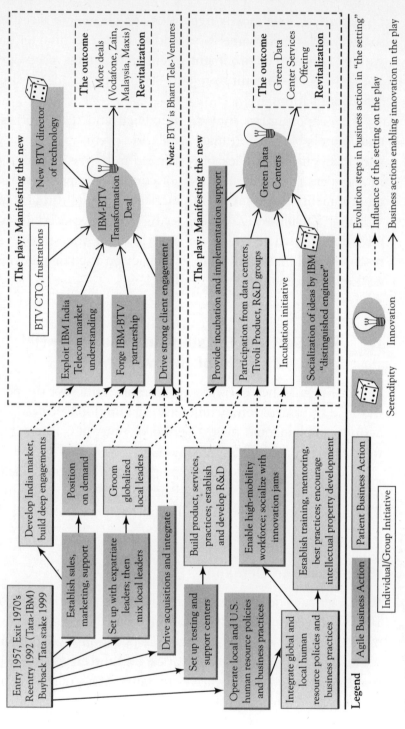

*Note:* BTV = Bharti

IBM's presence in India is a story of patience that has spanned five decades. It first entered India in 1957, only to find itself departing during a wave of Indian nationalism around 1970. Not to be deterred, IBM returned in the 1990s, initially through a partnership with Tata, converting that to full autonomy some years later. Since then, IBM has patiently developed deep engagements across Indian industry, offering computing hardware and, increasingly, services.[15]

Top-notch R&D labs, mirroring established practices in the United States, were incrementally built in India, almost one researcher at a time, by relocating IBMers from overseas and culling top-rated India-based talent. Its India human resource, training, and development policies are a fusion of global practices of aligning with local practices and sensitivities.[16] During an earlier period, Rajendra Bera, a senior research scientist hired away from a prestigious government lab in India, mentored select employees and provided them a trusted environment for sharing novel technical ideas that led to a record number of patent filings from IBM India.

Examples of IBM's agility are equally evident. Encouraging a globally mobile talent pool, IBM has integrated its workforce well beyond the organizational level by fostering personal connections and trust across disparate cultures. Experimentation and individual initiative consistent with overall business contexts are encouraged. As P. Gopalakrishnan, vice president of India Software Lab, said in an interview, "People who shut themselves in their room on a Friday afternoon and think up new things usually don't get anywhere because it is not relevant to the business, or doesn't have a delivery vehicle, or doesn't have a market need, or doesn't do something new."

On the business process outsourcing (BPO) side of the business, once the imperative for scale-up became evident, IBM chose an inorganic route by acquiring a six-thousand-person Indian company and setting a new trend of mergers and acquisitions in India.[17]

New ideas to implement and new approaches to old problems are regularly generated through synchronized "innovation jam" sessions across the networked global enterprise.[18]

## Sasken: Embedding Connectivity

Now consider Sasken, a publicly owned SME Indian enterprise with around thirty-five hundred employees spread across India, Europe, and the United States. It has been nimble since inception in 1989, focusing on software intellectual property and services in embedded systems, with a specialization in telecom. Figure 8.2 traces our understanding of the setting in their case.

Recognizing that embedded systems of the future would become dominated by software, Sasken set out over the years to patiently build this into a core competence. As expected, companies in the Japanese market began the trend of vertical integration and were thus in need of software expertise. Sasken was well positioned to fill this void and by 1999 had 30 percent of its revenue from software contracts in Japan.

Sasken invested in technology early. It also nurtured a corporate product management practice with expertise to track opportunities in telecom markets and thereby guide technical development to spawn new market offerings, new business units, or even spin-off companies. A multiyear program to build a complete wireless handset protocol stack for a major U.S. organization was one of many outcomes. T. K. Srikanth, head of the product management group, says, "This is all about incubation. It is identifying new opportunities and taking them through analysis, prototyping, and execution. For example, we were tracking technologies like Android and later NFC [near field communication] from the time when people barely knew what it meant."

Faced with talent attrition that was rampant within the Indian workforce, it chose the slower but surer path of training

# Figure 8.2 The Setting: Sasken's Potential Field of Innovation

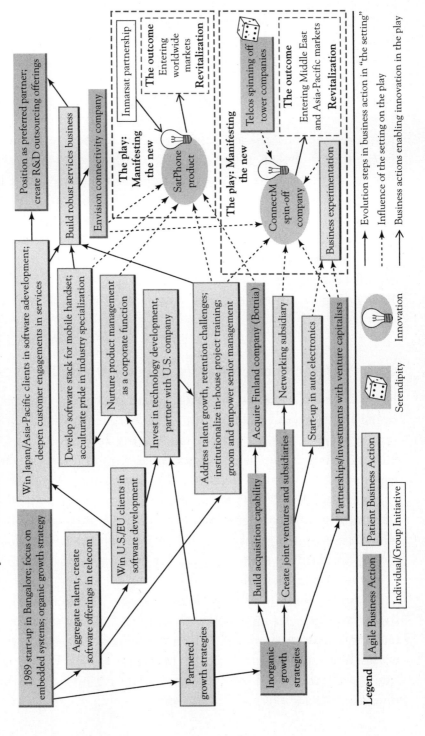

**Legend**  Agile Business Action  Patient Business Action

Individual/Group Initiative

→ Evolution steps in business action in "the setting"

- - → Influence of the setting on the play

⟶ Business actions enabling innovation in the play

Serendipity   Innovation

fresh recruits in-house over several months rather than seeking hard-to-find expertise to hire. Senior management was similarly groomed into a unique corporate culture. All of this takes patience.

Sasken, like IBM, has acted with agility when needed. It turned its brand advantage in the telecom ecosystem into a robust services business and repositioned its role as a technology integrator of choice. It acquired a Finnish wireless company during an economic downturn, giving it immediate access to European markets and advanced wireless communication technology. It further transformed to a connectivity company and leveraged its position in wireless and multimedia into newer areas such as satellite technologies and consumer electronics. And it has tested the viability of inorganic growth through subsidiary formation, joint ventures, and partnerships with venture capital.

## Strand Lifesciences: Interdisciplinary Discipline

Finally, consider Strand Lifesciences, a privately held computational life sciences organization and an excellent example of a new-generation scrappy start-up navigating through a choppy business environment with perseverance. Strand develops software products for key life science markets including drug discovery. Founded in 2000 by four computer science professors at the Indian Institute of Science (IISc), Bangalore, Strand now employs about one hundred people, many of them computer science doctorates and medical doctors. Figure 8.3 traces our understanding of the setting in their case.

Strand's genesis is an example in patience. The four founders shared a passion to apply computational techniques to biology, medicine, and, more broadly, the life sciences. Buoyed by the excitement gathering around the Human Genome Project in the United States and the entrepreneurial buzz in India at the time, they decided to form a company.

# Figure 8.3 The Setting: Strand Lifesciences' Potential Field of Innovation

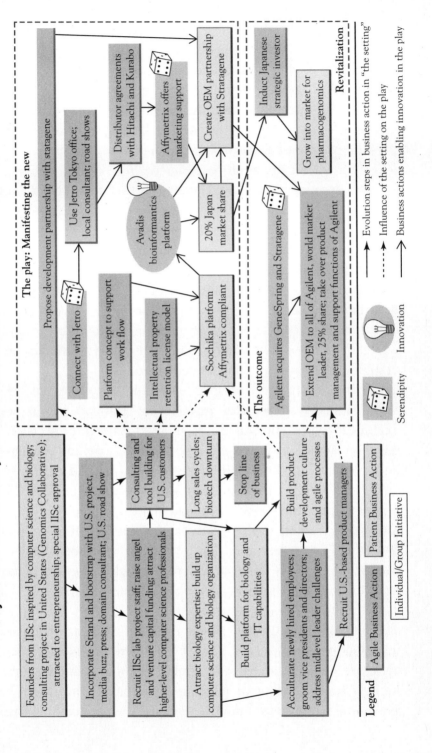

**Legend**   Agile Business Action   Patient Business Action

Individual/Group Initiative

⚅ Serendipity   💡 Innovation

⟶ Evolution steps in business action in "the setting"

┄┄► Influence of the setting on the play

⟶ Business actions enabling innovation in the play

While the potential of new computational approaches to this interdisciplinary field was clear to see, there was a daunting barrier to cross: IISc is an academic institution and did not welcome this entrepreneurial instinct from full-time faculty. It required the intervention of Ratan Tata, the head of the Tata Group, who also serves as the head of IISc's governing council, plus the passing of an entire year to approve "entrepreneurship leave" for the faculty as an "experiment."

The decade that followed offered further tests of patience, starting with attracting and nurturing the top talent essential to a strong foundation of interdisciplinary expertise in the computer and life sciences. Focusing on software product development, Strand painstakingly built cross-functional teams embodying state-of-the-art software technologies, development methodologies, and life science expertise. Along the way, it developed the organizational practices it needed to retain and motivate a highly educated and qualified workforce unaccustomed to the business of high-end software product development.

There are examples of agile leadership as well. Strand initially launched a services practice for start-up sustenance. Technical competence rapidly established through projects executed under this initiative, along with the aura behind academic entrepreneurship, drew positive media attention and vital initial publicity. This led to angel and, later, venture funding. The lackluster performance of direct sales to the biotech and pharmaceutical markets in the United States was recognized in time and scaled down before it depleted scarce resources. Business strategy was quickly changed toward original equipment manufacturing and distribution partnerships in major markets.

This example and the two others illustrate that each company shapes its potential field of innovation differently. Nevertheless, there are common themes: leadership guiding business actions strongly toward agility or patience covering all the factors of market, talent, business infrastructure, and the sociocultural base.

# The Play: Manifesting the New and Getting to Revitalizing Outcomes

Having set up and maintained a potential field of innovation, one might think innovation will automatically result or at least can be made to occur. Unfortunately, it does not seem to be something that can be forced, driven, or mandated by management. In contrast, the occurrence of innovation appears to depend on the initiative and ideas of individual employees, no doubt encouraged by the favorable climate of a potential field of innovation. It also depends on a combination of serendipitous events catalyzing the processes that could result in sparks of something new.

Even when something new gets established, the enterprise faces the subsequent challenge of monetizing the value of the object of innovation and reaping the business benefits as rapidly and quantifiably as possible. These new objects of value can be new kinds of products, processes, business deals, organizations, or even new business strategies, or new management and leadership practices.

We return to the examples of IBM, Sasken, and Strand to illustrate actions and events manifesting something new in the potential field of innovation and then ensuring that business benefits are reaped.

## IBM: Beyond Blue

Two examples of IBM's innovations arising from a potential field of innovation in India are shown in Figure 8.1 (see the boxes labeled "The Play" and "The Outcome"). IBM's deep engagement with Indian firms resulted in a first-of-a-kind on-demand business transformational engagement with Bharti Airtel, the leading telecom player in India. Under the terms, IBM provides all IT services driving Bharti Airtel's business, but unlike a typical client-customer contract, it is paid a proportion of the client's revenue. For IBM, this represented a high-profile example of its trademarked on-demand model of business, with the scope for a significant upside over a traditional pricing model. For Bharti Airtel, this offered continuous access to state-of-the-art IT systems and services at a predictable cost and limited capital outflow.[19]

The sparks for this innovation were twofold. First, there was growing frustration at Bharti Airtel in managing multiple IT vendors under intense industry and technology dynamics. Second, there was the serendipitous arrival of a key Bharti Airtel executive who, besides being an ex-IBMer, brought in new ideas and global IT experience.[20]

The revenue from this to IBM was initially estimated at around $750 million over a ten-year period. It turned out that by 2009, the halfway mark, the deal had already generated about $2.5 billion in revenue for IBM driven by the growth of Bharti Airtel's subscriber base from 10 million to an astounding 94 million in this period.[21] As a further revitalizing outcome of such innovation, IBM has engineered similar engagements with other Telecom providers in India, like Vodafone and Malaysia's Maxis. Furthermore, when Bharti Airtel acquired Zain in Africa, it contracted IBM to extend its services across Africa.[22]

Consider now an innovation in systems integration. IBM's prowess in R&D, and its hardware products and software services have combined to create multiple green data centers in India.[23] These are data centers turned green through radical and innovative approaches to energy conservation. The computing hardware stack is instrumented with a variety of energy-monitoring sensors, integrated into a building management system. Sensors along aisles, active floor tiles directing cool air to heated zones, and coldwater heat exchangers designed into hardware units are some examples. Predictive analytics estimates patterns of energy demands and drives the systems toward optimized energy expenditure. Web-enabled dashboards facilitate central management across multiple centers.

This came about through a culmination of favorable events. A senior executive brought up the idea in personal and professional networks. Through this, R&D researchers began to explore analytics in green technologies. Product and service divisions suggested IBM-Tivoli for implementing energy management rules and actions. And facilities management in several Bangalore centers worked out the physical implementation.

Green data centers, first conceived and proven within IBM's own facilities, are now offered as energy management services to IBM's customers in India. Furthermore, they have catalyzed enhancements to software and hardware products and spawned patent applications and research publications.

There are other examples as well. The adapter component to WebSphere, IBM's leading Web application server, now offers easier implementation, mainly for emerging markets where higher-end in-house IT skills are not easily found. As product director Kalpana Margabandhu emphasized in an interview, "A big focus at IBM is 'consumability,' how easily and quickly can consumers adopt your product."

Serendipitously, at that time, U.S.-based leaders were seeking to demonstrate the value of distributing product development across continents, while India-based leaders and managers aspired to take over complete product development and product management responsibilities. This project showed agility in the way U.S. and India leaders coordinated business and staffing decisions. Patience was demonstrated in launching the final product after many development cycles with work distributed among U.S., India and China teams.

## Sasken: New Spins

What enabled Sasken's innovative Inmarsat-linked satellite phone (see Figure 8.2)?

Years of patient technology investments in telecom and the accompanying expertise in handset protocol stacks were finally exploited. Senior management, groomed in such initiatives, compressed the development cycle to a mere eighteen months. The earlier acquisition of the Finnish company provided crucial technology for satellite phone antenna design.[24]

Another notable Sasken innovation is ConnectM, its spin-off company that offers wireless machine-to-machine (M2M) connectivity for monitoring and management. Application areas include building energy controls, wireless telecom tower operations, and life cycle monitoring of industrial equipment. All of these applications employ physical sensors placed on the asset to wirelessly transmit operational data to a gateway and then to data centers for aggregation, analysis, and reporting.

Several business actions led to ConnectM. Start-up risks were shared with a venture capital investment partner. Earlier start-up experiences helped expose viable market segments. Sasken's G. Venkatesh, chief technology officer, acknowledges, "We worked on seven ideas and picked M2M. The process of discovery of the solution areas for ConnectM was a huge effort." An existing networking subsidiary provided ready expertise for faster field implementation. In-house leadership talent was groomed and readily available to transfer to this new opportunity. Most important, recasting Sasken as a connectivity company rather than just an IT or telecom player resulted in a novel spin-off beyond the obvious.

## Strand Lifesciences: Platform Leaps

Strand's eureka moment came with its realization that the disparate software platforms available around the turn of the century would not interoperate or scale to handle the prodigious amounts of digital data being produced through newer-generation instrumentation at life science labs around the world. As Vijay Chandru, CEO, says, "Like good computer scientists, we took a step back, abstracted the problem and realized the need to build a software platform." They did this by creating robust contemporary and legacy-free software architectures ground up. (See Figure 8.3 for Strand's innovation play and outcome.)

The AVADIS platform was realized over multiple prototypes with tight client-centered feedback loops and now offers a complete work flow for domain researchers from data access, visualization, analysis, and discovery.

When chance events provided an entry into Japan, Strand was quick to turn this into distribution agreements with established Japanese players. To address the U.S. market, it audaciously approached a competitor, Stratagene, for a partnership, realizing that Stratagene's products had not kept up with emerging technologies. Stratagene was initially reluctant to engage, but warmed up once Strand's success in Japan became evident. Stratagene agreed to license and embed Strand's software platform into its own product suite.

The events in Japan then attracted a strategic investor who offered both reserve capital and further access to the Japanese market. By a curious turn of events, Agilent, the U.S.-based market leader, acquired Stratagene and another competitor, GeneSpring, which led to Strand's OEM partnership covering all relevant Agilent products. As a result, Strand's market share grew to 25 percent worldwide. With growing confidence in Strand, Agilent entrusted Strand with product management and support for its products.[25]

## Insights and Recommendations

What does the pattern of enterprise innovation uncovered so far and illustrated through examples and cases tell us? It is essentially that there may be a way to churn innovation out of the vortex of radically new business experience in India. In Table 8.1, we summarize this pattern by looking at the guidance that leaders can provide, the business actions they need to take, and the innovation possibilities they expose. This is examined across the

**Table 8.1 Patterns of Leadership Guidance for Enterprise Innovation in Emerging Economies**

| Factor | Guidance for Agility | Guidance for Patience |
|---|---|---|
| Market | *Business actions*<br>Focus on the known.<br>Cherry-pick.<br>Retro-fit or strip down.<br>*Innovation opportunities*<br>Recast tested business models: pricing, packaging, market positioning, branding, deal structuring, acquisitions. | *Business actions*<br>Develop new markets and segments with understanding.<br>Build deep client relationships and business partnerships.<br>Reverse-innovate; codevelop new products and services with fresh eyes and with the participation of stakeholders.<br>*Innovation opportunities*<br>New business strategies, new market segments and products, both global and geography specific.<br>Forge new business models. |
| Talent | *Business actions*<br>Recruit aggressively from available talent pools.<br>Scale up at lower talent levels.<br>Acquire organizations.<br>*Innovation opportunities*<br>Repurpose talent for higher value.<br>Change work flows for higher productivity.<br>Adopt technology to deskill jobs and enable new capabilities. | *Business actions*<br>Discover new sources of raw talent.<br>Incrementally build competence and scale, infusing new work cultures and practices.<br>Blend skill levels, and promote opportunities for interaction across geographies, functions, and cultures.<br>Direct capabilities to high-value business opportunities.<br>*Innovation opportunities*<br>Set up "finishing schools" for recent college graduates to close skill gaps with respect to industry expectations.<br>Uncover hidden talent pools. |

**Table 8.1 Patterns of Leadership Guidance for Enterprise Innovation in Emerging Economies (continued)**

| Factor | Guidance for Agility | Guidance for Patience |
|---|---|---|
| Business infrastructure | *Business actions*<br>Align with local practices, even if they are inconsistent with global practices.<br>Develop local partnerships to broadly delegate responsibilities.<br>*Innovation opportunities*<br>Very limited. In fact, the purpose is to avoid innovation in this dimension.<br>Some special cases of innovative local practices (for example, the celebrated logistics excellence of Mumbai *dabbawallas*[a]). | *Business actions*<br>Build up local organization, imbuing company's global experiences and best practices.<br>Establish network of vendors and partners, and attempt to propagate company practices into a network.<br>Integrate the best of local and global practices.<br>*Innovation opportunities*<br>Build open innovation with local and global universities, start-ups, and venture capitalists.<br>Transform supply chains and other support services for major productivity gains. |
| Sociocultural base | *Business actions*<br>Leaders are "informed tourists." They seek to understand cultural essence but rely on intermediaries for execution.<br>Operate from zones of safety and familiarity (e.g., offices in metropolitan areas, only English-speaking staff, living in sequestered communities).<br>*Innovation opportunities*<br>Limited, if at all. The goal is to minimize cultural faux pas and unfamiliar local interaction. | *Business actions*<br>Leaders immerse themselves in the regional and local culture, aspiring for familiarity.<br>Leaders develop firsthand familiarity with cultures and lifestyles across metropolitan, small town, and rural settings.<br>*Innovation opportunities*<br>Inspire new technologies, products, and distribution models with global relevance.<br>Customize work practices with deeper understanding of local attitudes, cultures, and behaviors.<br>Devise culturally aware practices of communicating guidance for agility or patience, and rewarding favorable outcomes. |

[a]*Dabbawalla* is a unique service industry whose primary business is collecting freshly cooked food in lunchboxes from the residences of office workers (mostly in the suburbs), delivering it to them their respective workplaces, and returning the empty boxes back to the customer's residence.

four factors underlying the business experience. Stark differences can be observed depending on the guidance chosen.

But to provide such guidance and execute business actions, companies and their leaders must prepare themselves afresh at a more fundamental level:

- *Expect the new:* Companies setting up business in India should anticipate being swirled into a vortex of new experiences that are quintessentially India.

- *Transcend dilemmas:* Leaders immersed in this vortex will indeed face dilemmas of action—a tension between ready opportunities and potentially larger opportunities to be uncovered with endurance. Leaders need to build a deep awareness of these dilemmas and opportunities before making decisions on allocating resources and calibrating expectations of outcome.

- *Aspire to be the "tour guide":* Organizations initially entering India will naturally delegate responsibilities to local entities. However, greater rewards await those who go beyond this, immersing and assimilating the local sensibilities and thereby graduating from hapless tourists to tour guides.

- *Unbalance guidance:* Choices of patience and agility abound in this business environment. But being equivocal here can be both wasteful and debilitating and must be overcome with clarity.

- *Keep the powder dry:* Organizations taking repeated and sustained positions of unbalance seem able to create a potential field wherein innovations can be sparked.

- *Fan the worthy sparks:* Flames of innovation are sparked by event synchronicity and individual initiative. Innovation is often spontaneous, serendipitous, and even unexpected. Leadership must recognize nascent signals and nurture those with high potential, some that may make a global impact.

- *Recognize leapfrogs and white spaces:* The emerging Indian economy has opportunities to leapfrog an entire generation of business evolution seen elsewhere. For example, the first banking encounter for many Indian consumers may be through a mobile phone. Similarly, white spaces, representing previously unrecognized needs, may suddenly open up. As G. Venkatesh, CTO of Sasken, puts it, "In between two boxes of opportunities that have some permanence, there is white space. When things are dynamic, white space increases."

In conclusion, companies must now learn vortex leadership, a new leadership practice for recognizing and realizing business opportunities in emerging economies like India. Leaders must be trained to exploit new vistas that get uncovered as in a kaleidoscope—small patches of light transforming to something much larger with a turn—and capable of seeing opportunity in complexity, able to transcend seeming opposites of agility and patience. They must be at ease combining an unhurried socio-cultural sensitivity with the business pragmatism of the immediate.

# 9

# PROTECTING INTELLECTUAL PROPERTY IN CHINA

## A View from the Field

## Andreas Schotter, Mary B. Teagarden

Intellectual property (IP) theft in China is a much bigger problem than simply knockoff Gucci purses, North Face jackets, or Rolex watches. The challenge in China ranges from copying toys and luxury goods, to copying automotive and aircraft parts, pharmaceuticals, and other cutting-edge high-tech products like medical X-ray machines.[1] It also includes copying business processes and even business or service models. The problem is amplified by the many actors who play a role in the proliferation of IP violations, including legitimate competitors, would-be competitors, national Chinese IP development policy, and local governmental practices that threaten companies' IP in China. While many companies remain vulnerable, some have developed IP protection approaches that allow them to thrive in China's dynamic environment.

For example, Apple Inc. has experienced IP challenges across its entire value chain. Its extraordinary popularity has led to considerable counterfeiting or copying of its prototypes, products, know-how, trade secrets, service model, and even store concepts.[2] Apple's products are predominantly contract manufactured in China; in addition, the rising middle class makes the company's products very popular with local consumers. The strong interest of this consumer group to show off with high-status consumer goods spurs the interest of counterfeiters.

Competitors use shipping information about Apple's supply chain activities that can be purchased from business intelligence companies to extrapolate potential sales data and product release details. As a countermeasure, prior to shipping its iPad in March 2010, Apple blocked its bills of lading and other import records from public access. Should we consider this excessive caution, maybe even paranoia? Or is Apple taking appropriate and successful steps to protect its IP? Before responding, consider the extent of the challenges Apple has encountered in China and beyond.

Apple sells its products globally through company-owned retail stores and value-added resellers and online. By the last quarter of 2010, it had 233 retail stores in the United States and 84 internationally, including 2 in Beijing and 2 in Shanghai.[3] The Apple retail store, a critical differentiator of the Apple experience, is being knocked off in China. By late 2010, fake Apple stores outnumbered real ones, and recently bloggers reported five new fake stores in Kunming, a southwestern Chinese city with a population over 6.4 million. The fake stores had Apple's iconic look, logo, store layout, and employee apparel. Tell-tale signs identified the fakes—including the words Store—and in one case Apple Stoer—beside the white Apple logo in the window, something Apple never does. According to some reports, staff members in these fake stores believed they were working for Apple.

Chinese authorities acknowledged these fake stores and in the process identified twenty-two fake stores in total. Consequently, these stores were prohibited from using Apple trademarks and symbols. However, only two stores were closed; the others simply changed their store names but retained the Apple retail look and service model. It should come as no surprise that almost all of the products sold in these fake Apple stores are knockoffs, mostly sourced from Hong Kong.[4] This problem has not stopped at China's borders. Apple seized unauthorized iPod, iPhone, and iPad knockoff accessories bearing the Apple logo for sale in the Chinatown section of Queens, New York.[5] While Apple's is a dramatic case, almost all innovation-driven firms face equally significant IP violation exposures in China daily. In this chapter, we discuss best practices surrounding IP protection that we identified in our extensive multiyear research project. The goal is to provide guidance for executives to increase their organizations' operational effectiveness in China.

In 2011, a decade after China's admission to the World Trade Organization, the ability to protect corporate know-how remains one of the most critical issues for multinationals that operate in or consider entering China. Protecting IP is especially challenging for multinationals from the high-tech and service sectors. Corporations that successfully operate in China have found that integrated dynamic approaches to IP protection that go beyond patenting and legal litigation are potentially the most important organizational capability for ensuring long-term firm performance in China. We studied what these companies actually do to protect their IP. Based on this, we developed a framework that details a best practice IP protection model for China including a range of defensive and offensive activities used to protect IP.

For this study, we conducted extensive field research in China using semistructured, face-to-face, and telephone interviews to answer three questions:

1. What are the key external issues and characteristics regarding IP protection in China?

2. How are foreign and local companies protecting their IP in China?

3. Are there best practices or common themes in IP protection among companies?

We set out with the objective of identifying critical issues surrounding IP protection and developing an as-complete-as-possible understanding of applied IP protection practices in China. Altogether we conducted sixty-eight one- to four-hour interviews between January and September 2010. We recorded and transcribed these interviews, took extensive notes, and collected quotes by hand. In addition, we collected secondary data through analysis of company reports, e-mail correspondence, court filings, newspapers, and research publications. We interviewed four types of experts from a diverse set of industries:

1. Consultants in risk management, business intelligence, accounting, strategy, market entry, and foreign operations management

2. Attorneys active as in-house counsel or in private practice focusing on IP

3. General managers in multiple industries including IT hardware and software, pharmaceuticals, telecommunications, automotive, health care, entertainment, electronic components, tools and some diversified manufacturers

4. U.S., European Union, and Chinese governmental agency representatives from these three countries

The interviews were recorded and transcribed. Transcripts were given to the interviewees for corrections, clarifications, and additional comments. We then conducted a content analysis on the transcripts. Based on that analysis, we developed a preliminary conceptual framework for companies seeking to protect IP in China. We presented this framework in a workshop at the Shanghai American Chamber of Commerce attended by more than fifty experts with IP protection responsibilities. We refined the framework based on feedback we received during this session. In addition, we presented the refined framework at several conferences to Japanese, German, and French executives and to academics with extensive China experience. Feedback from workshops at these conferences was then incorporated into the framework presented in this chapter.

## The Chinese IP Protection Challenge

Over the past decade, foreign direct investment (FDI) trends in China have changed significantly from low-cost manufacturing to a proliferation of high-tech manufacturing and high-tech service activities. Exports from China's high-tech industry grew to over 30 percent in 2009, up from 6 percent in 1992. The trend is expected to accelerate, especially in areas like renewable energy, information technology (IT), and urban and professional services. This shift in FDI has provided Chinese companies with access to world-class technology, but it has not necessarily improved the ability of Chinese companies to build the capabilities necessary for innovation. In a recent *Wall Street Journal* editorial, Gupta and Wang discuss modern China's newness to the innovation game, the government's penchant for "picking winners" for R&D investment funding without peer review, and the educational system as barriers to building innovation capabilities.[6] For many executives, China's lack of innovation capabilities creates a serious dilemma. In China, foreign multinationals can no longer compete with offerings based on previous-generation (dated) technology or service know-how. The China market is much more sophisticated than it was in the recent past. Today foreign companies have to compete with their most advanced know-how despite the fact that for many executives, China is perceived as synonymous with counterfeiting and IP theft.

The traditional approach that manufacturing firms use to fight product counterfeiting relies mostly on patents, enforced through the international legal system or, more recently, the immature but gradually improving Chinese legal system.[7] This approach appears to be an uphill battle with mostly after-the-fact damage control measures that provide limited benefits—and those after the damage has been already done. Pfizer's long-running battle with Chinese copycats is an example. Pfizer obtained a Chinese patent license for Viagra in 2001. Following complaints by twelve Chinese pharmaceutical companies, this license was revoked in 2004 based on a claim that it did not accurately explain the uses of the pill's key ingredient. Pfizer persisted and took several infringement cases to Chinese and international courts. Some legal observers claimed that the Chinese State Intellectual Property Organization was not meeting its intellectual property protection obligations under World Trade Organization membership. In 2006 Pfizer received a ruling in its favor. Subsequently the court ordered two Chinese companies to stop producing counterfeit pills. Pfizer still struggles with enforcement of the ruling through local authorities. Meanwhile, Chinese drug companies from around the country claim to have invested over 100 million remimbi in less expensive imitations of Viagra, and seventeen of them formed a joint venture to produce a generic version of the drug.[8]

The Pfizer example shows that while the legal route does lead to some success, the enforcement of legal rights is not yet effective. Furthermore, we found that multinationals that rely on IP in areas such as organizational and operational processes and service capabilities find it much more difficult to protect IP than do manufacturers with simpler processes. Nevertheless, foreign multinationals have not given up on the fast-growing and large China market, and the successful ones have developed unique approaches for IP protection often based on trial and error to address the IP challenge.

The prevalence of IP theft in China arises from several unique sources. China's idiosyncratic social and cultural history is one source of the problem. The Mao Zedong era (1949–1976), characterized by extreme communism and absolute poverty, ran counter to property rights protections. Antiproperty ownership was a theme incorporated into all four Chinese constitutions written since 1950, and the legacy of this ideology lingers and subtly influences attitudes toward IP protection.[9] Although Deng Xiaoping introduced economic reforms, institutions that support these reforms, such as a business-supportive legal system, have evolved slowly. China's legal system is widely regarded as immature, lacking an adequate legal framework and riddled with spotty enforcement. The extreme variability or apparent randomness of enforcement outcomes is the most vexing problem associated with this slowly evolving legal system. Hence, executives have to accept that, for the time being, legal IP protection systems are evolving but that these will not soon reach standards similar to those in the United States, Japan, or Western Europe.

Another social factor is the approach to education in China that contributes to IP theft.[10] Chinese education emphasizes rote memorization, a bias or distinct preference for and exact copy of the expert or master, and team-based problem solving versus individual work. The managing partner from a market-entry consulting firm commented, "Chinese are taught to copy the master. The Chinese culture does not value IP rights and therefore does not see stealing IP as theft but as a compliment to the originator." Consequently, the problem needs to be addressed partly from an educational perspective. Companies like Microsoft, Intel, and Baxter make significant investments in training their high-tech knowledge workers to value independent thinking and problem solving, especially in China. However, social and cultural dynamics do not change quickly. Although there was broad-based consensus among the executives we interviewed that the institutions that support IP protection are improving, this is happening much more slowly than business executives would like.

Another factor is that there are very low costs for IP theft or copying when compared to the costs associated with innovation. A Shanghai-based manager at a business intelligence company drew a parallel between the business environment in China today and in the United States at the turn of the twentieth

century when companies like Coca Cola were able to slow counterfeiters with their iconic bottles that were complicated to
manufacture, but they could not stop counterfeiters entirely. She
observed, "Most copied products are foreign branded. . . . It is
easier to copy than to come up with an idea of your own." The
current stage of China's development relative to innovation
capabilities, or lack thereof, conspires against robust IP protection values.[11] In response to a question about protecting Chinese
IP, this manager concluded, "The more IP there is to protect,
the more a given industry will want to enforce IP protection."
A general manager in our study stated, "Widespread IP leakage
will persist until it is more expensive to copy than it is to
innovate." Everyone we interviewed expressed a belief that it
will be a very long time before copying is more expensive than
innovating.

Finally, there is an extremely high turnover of well-educated
middle managers and engineers, often the keepers of a company's
IP, in China. According to a recent McKinsey & Company study,
annual staff turnover rates in high-tech industries in China have
reached over 20 percent, effectively causing a constant bleeding
of talent and the IP that is in the heads, computers, or files of
those who leave.[12] A senior executive from an American Fortune
100 company commented, "When I came to China two years
ago, I was taking the protection of our patents and processes for
granted. I felt comfortable about my experience with the legal
IP protection mechanisms back in the USA. I never imagined
that I would have to include IP protection management in almost
all of our business processes. I think about the issue actively every
day, yet we are still not able to prevent leakages that are often
simply based on staff turnover."

The unfortunate reality is that, in China, eventually all IP
leaks. Some leakage is faster and some is slower. We note that
IP leakage is one reason for early-stage industry growth and evolution but that, once the tipping point has been reached, it
becomes a major impediment to innovation. The problem in

China is that industries do not evolve in the same linear fashion as they did in North America, Europe, and Japan during the twentieth century. In China, industry development is asymmetric, with rapid increases at the bottom and at the top, often driven by leapfrogging of certain development stages based on substantial rather than incremental advances. Staying on top of the speed-to-market game is essential to survival for many local firms. Copying proven high-tech know-how from foreign multinationals, especially with little worry of punishment, becomes not only the most attractive but also the least risky strategy.

For foreign multinationals and local innovation leaders, a key capability for successfully operating in China is proactive and dynamic management, control of IP leakage, and use of an IP protection strategy that goes on the offensive. A defensive IP protection strategy rooted in overreliance on an immature and only gradually developing legal system is less effective. As an executive from another American Fortune 100 company observed, "It is not only the process of protecting IP and all kinds of know-how from externally driven theft that needs to be managed in China, it is equally important to control IP leakages from the inside out. Firms need to be very diligent and never tolerate a violation without reacting with severe and explicit punishment."

Protecting IP is a challenge in any market, but it seems especially complex for companies from industrialized countries including the United States, Japan, and the European Union when operating in emerging markets. The reason for this is a prevailing static view of the role and the execution of IP protection activities. Often multinationals from these countries base their activities on their own understanding of the effectiveness of legal systems in their home countries. A Beijing patent attorney commented, "Many companies believe that IP filings in the US and EU are enforceable in China. They are not." Most express a belief that a patent, copyright, or trademark is adequate protection. In China these are not, at least not yet.

## What Works in China?

Despite all of the threats to IP in China, the majority of companies we interviewed learned to protect their IP, often through trial and error. They discovered unique combinations of practices and activities that worked for each of them. Those companies that have developed a mind-set of moving through continuous IP protection process improvement have more successfully protected IP than those that have not. The operations manager of an automotive component company told us, "IP protection in China is not just another process or efficiency system that you set up which then runs itself. IP protection is a constant adjustment. You have to expect new kinds of threats every day. It concerns every decision. Change has to become second nature. Do not ask what the best protection practice would be today, but try to develop the best practice for tomorrow, and then the day after tomorrow, and so on."

We believe that the lessons learned by the companies we studied apply more generally and are the basis of best practices for IP protection in China. Effectively protecting IP in China depends on a dynamic combination of simple and complex, static and flexible practices. The relationships among these activities and practices are shown in Figure 9.1. We address these activities and practices next, which range from basic to complex.

### Begin with Low-Hanging Fruit

There are three obvious simple core defensive practices that companies should follow:

- Managerial and organizational clarity on the China strategy
- Robust business intelligence for deep understanding of the local context
- Adherence to solid legal fundamentals

## Figure 9.1 Activities and Practices for Protecting IP in China

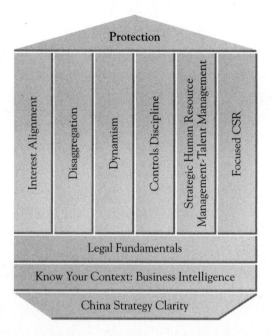

Strategic Clarity. While having a clear China strategy might seem obvious, we found that this is frequently a missing link for multinationals operating in China. The CEO of an electronic games company with years of China experience commented:

> Nowadays, everybody who knows how to eat with chopsticks believes he/she is a China expert. It is quite scary. There is no doubt that China is very important and that multinationals can't ignore it. Sadly, few companies understand why they are in China and even fewer companies have a real China strategy. However, all have an execution or operations plan. Those who have a strategy are successful and those who just operate in the country without proper strategic alignment will eventually fail. I have seen it over and over again.

In practice, this means that multinationals must have China-relevant corporate and business strategies that are aligned with the key objectives for operating in the country. A CEO of a European manufacturing company told us:

> It is critical to have a clear understanding of why you are in
> China and what you want to achieve. Too many times
> companies rush into the country because they believe they have
> to be here for cheap labor or the large market. Then they find
> out that they do not have the organizational skills to operate
> here and that the assumptions they made in fact do not hold.
> Those who figure out quickly that they need to reset or adjust
> might eventually succeed. Those who do not understand this
> will fail quickly and expensively.

Furthermore, through a clear and focused strategic lens, companies must identify the critical IP required to execute their China-relevant strategies. And building on this, they must identify the right people (internally and externally) to staff the venture. They must explicitly formulate operational, management, and contingency processes to guide implementation. Finally, they must develop an explicit awareness of timing and its impact on the other factors we have mentioned. Although these practices seem obvious and relatively simple, our research indicates that companies more often than not rush into China without considering these obvious measures. We collected overwhelmingly rich evidence for the fact that this negligence in almost all cases leads to significant IP leakage, often by bringing "too much" or "too advanced" IP to China or sharing it with unvetted partners. Incorporating IP protection tools and practices during the development of the business strategy provides the critical foundation on which to build a robust IP protection strategy.

***Business Intelligence.*** Understanding regional variations in China is critical. Markets in China offer a range of opportunities and threats, including how IP is viewed and how IP infringements are addressed. A risk management consultant in Beijing commented, "China is many markets, not just one market. Your location matters. Some locations like Shanghai enforce IP protection more vigorously than others." This is a comment that we have heard often. Stories abound about difficulties in running businesses in China. An old China hand, the first foreign certified public accountant in China, shared three rules: "Be suspicious—be especially vigilant if you outsource; Be realistic—piracy is a universal truth; and Be on site—remote management does not work in China or any other part of Asia for that matter." There are many formal and informal ways to collect business intelligence that range from doing it in-house (recommended only for China-experienced companies) to hiring professionals. Regardless of the approach chosen, it is critical to understand the very important and highly localized rules of the game before diving into China.

*Legal Fundamentals.* One of the most often cited mistakes that companies make in China is a belief that IP filings in the United States and the European Union are valid in China. They are not. In China, legal advisors and operations managers must coordinate activities. A manufacturing CEO in Hangzhou stressed, "The legal side of your China operation must work hand in hand with your operations." When retaining legal counsel, it is critical to hire an attorney with the right expertise. An IT CEO learned from experience that "not 'just any' attorney will do. Select an experienced expert in China in your specific technical domain." Many of the executives we interviewed had examples of multinationals using a local legal firm that knew the Chinese legal system but did not have industry or product-specific technical expertise, or, worse, using a lawyer from San Francisco, Washington, D.C., London, or Hamburg who does not know the Chinese legal system. These are common mistakes multinationals make by trying to maneuver around the legal system in China.

The CEO of a diversified conglomerate in Shanghai stressed, "Use the legal system actively, that is, strategically—consider image, potential gain, rationale, and timing. But use the system." For example, Cisco overestimated the potential gain from suing Huawei for IP infringement while underestimating the negative effects. Public sentiment was with Huawei—the home-town competitor—seen by local Chinese as the little guy. Examples like this only reinforce the growing nationalism reflected in the growing "buy Chinese" sentiment. Furthermore, a Shanghai-based management consultant advised, "Use the right legal tools for the individual job—administrative actions, judicial actions and so forth. Each case might vary based on the contextual circumstance."

The 2003 landmark Lego case is an interesting example. The Swiss company Interlego AG sued Tianjin's COKO Toy Company for copyright infringement of Lego bricks. The Lego Company is a Danish toy company well known for its interlocking plastic brick toys. Interlego AG began importing Lego toys into China in 1992. Subsequently it discovered that similar interlocking bricks were being sold by COKO Toy Company in large department stores in Beijing. Interlego AG sued COKO for copyright infringement. The trial court agreed that as a member of the Bern Convention for the Protection of Literary and Artistic Works, China was obligated to protect Lego bricks. The trial court recognized fifty of the fifty-three pieces of Lego bricks submitted as works of applied arts. They found that thirty-three of the fifty pieces of Lego bricks were infringed since COKO's bricks were substantially similar to Lego's. The court did not find substantial similarity in the remaining seventeen pieces. The trial court ordered COKO to stop manufacturing and selling the infringing products. COKO was also ordered to publish an apology in the *Beijing Daily* newspaper and pay the equivalent of $6,000 in damages to Interlego.

COKO appealed, arguing that patent law, not copyright law, should protect industrial design. It also argued that there was no precedent for dual protection of both copyright and patent law in China's judicial history. Beijing's High People's Court found against COKO and upheld the lower court decision.[13] Although it is not yet perfect, China's legal system is slowly improving. Unfortunately, use of the legal system is beneficial only after the IP has been infringed or stolen, and "winning" may be a hollow victory. This is why we recommend a less obvious, more complex approach to protecting IP. In essence, we urge companies to embrace a set of dynamic practices that slow the inevitable leakage of IP from the start.

## Shift to Complexity: An IP Strategy on the Offensive

Once companies have a clear China strategy, a deep understanding of the rules of the game, and their legal fundamentals in order, IP protection can shift from relatively defensive activities to offensive activities aimed at throwing up barriers that are difficult for would-be IP thieves to penetrate. The key is the complexity that results from combining six distinct activities in a multilayered, interlocking network of IP protection. The effect is a significant slowing of both opportunistic would-be IP thieves (including departing employees, suppliers, and customers) and organized IP theft through espionage. Finally, the use of socially complex processes like talent management—an important part of this safety net—extends the reduction of IP theft to the employee level, the most common source for IP leakage.

We identified six IP strategy best practices that contribute to effective IP protection, especially when used in combination to form an interlocked barrier:

1. *Proactive interest alignment* with regulatory institutions and individual government officials in the localities where the company operates

2. *Disaggregation* of IP components and core processes through organizational and physical separation of activities, technology, vendors, and clients

3. *Dynamism* through continuously improving products and processes in order to stay at the leading know-how edge, forcing the competition to continually play catch-up

4. Use of a *controls discipline* that rests on and is embedded in a strong organizational culture

5. *Strategic human resource and talent management* that make the company a great place to work

6. Focused *corporate social responsibility* activities that make the company a valuable part of the local community

No company we spoke with uses all of these practices. However, most use at least three of them to weave a web of IP protection.

## Interest Alignment

The Chinese term *guanxi* is now commonly used in English. At its core, *guanxi* is a form of favors reciprocity: you scratch my back, and I'll scratch yours. An operations executive from an American automotive company commented:

> In China, nothing happens without self-interest. This might sound surprising, especially for those who heard about *guanxi*. In order for you to protect your IP against leakage you need to make sure that everyone who has access to your IP knows that it is for his/her best interest not to violate it. Your customers, your suppliers, and explicitly your employees. Do not rely on your own perception of a win-win situation. In China, IP loss is not necessarily seen as a problem. You have to be explicit and active in managing interest alignment.

This sentiment was echoed by an IP protection officer in a world-leading American electronics manufacturing company who said, "We constantly work with our local staff at all levels to make them aware that protecting IP pays off. We reward those who make us aware of leaks, and we immediately fire those who violate our interest, even if it is a minor issue. We have a zero tolerance policy."

The CEO of a European high-technology manufacturing company discussed the extension of interest alignment to his suppliers:

> Our suppliers have to go through rigorous and continuous checking procedures. One of the things we are looking for is fit. How much can we make them dependent on us, and how dependent do we become on them? We keep a constant eye on these relationships since formal contracts are not necessarily regarded as binding. We sometimes go with the second- or third-best supplier in terms of price or other terms if we feel that the first-choice candidate would make us too dependent and their interests could shift away from those that are aligned with ours.

In this case, interest alignment serves as an effective strategic substitute for China's immature legal system.

An executive from a Japanese electronics firm described how it extends interest alignment to the local community level:

> Last year we donated funds to the local community for a new elementary school building. We invited all our staff to the opening ceremony. We made it very clear that we could only give if it is worthwhile for us as a business to operate here. We created a flyer saying that IP theft takes money directly away from those donations. It was amazing to see the reactions. While some did not understand what the big deal was, others jumped right on the bandwagon. We now have a monthly

meeting with the local authorities when we talk explicitly about those issues. We also make any violation public amongst all levels, down to the last factory worker.

A joint venture consultant in Chengdu advised, "It is important to create local relationships as a company. Not just business relationships but relationships with your employees and with the community at large. If they see that you do something for the community over and above others, you will get support." The underlying logic here is that companies that are seen as good citizens in local communities enjoy more favorable local treatment regarding IP infringement threats. As we discuss later, they also become more attractive to the best talent.

Finally, the country manager of a European industrial equipment manufacturing company emphasized the importance of location. He recounted, "We moved our production from Shanghai to Shandong. People here are more honest and less transient. It feels like they understand better why we protect our IP. Shanghai has great talent but little commitment." This comment highlights another theme that emerged regularly in our interviews: IP leakage through employee turnover is much more prevalent than through any other way.

A comparison of Nissan and Toyota's approach to interest alignment illustrates how this works in practice. The Chinese government changed its policy to require electric vehicle IP technology transfer from foreign carmakers selling electric cars in China. Toyota pushed back vigorously against the policy changes, while Nissan embraced the change in policy regarding required electric vehicle IP transfer. Nissan, along with Renault, helped form the Greentech alliance to partner with the Chinese government to build a plan for mapping out a battery-charging network and a marketing program.[14] Toyota has never enjoyed the same brand image in China that it has in the United States, and the IP push-back reaction has not helped. Consequently, Nissan is winning in the fast-growing, lucrative, and future-oriented China auto market.[15]

## Disaggregation

Disaggregation or compartmentalization focuses on where work is done, how work is done, and who is doing it. Basically, do not put all your eggs in the same basket. Many of the executives we interviewed, especially those in high-tech industries, emphasized the importance of the disaggregation of processes and the compartmentalization of know-how. A senior executive of a U.S.-based IT component manufacturing company told us:

> We make sure that no single person knows everything about our processes and that product know-how and processes are as disaggregated as possible. We specifically utilize our plants in Vietnam and Malaysia for subcomponent manufacturing. The plants do not communicate directly with each other. The R&D integration happens in the U.S. The logistics between the plants is different too.

Another example mentioned by a management consultant is Dura-line. The company produces special silicon materials in one location outside China and ships it into China where it is then used in the finished product manufacturing process.

World-class golf club manufacturer Callaway approached this issue more along its downstream activities. After initial problems with counterfeited products, the company implemented a series of unique testing procedures, which it keeps changing. Callaway works closely with key distributors and checks its own channel partners often but irregularly. Callaway disaggregated testing procedures and made each channel partner play a key role. This created a self-enforcing system in which distributors and legitimate retailers alert the company of the latest counterfeit strategies. Finally, an R&D executive of an American industrial equipment manufacturing firm commented, "If you have valuable prototypes or models, have them hand-carried over [from overseas] and keep them in a vault all the time. In addition, you must license their IP correctly—including licensing it to yourself in China. At the same time, keep all patents and brand [materials] offshore; keep [them] in a country that cares about intellectual property." This strategy ensures that if would-be IP thieves access a piece of the puzzle, they rarely can access all of the pieces needed to replicate the IP.

Finally, locating work where there is better IP protection is always a disaggregation option. As a CEO of a U.S. manufacturing company in China observed, "If I wanted to create IP with my Chinese talent, I have to bring a variety of bright minds to the U.S. where their 'non-competes' are enforceable." Disaggregation can be implemented at the work process level such as placing activities in multiple locations. It can be implemented at the supply chain level, as the Callaway example illustrates. IP protection can also be achieved by moving talent to locations where IP protection enforcement is more favorable.

## Dynamism

The business environment in China changes rapidly. Companies that are effective in protecting their IP are also companies that keep discovering new solutions to this challenge. A subsidiary manager from the IT industry told us, "In China things happen so fast. One cannot trust that everything is okay today just because it was yesterday. Things can change so rapidly overnight that, for example, your trusted supplier might score a big contract with another firm and despite a good relationship before, he could leave you behind without notice. If you are not careful, your IP will be a bonus for the new client." This environmental dynamism makes it essential for companies operating in China to embrace an equally dynamic stance toward IP protection since constant change is difficult to replicate.

In essence, companies that embrace dynamism stay one step ahead of the competition. The CEO of an IT services company emphasized, "If you keep changing, you are harder to figure out. Sure, this might cost you some efficiency, but the extra complexity is worth a lot if it reduces IP leakage." A European manufacturing firm's subsidiary manager cautions, "Never feel comfortable! I hate to say it, but paranoia is a good quality in China when it comes to IP protection. Keep things moving and hard to figure out. Do not include your critical knowledge in standard routines. Instead deliberately change things up." Developing the capability to stay at the leading edge of innovation and innovating with a focus on speed requires considerable managerial and capital investment. It is inherently high risk. However, for companies that compete in high-technology domains, this is often the best defense against IP theft. Their products can be copied, but their innovation or speed capabilities are much, much harder to copy. Hence they stay ahead of the game.

## Controls Discipline

Everyone does not need to know everything. A corporate culture that is infused with a controls discipline is key to setting the corporate context for IP protection. A subsidiary manager in an IT company stated, "Companies need to consider what they deem proprietary information areas. Not everybody needs to have access to all knowledge. You may feel comfortable allowing access to your secretary in the United States; however in China, you have to be very vigilant in terms of system access." A senior executive from an IT services firm added,

> It is not so much that you have to protect your IP from intruders. It is more critical to control that those who are inside do not take anything out. Check everything. Even as the highest-ranking executive, make yourself subject to diligent and regular bag and jacket checking procedures. Make sure that you check the checkers. Make a personal effort to make the process the most important responsibility for yourself. Do not allow cell phones or keys in the office. Make sure that people enter a room with their own key card, not someone else's. Each employee has to enter individually, not in groups.

This attention to detail encourages what scholars call behavioral control, or changes in employee conduct that align with the company's IP strategy.[16] Inside the bathroom stalls in the offices of one high-tech multinational operating in China is a sign that provides specific guidelines on the use of the Internet and discussion boards outside work. Employees are cautioned not to mention things like having to work on the weekend to, for example, correct a production problem. They are advised that this could give valuable information to competitors who might be monitoring the discussion board. When employees are surrounded with practices that emphasize the importance of IP protection, they are more likely to pay attention to the issue and behave in ways that support their employer's IP.

A second form of controls discipline that was discussed in our interviews is alliance or partner control. The CEO of a European manufacturing firm explained,

> We set up a joint venture in China on behalf of our headquarters. We paid a lot of attention to partner selection beyond what we had been used to back home in the United States. The most important questions for us were: Who is the [local] partner really? Who is behind the company name? What will and what could they be doing with our technology? We determined that the best way to protect the IP was to control things centrally. We literally installed counters on the production equipment to verify the number of product units coming off the production line. We also had our own guy running the item counters.

These changes in business procedures may seem to be over the top and to some even offending in the U.S. context, but they are critical in China.

Finally, several executives highlighted a variety of managerial practices that reinforce controls discipline. An auto company's China CEO stressed, "Finance controls and risk management are

[also] key. Successful firms will compartmentalize their processes and have controlled copies of their key IP materials. Never have only one-person sign off. Always have at least two people sign off, best if they come from different backgrounds or different parts of the company." This same CEO emphasized the importance of presence: "It is key that you show presence. You can't manage China from Detroit. You can't manage the manufacturing line from your executive office. Make it a habit to show physical presence all the time right where things happen, including the manufacturing floor and the R&D lab." Both internal, visible controls discipline and extension of that discipline to supply chain partner operations can add critical layers of security and complexity to the IP protection safety net.

## Strategic Human Resource Management and Talent Management

People are the primary source of IP leaks. Consider the following highly publicized IP leak incidents:

- In 2006 a former General Motors employee in China was convicted of stealing trade secrets related to hybrid vehicle technology valued at $40 million and selling them through her husband's company to Chery Automobile Company, a GM competitor. Not only did GM lose this technology; it had to make significant investments in its security system to prevent such thefts in the future.[17]

- In 2007, a Ford employee who worked as a product engineer from 1997 through 2007 in the United States took more than four thousand confidential trade secret documents and used them to secure a job with a Chinese auto manufacturer. On the eve of his departure from Ford, he copied the documents. He was sentenced to seventy months in U.S. federal prison and ordered to pay a fine of $125,000. He will be deported from the United States once he completes his sentence. Ford estimates the value of the stolen design documents in the multimillion-dollar range.[18]

○ In 2008 an Intel employee in China took intellectual property to AMD, the company's main competitor. While on vacation, he accessed Intel's network and downloaded over a dozen documents, including processor designs. The employee then left Intel and said he was going to work at a hedge fund. Instead he took a job at AMD. Intel estimated the value of the information theft to be close to $1 billion. The employee was indicted on five counts of stealing IP and wire fraud. AMD was reported to be aiding authorities in the investigation.[19] However, nobody knows the real monetized damages of this incident, and we do not want to even imagine the damages that could have occurred if the IP had been leaked to a less honorable company.

○ During the same time period, an IBM China executive was caught e-mailing trade secrets to HP. Court documents claim that two months before he moved to HP, he requested and received an internal memo marked "IBM Confidential" and that an IBM pricing coordinator informed the employee not to distribute the memo. When he joined HP, he e-mailed the document to an HP senior vice president (who has not been indicted). The employee was found guilty.[20]

Intel, IBM, Ford, and GM were all victims of IP leakage through former employees. Better strategic human resource practices, specifically in attracting, development, and retention, might have proved useful in hindering these incidents. For example, a stringent background check is critical for any employee who will be working with IP. A business consultant in Beijing commented, "Make it a habit to conduct background checks on everybody. Employees should be checked not only when they join the company, but also when they are promoted. Checks should include risk control items such as conflict-of-interest and code-of-conduct declarations. Make sure the employee doesn't have relatives in a competing company and that your company is aware of the risks of every single current and potential employee." Employee background checks are a first line of defense against IP leakage. They are more difficult to conduct in China than in most industrialized countries, but there are organizations that specialize in this type of business intelligence. It is wise to use them.

The results from this research strongly support the argument that staff turnover is likely the most prevalent cause of IP leakage in China. An American IT entrepreneur in Shanghai advised, "In my operations I tend to hire women and people who are not originally from Shanghai as they are more loyal and usually work a lot harder compared to most Shanghai returnees. These returnees want to work for a multinational and be the big shots in town, but they are foremost opportunistic and want to take advantage of their local connections for personal gain."

In addition, reward systems are effective in driving aligned behavior and to reinforce controls discipline. A software executive recommended, "In China you have to manage with carrots and sticks. Reward those who make you aware of violators generously without exposing them and at the same time rebuke violations without mercy." One of the less obvious rewards is training and development since many local employees consider it highly valuable. Training and development that focus on improving technical skills are key for high-tech employee motivation, which underlies commitment and retention in China. The reason is that outside training and development are not readily available. This presents an opportunity to link rewards with dynamism. When employees have advanced technical skills, they can contribute to the acceleration of innovation in a company and help keep competitors in a catch-up position. They are also more likely to stay with the employer since only employees who are considered loyal and valuable enjoy the training awards.

Training and development should also be used to reinforce a controls discipline culture. A management consultant in Shanghai observed, "The employee risk is not just related to retention issues, but instead it is about [managing] people in general. For example, we will conduct integrity training, which covers such topics as bribery rules in China and Sarbanes-Oxley regulations. What we have found is that most companies do have training [on risk issues and bribery], but their training material is not detailed enough or not relevant in the China context." Do not assume that your Chinese workers are familiar with your home country standards regarding IP or integrity issues. Unless they have significant experience with other foreign multinational employers, they are not likely to understand your perspective.

Finally, a focus on retention of key employees is critical. A subsidiary manager in an IT company in Beijing made an important observation about talent: "Not all talent is equal. Make sure that you identify the critical people. Some companies are obsessed with staff turnover rates. In China, the rate is high and you can't do much about it. You need to identify who is really important to your organization and try to reduce turnover of these high-value employees." This focus on retaining employees who are critical to the company's operations and not just everyone is an essential best practice in order to slow IP leakage. The critical talent should be carefully selected, developed, rewarded, nurtured, and retained. They are the ones who are the keepers and creators of the company's IP.

Consider the case of Cisco in China. In 1994 Cisco started operations in China and found an extremely challenging environment because of high employee turnover and a shortage of managerial talent with experience in both Western and Chinese business practices. To address this issue, Cisco began to focus its high-tech talent attraction and retention efforts on recent college graduates from the top Chinese universities and provided them leadership and technical development opportunities. According to Cisco's head of human resources in China, "We are developing and nurturing talent, not waiting for the education channels to provide it to us." One of Cisco's flagship sales programs in China sends about twenty newly hired employees a year, for nine months at a time, to the company's training center in Raleigh, North Carolina, to study Cisco's culture, values, and skills such as proposal design, presenting, teamwork, and product knowledge and sales. When they return to China, they receive an additional year of coaching under senior staff members.[21] Cisco has found that this proactive stance to talent development helps it attract, retain, socialize, and screen the talent who will ultimately have exposure to their IP, thus stemming the constant bleeding of talent. Successful multinationals find strategic human resource and talent management important tools in the fight for IP protection in China. A proactive, integrated, and selective approach to talent management works best.

## Focused Corporate Social Responsibility

Multinationals in China report that their corporate social responsibility (CSR) reputation attracts talent, especially younger knowledge workers. However, the CSR practices and what they actually do matter even more. A product management executive in a toy manufacturing company observed, "Doing good in China has to be connected with direct relationship development. Everything else feels good but is a waste of time and money." Another executive describes this as "walking the CSR talk" and contends that CSR is the glue that binds the individuals of the millennial talent pool to the organization. In addition, a positive reputation influences the community in which the multinational operates and aligns internal and external interests. The most critical challenge for foreign multinationals when it comes to CSR in China is that CSR is not being deployed as an instrument on the offensive. Often CSR is departmentalized and strategically detached from operations, making it less effective. In China, it is a critical legitimacy builder that turns internal and external stakeholders into the first line of defense against IP theft. CSR has be proactive and targeted.

These six practices contribute to effective IP protection by slowing or preventing leakage. Individually each makes a contribution, but used in combination, they help a company develop a powerful barrier to IP theft that is difficult for would-be copycats to penetrate. We have demonstrated where some of the practices can be linked together. However, each multinational brings its unique set of capabilities to the table, so each will have to find a combination of activities that makes sense for their respective operations in China.

## Conclusion

Based on our data, we argue that in China, IP protection that goes beyond patenting and legal litigation is potentially the most important approach for ensuring long-term performance in high-tech and service firms. China's slowly maturing legal and economic environment will one day provide the IP protection that foreign investors seek. But if multinationals wait for this maturation to enter China, they will miss profitable business opportunities. Although these opportunities certainly are not without risk, we have illustrated a series of best practices that reduce and manage this risk by erecting complex, integrated, multilevel, socially based IP protection barriers. We suggest that these best practices can be used to guide IP protection activities in other emerging markets where there is similar risk of IP leakage.

Multinationals must have a well-focused China strategy. This will guide the choices they make about the transfer of IP to China or the creation of IP in China. It is inadequate to move operations to China simply because it is a large or fast-growing market. Investment in China must be part of a larger global strategy, and the role of China in this strategy must be clearly defined. This strategic clarity will guide the identification of which IP should be transferred. A general rule is to transfer the most appropriate IP to achieve strategic goals in China but not necessarily to transfer the most advanced technology if a less advanced version will create equal value for customers in China.

Multinationals must understand localized rules of the game for their industry in its specific location. These rules vary by business, industry, and in-country location. When choosing a location, seek one that is more favorable to IP protection; not all locations are equally favorable. Seek a location where there is opportunity to align your interests with the interests of local officials through jobs, training, and community relations.

Next, it is important to get the legal fundamentals right. This includes using legal counsel with specific expertise in Chinese IP law, specific expertise in the location where you will operate, and specific expertise in your industry or line of business. Do not use counsel without these detailed levels of expertise just because you know them from your home country. If you decide to use the legal system in China, do so proactively. Pay attention to the unintended consequences of doing so, and use the jurisdiction closest to where you have the best interest alignment to increase the likelihood of a positive outcome.

Once multinationals have made sure they have these basics right, they can begin building a network of activities that will create a complex, multilevel barrier that keeps would-be IP thieves out and the IP in the heads, computers, and files of company employees. We discussed six activities identified by the multinationals as IP protection best practices:

- *Interest alignment* with regulatory institutions and individual government officials in the localities where the company operates
- *Disaggregation* of IP components and core processes through organizational and physical separation of activities, vendors, and know-how

- *Dynamism* through continuously improving products and processes in order to stay at the leading edge—forcing the competition to continually play catch-up
- Use of a *controls discipline* that rests on and is embedded in a strong organizational culture
- *Strategic human resource management and talent management* that makes the company a great place to work
- Focused *corporate social responsibility* activities that make the company a valuable part of the local community

We urge multinationals seeking to protect IP in China to develop and reinforce these six capabilities. The more interlinked activities a multinational can deploy, the stronger the IP protection will be.

China is an important market for many global firms, and its lure is hard to ignore. But the challenges it presents, especially to a foreign multinational's IP, is significant. Ultimately it is a multinational's corporate culture, process complexity, and speed that will keep copycats at bay in emerging markets like China.

# 10

# COMPETING IN EMERGING ASIA

## Reflections and Conclusions

### Anil K. Gupta, U. Srinivasa Rangan, Toshiro Wakayama

Emerging Asian markets have become the next battleground for multinational companies in every industry. Asian countries stretching from Turkey on the shores of the Sea of Marmara to Japan on the Pacific Ocean and from landlocked Kazakhstan to the island nation of Indonesia are among the fastest-growing economies in the world. In terms of purchasing power parity, as of 2011, seven of the world's ten largest emerging economies are in Asia; of these, two (China and India) rank among the four largest economies in the world.[1] As these economies keep registering high and sustained economic growth, they have become the engines of growth for both multinational firms and domestic companies. Be it automobiles, scooters and motorcycles, pharmaceuticals, consumer electronics, information technology services, telecommunication equipment, or mobile phone services, no company can afford to ignore the market opportunities that the emerging Asian markets offer.

These national economies are also developing their resource bases. Whether it is natural resources like iron ore, oil, or rare earths, Asian nations possess large shares of global mineral wealth. With their emphasis on and investment in education and health services, these countries are also developing human capital capabilities that are the foundation of future innovation. Many multinationals have found it critical to offshore as well as out-source parts of their value chain to Asia. Indeed, multinationals have come to recognize that emerging Asian markets are places where new innovations can emerge.[2]

The combination of growing markets and maturing resource bases also means that in many Asian countries, local firms have begun to develop global ambitions. Firms from emerging Asia—Tata Steel, POSCO, and Baoshan in the steel industry; Tata Motors, Hyundai, and Geely in the automobile industry; Samsung in consumer electronics; and LG and Haier in home appliances—are not only challenging established multinationals at home but are also seeking to compete in the rest of Asia as well as globally.[3]

As emerging Asia increasingly offers lucrative and growing market opportunities; provides the base for sophisticated products, services, and innovations; and becomes the home of new and vigorous competitors, it becomes necessary to understand how businesses are trying to position themselves to compete successfully in emerging Asia. The questions range from how one conceptualizes global strategies in the light of emerging Asia's promise and potential to how local players are seeking to compete with the players from outside. The chapter authors in this book have sought to address many such questions. At the same time, they raise new and profound questions for managers as well as researchers. In this concluding chapter, we take a look at the key arguments and conclusions the authors have arrived at.

The authors in this book touch on five themes explicitly or implicitly:

*Theme 1:* How should firms moving into emerging Asian markets as well as aspiring globalizers from Asia deal with the rise of Asia? In other words, how should managers reconceptualize their global strategies to compete better in Asia and against Asian firms?

*Theme 2:* How should senior managers in global as well as Asian firms factor in the role of innovation in their strategic calculus to compete in Asia or elsewhere?

*Theme 3:* What are the organizational imperatives of the strategic and operational challenges that emerging Asian markets pose? In other words, how should global firms reinvent their organizations to compete better in Asia?

*Theme 4:* How do firms use strategic tools such as alliances and acquisitions in order to compete better in and out of Asia?

*Theme 5:* What are the mind-set transformation issues that firms face when they seek to enter and do well in Asia or when firms seek to go global by leveraging their Asian base?

## Theme 1: Reconceptualizing Strategy

In Chapter One, Gupta and Wang set the stage for this theme when they set out the challenge of building the next generation of global enterprise, especially in light of the emerging challenge of competing in and competing for Asian markets. They make a strong argument that the new global reality of emerging markets is forcing firms to do some fundamental rethinking of their strategy. And that calls for willingness to plan for recognizing the market needs of emerging markets, the opportunities for disaggregating the value chain across the globe, and the need to think in terms of global platforms that permit local solutions. All of the other authors elaborate on each of these points.

Dawar and Bagga follow up on the question of how strategy needs to be thought afresh as firms seek to conquer emerging Asian markets. Increasingly the potential of emerging markets may reside in the broad swath of middle-income consumers who account for more than half of the consumption in such markets. They call this large segment the core of the diamond of market opportunities in emerging markets and identify a major challenge for traditional multinationals: "The MNCs have the organization, the infrastructure, and the know-how to capture large opportunities. On the other hand, emerging market firms are better placed to understand the needs of local consumers and address them." The question facing MNCs is this: Will they be able to come up with a new business model that can simultaneously win the middle-class market in emerging markets and keep the emerging market rivals at bay? Here the authors use a case study to illustrate how this issue may play out. Their chosen setting is India, and the market they focus on is automotive.

The tale they narrate is instructive. India's auto industry was opened up for foreign firms starting in the early 1990s, and almost all global firms—Toyota, GM, Honda, Fiat, Ford, Volkswagen, BMW, and Peugeot—rushed in. All faced a dominant domestic player, Maruti, a joint venture of Suzuki that held more than half the market in the mid-1990s. By 2010, a newcomer, Hyundai of Korea, had captured 25 percent of the market—greater than the combined market shares of Toyota, Ford, GM, and Honda. How did Hyundai do it? First, instead of pushing older models from elsewhere into the small, midsize, and premium car segments as the MNCs did, Hyundai decided to go after the developing middle market with newly designed cars, taking on Maruti in the marketplace. Second, its product positioning emphasized its appeal to the aspiring and upwardly mobile Indian middle class. Third, unlike its global rivals, which were trying to minimize investments in a new market, Hyundai was willing to make a big commitment to a new market with an intent to capture a large part of it before its rivals established a foothold. Fourth, to exploit the scale efficiency that comes with large investments, it also made provision for exports of cars from India. Finally, to keep ahead of its rivals, it invested in a new R&D center in India "to inject local understanding and talent to customize product design" to suit Indian consumers. In sum, Hyundai was willing to reinvent its strategy for the sake of winning the race in India.

In Chapter Three, Wakayama, Shintaku, Amano, and Kikuchi use the experience of consumer electronics and home appliances giant Panasonic in China to illustrate a similar strategic evolution. When Panasonic entered China in the late 1980s, it started, like any other multinational, with its successful products and processes. In addition to catering to local market needs, the China operations served as a global manufacturing base for Panasonic. By the late 1990s, it became clear to senior managers in Japan that the company needed to do more by way of localization of product to succeed against local competition. It opened the China Lifestyle Research Center, patterned after its similar corporate center in Japan. The China center began with collecting data on local lifestyles and gradually began to contribute to new product concepts. The interaction with its counterpart in Japan also allowed it to gain technological knowledge and cost considerations to help further in localizing products for China. As the China center built up its local R&D capabilities, a host of local product introductions took place.

According to Shintaku and Amano in Chapter Four, Japanese firms find that their products do not fit the needs of emerging markets. But wedded as they are to satisfying the quality and innovation needs of developed markets and the resultant deployment of firm-level assets and capabilities, they are in no position to tackle the needs of emerging markets. Staying with the current approach would inevitably doom them to competitive outflanking by their newer rivals.[4] Faced with this dilemma in the Vietnamese motorcycle industry, where Honda had long been dominant with versions of its long-lived product developed over fifty years before and sold at somewhat premium prices, Honda had to rethink its product development and planning processes.

In the early 2000s, Chinese manufacturers came roaring in with products priced at a third to a quarter of the Honda products. It had two effects on the market: it dramatically expanded the primary market, especially at the low end, and it cut Honda's market share drastically to less than 10 percent. To its credit, Honda responded effectively by moving on two fronts almost simultaneously. It repositioned its product by reviewing its quality design standards, revamping its cost and price approach, and by opting for reductions in quality and functions as needed. Then it reallocated resources and capability to the member states of the Association of Southeast Asian Nations (ASEAN) by taking steps to locate motorcycle models and mechanical parts development to Thailand and locate product planning and exterior design responsibilities to Vietnam and Indonesia, two of the fastest-growing motorcycle markets in the ASEAN region. Honda had to revamp its entire Vietnam strategy and, over time, its ASEAN strategy because of the Chinese challenge. Key to its success was its willingness to reexamine its business model and change its resource allocation and strategic positioning approach to suit the needs of the emerging markets.

In Chapter Seven, Rangan and Hariharan come at this issue of global strategy rethinking from a different angle when they take a look at Indian and Chinese firms' overseas acquisitions and assess their implications. Using four in-depth case studies— Bharat Forge and Bharti Airtel from India and Lenovo and Geely from China—they argue that acquisitions by emerging Asian firms have a significant impact on the competitive landscape and so need to be taken seriously by incumbent multinationals. In each of these acquisitions, the authors point out, the acquiring firms sought to use the acquisitions to achieve a number of things: they have overcome the mobility barriers to join the global industry players, gained access to new strategic assets and capabilities, and used the new capabilities in combination with their home-based assets and capabilities to offer new value propositions to potential customers. This approach has allowed these firms to rewrite the rules of the game in their respective industries, forcing the incumbent firms to react to new business models. In sum, the acquisition approach has allowed the Indian and

Chinese firms to scramble the global competitive landscape to the disadvantage of incumbent firms.

## Theme 2: Rethinking Innovation

Innovation is the lifeblood of any company's competitive success today. Every chapter in this book touches on the topic of innovation. Right at the outset, Gupta and Wang suggest that in the future, as in the past, global strategic success will go to the company that is able to outinnovate its rivals. Given the rapid advance of technology, the transparency imposed by the growth of the Internet, and the emergence of new rivals from emerging markets, the need to rethink how and where innovation would occur in global organizations has become paramount. The rethinking of innovation in turn calls for developing the desire to foster innovation in all aspects of the business, a passion for frugal innovation, and a willingness to work collaboratively with other firms to innovate faster.

Chapter Two on how Hyundai outcompeted its global auto rivals in India is actually a paean to the innovative capability of the Korean company. Dawar and Bagga's description of how Hyundai did it is as much a description of its strategic rethinking as it is about its ability to outinnovate its rivals. At one level, Hyundai's success story simply suggests rethinking the familiar strategic and marketing aspects—positioning, product, price, promotion, and placement—in emerging markets. At another level, such rethinking implies a willingness to entertain a new business model for emerging markets. A refusal to rethink the business model and adherence to old developed market business models may well spell disaster in such markets. Such rethinking of the business model means that Hyundai was able to introduce pervasive innovation in all activities at all levels of the organization; without that innovation, the company would not have succeeded to the extent it has.

Wakayama, Shintaku, Amano, and Kikuchi illustrate another way of thinking about innovation in a large multinational company. Historically multinationals have followed what is often referred to as the waterfall model of innovations: innovations occur at the research labs in multinationals' home countries, and over time the innovations are introduced, first to other developed countries and then later to less developed countries. The growing importance of emerging Asian markets and, as we saw in the case of the automotive industry in India, the challenge of meeting their requirements is forcing multinationals to rethink the waterfall paradigm. Faced with declining market share in the Chinese appliances market, Panasonic sought to innovate its way around the problem. Its willingness to open the China Lifestyle Center was an acknowledgment of the fact that innovations can happen away from the home country. As the China center built up its local R&D capabilities, a host of product introductions took place, and an interesting thing happened on the way. As the company began recognizing the value of new knowledge generated by the China center and its impact on product development, it began a deliberate process of including the China center in its global plans for new centers in Europe and for help in the development of the next generation of global products. It seems that Panasonic has come to rethink the way it innovates for the global marketplace.

Shintaku and Amano's work dealing with Honda's fall and rise in the motorcycles market in Vietnam offers an instructive lesson on how multinationals could rethink the way they go about promoting innovations in their organizations. Historically Japanese firms in many industries, ranging from consumer electronics to automobiles, have succeeded by systematically augmenting their quality image and adding more features for less cost or at a cost comparable to their rivals' products with fewer features. This approach of value creation based on quality and features had allowed Japanese firms to outcompete American and Western European rivals in North America and Europe. But the emerging markets pose a different strategic dilemma for Japanese multinationals. These opportunities in emerging markets are in rapidly growing middle markets that require good quality, but not exceptional quality, and at the same time look for relatively lower prices compared to those of developed country markets. Akin to the innovator's dilemma that innovation-based firms face,[5] Japanese firms find that their products do not fit the needs of emerging markets, wedded as they are to satisfy the quality and innovation needs of developed markets. In other words, the waterfall model falters as Western and Japanese multinationals enter the rapidly growing emerging markets of Asia. To its credit, Honda reexamined its product innovation strategy and made the appropriate changes.

Rangan and Hariharan tackle the innovation issue at the intersection of global strategy and local needs and capabilities from a different angle. Although primarily concerned with the acquisition-based strategies of Indian and Chinese firms, their work takes them to look at how Indian and Chinese companies may be coming up with newer innovation approaches. These firms' strategic approach combines their access to low-cost talent in their home bases and their exposure to the sophisticated needs of their customers in the developed countries. For example, the Indian company Bharat Forge Limited (BFL) in the auto components industry has leveraged its frugal innovation capabilities, access to low-cost talent, and customer-facing interface in the West to come up with a new innovation model to serve its clients better. BFL developed a strategic positioning that combined some differentiation based on speed to market and technology with low-cost production. For instance, it produces a new part for its German and U.S. customers with excellent quality within three weeks of being requested to do so.[6] Then it exploited the complementary competences located in the different parts of its global operations with a skillful distribution of roles and responsibilities. Its German operations, for example, are used to work closely with customers using its strong design and engineering capabilities, whereas its Indian operation is leveraged as a low-cost manufacturing base. Finally, over time, BFL has evolved what it calls the "dual-shore" capability to serve its global customers better. Under this approach, BFL has a design, forging, and manufacturing capability, "one close to the customer and one in a low cost but technologically competitive destination" such as India (and perhaps, in the future, China).[7] Backed by a full-service capability and dual-shore model, BFL has become a provider of end-to-end solutions from product conceptualization to designing and, finally, manufacturing, testing, and validation to customers that now include the top five passenger and commercial vehicle manufacturers in the world and a large number of automotive original equipment manufacturer (OEM) and tier 1 auto components firms. Rangan and Hariharan suggest that other firms, such as Bharti Airtel from India and Lenovo and Geely from China, are following a similar distributed model of innovation and customer service.

In Chapter Eight, Kannapan and Lukose use India to illustrate how the environment in emerging economies can spur corporate imagination and serve as fertile soil for innovation. Their corporate examples come from mobile telephony technology and life sciences. It is clear, however, that other industries can also serve up similar experiences. Kannapan and Lukose identify four factors that they believe largely determine business experience in an emerging market and thus have an impact on the kinds of innovations they give rise to: market, talent, business infrastructure, and sociocultural context. They illustrate the role that these factors have played in creating an environment for innovation in companies like IBM (in information technology), Sasken (a medium-sized public company focused on embedded systems), and Strand (a small, privately held firm focusing on computational life sciences). IBM has leveraged the talent pool available in India to create an R&D center that is closely aligned with its other global R&D centers, which has allowed IBM India to create a record number of patent filings. IBM's bet on Indian talent paid off when the mobile telecom business began to take off in India. It crafted an innovative business arrangement with Bharti Airtel, the leading telecom service provider in India, whereby it shares in the upside revenue potential of Bharti Airtel instead of a traditional fee-for-service model. Now IBM is following Bharti Airtel into Africa with the same service provider model. In other words, the business model innovation pioneered in India is going global. Sasken leveraged the talent pool in India and the fast-rising penetration of mobile phones to position themselves for leading innovation in their chosen field. Such an early focus led them to come up with a new application, machine-to-machine connectivity, that seeks to solve the problem of remote monitoring and management for firms in industries, such as telecom tower operations and life cycle monitoring of industrial equipment. Strand, established by a group of highly talented professors from a leading institute in India, also leveraged the talent pool in India to focus on the computational needs of life sciences firms.

If innovation is to be the lifeblood of commerce, intellectual property rights need to have strong protection. Chapter Nine by Schotter and Teagarden focuses on a widely perceived and extremely urgent managerial challenge relating to protection of intellectual property in emerging markets in general and China in particular. Even the most casual observer of China's business scene is aware that intellectual property (IP) theft is a major issue not just for foreign firms but increasingly for domestic Chinese firms. The IP theft issue ranges over the entire gamut of illegal usurpation of patents, flagrant violation of copyrights, and utter disregard for trademarks. Even as managers are urged to recognize that innovation is the lifeblood of a company's competitive success, violation of intellectual property rights has become a major managerial concern for firms operating in China. Schotter and Teagarden take a workmanlike approach to the topic of how firms seek to deal with this urgent issue. Based on their fieldwork, they suggest that firms need to take proactive efforts based on strategic clarity, business intelligence, and knowledge of local legal fundamentals to protect their intellectual property.

## Theme 3: Reinventing the Global Organization

If firms have to rethink their global strategies in the context of emerging markets and their rising importance and if they also have to rethink how they pursue innovation efforts, it cannot happen without reinventing their global organizations as well. Gupta and Wang identify this critical theme in Chapter One. Here, the authors argue, the need is for firms to move away from the old paradigm of a global headquarters to a new one of a network of global hubs, underpinned by the twin themes of connecting and coordinating instead of commanding and controlling, and an actively fostered one-company culture. Several of the chapters that follow Gupta and Wang's chapter touch on this theme of organizational renewal or reinvention.

Wakayama, Shintaku, Amano, and Kikuchi tackle in Chapter Three the old question of local adaptation versus global integration but in the new context of emerging markets, especially in Asia. As they point out, the management literature and lore have it that there is a trade-off between national responsiveness and global integration. Indeed, the global auto firms that lost out in the Indian automotive market to Hyundai were acting on that premise, unwilling to adapt to local needs at the cost of global integration. Taking a contrarian approach, Hyundai was willing to move much further in the direction of local adaptation. Wakayama and coauthors ask a more fundamental question: Is the trade-off between local adaptation and global integration real? Surprisingly, their response is that such a trade-off is not so much imposed on multinationals as it is assumed to be so by managers. In their view, it is more constructive to view the two themes of local adaptation and global integration "as dynamically coevolving competitive dimensions." In other words, as they suggest, deeper localization invites greater global integration, which in turn enables yet deeper localization. As firms realize the advantage of taking such a coevolutionary perspective, they are able to use the adaptation-integration tension as a driver for creating competitive advantage though innovative products, new organizational processes, and even business models. This is precisely what Panasonic did after a period of trial and error and scored a big success in China. Because of that, instead of viewing local adaptation and global integration as either-or choices, Panasonic began to recognize and then build on a coevolutionary approach by taking advantage of the knowledge network that local adaptation efforts gave rise to. Wakayama and his coauthors identify some key lessons for multinationals. One is that it is critical for MNCs to develop a coevolution mind-set by locating the issue of local adaptation versus global integration within a tension-embracing structure and processes rather than through trade-off choices in structure and processes. Another lesson is that global firms need to consciously create and sustain strategic coevolution outposts, especially in emerging markets.

Shintaku and Amano's chapter dealing with Honda's initial stumbles and its later recovery also touches on organization issues. As we saw, once Honda realized that its strategic and operational decision making centered in Japan could not help it regain its footing in places like Vietnam, it began to move away from a single location-dominated organizational approach toward a network of regional hubs that are situated in a small number of carefully chosen countries. For example, it reallocated resources and capability to the ASEAN region by taking steps to locate motorcycle models and mechanical parts development to Thailand and to locate product planning and exterior design responsibilities to Vietnam and Indonesia, two of the fastest-growing motorcycle markets in the ASEAN region. Honda revamped not only its strategy but also its organization. From a command-and-control model of managing the global strategy formulation and implementation, it moved to a more collaborative model in which regional hubs are increasingly listened to by the center. This was facilitated by Honda's willingness to shift resources away from headquarters to the regional hubs.

Chapter Eight by Kannapan and Lukose hints at this kind of global organization change when they explore how IBM integrated its India operations tightly into its global network. IBM patiently developed deep engagements across Indian industry, offering computing hardware and, increasingly, services. Top-notch R&D labs, mirroring established practices in the United States, were incrementally built in India, almost one researcher at a time, by relocating long-term IBM employees from overseas and culling top-rated India-based talent. IBM's human resource management, training, and development policies in India were a fusion of global practices with local needs and sensitivities. Encouraging a globally mobile talent pool, IBM integrated its workforce well beyond the organizational level by fostering personal connections and trust across disparate cultures. Experimentation and individual initiative consistent with overall business contexts are encouraged. As we can easily see, IBM's approach was to follow Gupta and Wang's advice to create a network global hub, allow them to connect and coordinate, and foster a one-company culture built on the shared vision of exceptional technological expertise.

## Theme 4: Globalizing Through Alliances and Acquisitions

As emerging markets grow in importance in the global economy and as traditional multinationals from developed countries as well as newer rivals from emerging markets compete intensely against each other, it is becoming clear that opportunities for both specialization and collaboration are rising. As Gupta and Wang point out, the ability to disaggregate the value chains, coupled with greater outsourcing, means that even as companies become more global and more diversified, they are becoming more focused regarding what they manage within their own boundaries. In short, companies are becoming embedded in ever larger interfirm networks. This development has meant that firms have to make selective acquisitions to augment their core capabilities even as they learn to collaborate with other firms to advance their global strategies. Many of the chapters in this book touch on the topic of alliances and acquisitions either implicitly or explicitly.

In Chapter Six, Karnani warns would-be acquirers by pointing out what could go wrong using Indian firms' overseas acquisitions as an example. After acknowledging the motivations behind these acquisitions, such as possible synergies between acquiring and acquired firms, opportunities for gaining new strategic assets or capabilities, and potential for exploiting firm-specific capabilities from the home country in a new country, he looks at the overseas acquisitions of Indian firms such as Tata Steel, Tata Motors, and Hindalco (an aluminum company belonging to the Birla Group) using well-known financial assessment techniques that call for measuring the value created by acquisitions through stock market returns. His conclusion is unambiguous: overseas acquisitions by Indian firms are unmitigated disasters for them because they have not created much value. What is worse, Karnani concludes, these acquisitions have actually destroyed value for the shareholders of the Indian firms. His focused case study of three such acquisitions suggests that the causes of such negative outcomes are too little integration effort by Indian firms to achieve synergies, managerial hubris that promotes acquisition at the expense of shareholder interests, and inadequate managerial discipline due to the availability of easy capital from global and Indian capital providers.

Rangan and Hariharan also look at Indian and Chinese firms' overseas acquisitions and assess their implications. After recording the rapid growth of cross-border acquisitions by Indian and Chinese firms in the past fifteen years and noting how opportunities to gain new capabilities, leverage existing capabilities, and accelerate globalization of the firm drive such acquisitions, they turn to two questions: How do these acquisitions affect the competitive landscape in global industries? and How should incumbent multinationals react to these acquisition moves? Using four in-depth case studies—Bharat Forge and Bharti Airtel from India and Lenovo and Geely from China—Rangan and Hariharan argue that acquisitions by emerging Asian firms have a significant impact on the competitive landscape and so need to be taken seriously by incumbent multinationals. In each of these acquisitions, they point out, the acquiring firms have sought to overcome the mobility barriers to join global industry players, gain access to new strategic assets and capabilities, use the new capabilities in combination with their home-based assets and capabilities to offer new value propositions to potential customers, and rewrite the rules of the game in their respective industries forcing the incumbent firms to react to new business models. The acquisition approach has allowed the Indian and Chinese firms to scramble the global competitive landscape to the disadvantage of incumbent firms. The authors suggest that in light of such acquisition-driven changes in the competitive battlefield, incumbent firms need to take steps to protect themselves. These steps can range from denial of advantageous acquisitions for emerging market firms to reactive efforts to change the rules of the game again in their favor.

Other chapters in this book also touch on how acquisitions play a role in firms' global strategies. Kannapan and Lukose suggest that the Indian company Sasken's global strategy included both acquisitions and alliances:

> Sasken, like IBM, has acted with agility when needed. It turned
> its brand advantage in the telecom ecosystem into a robust
> services business and repositioned its role as a technology
> integrator of choice. It acquired a Finnish wireless company
> during an economic downturn, giving it immediate access to
> European markets and advanced wireless communication
> technology. It further transformed to a connectivity company

and leveraged its position in wireless and multimedia into newer areas such as satellite technologies and consumer electronics. And it has tested the viability of inorganic growth through subsidiary formation, joint ventures, and partnerships with venture capital.

Shintaku and Amano's chapter on Honda's evolving strategy in the ASEAN region also suggests that global firms have learned to look to alliances as the way forward. Honda's revamped ASEAN strategy included considerable movement toward outsourcing. Its new R&D and production strategy enabled mass production of products with reasonable quality. This allowed Honda to increase its local procurement ratio for parts in Vietnam from 53 percent in 2001 to 76 percent in 2003. In Indonesia, the number of suppliers increased to 130 with Honda's technological assistance.

Tanaka and Wang show how global firms have to work patiently with local firms to take advantage of alliances. Toyota started its alliance with the Tianjin Automobile Group (TAG) in China in 1994, cooperating with TAG in parts manufacturing with the hope of converting the alliance into a full car production joint venture later. Toyota's plans did not go smoothly. The institutional barriers due to the joint venture structure and the regulation of state-owned enterprises, difficulties in getting the dealer network to change their poor practices, and the problems posed by the parts management practices of TAG combined to frustrate Toyota's efforts to upgrade TAG's supply chain management approach. But Toyota's persistence eventually paid off when some external developments persuaded the Chinese government to allow a car production joint venture. This development allowed Toyota to pursue the transfer of its management practices and the famed Toyota Production System as an integrated package to the joint venture. A key lesson emerges from this chapter: it is critical for managers of MNCs to recognize the constraints posed by institutional arrangements and policy choices of host governments in making local operations conform to its global norms and practices. Moreover, multinationals have to carefully calibrate the timing of such efforts to take advantage of changes in the market conditions and partner desire to collaborate more effectively.

## Theme 5: Fostering a Global Mind-Set

As firms consider revamping their global strategies, rethink their global innovation approaches, reinvent their global organizations, and reevaluate the use of alliances and acquisitions in the face of emerging market challenges, an important question arises: Can aspiring global firms go through a metamorphosis without fostering a global mind-set among its managers? Gupta and Wang say they cannot. They posit that the most critical challenge for organizations aspiring to build the next-generation global enterprise is the need for globalizing the corporate mind-set—the cognitive lenses through which managers seek to make sense of the world around them. As globalization gathers pace, a global mind-set that simultaneously recognizes the existence of differentiation across countries and markets and the need for and possibility of integration across countries and markets is becoming required for managers.[8] In this context, the emergence of Asia as an economic engine poses an important challenge to Western multinationals since the Asian markets tend to be psychologically, cognitively, and physically far removed from corporate headquarters. As the authors point out, such distance tends to result in an organization that is wedded to the past rather than the future.

Several chapters touch on this theme and suggest that successful firms are those that manage to develop a global mind-set and unsuccessful ones are those that remain mired in past thinking.

Dawar and Bagga show how the major auto multinationals like GM and Toyota lost ground in India due to a mind-set that advocated pushing older models from elsewhere into the small, midsize, and premium car segments to minimize investments in a new market. Such unimaginative efforts to be content with skimming the narrow sliver of the high-end segment allowed an upstart firm from Korea to steal a market. If Hyundai's experience in India shows how approaching the emerging markets in Asia with a different mind-set can pay off, the experience of mature multinationals from Japan demonstrates that even established players can learn to play the game better by developing a more flexible global mind-set.

As Wakayama, Shintaku, Amano, and Kikuchi recount, Panasonic started to develop a global mind-set as it began to respond to the challenges of operating in the Chinese white goods market. Such a global mind-set implies a willingness to go beyond the traditional trade-off perspective to a coevolution perspective.

Shintaku and Amano approach this issue of changing the corporate mind-set to fit the needs of the emerging markets from a different angle. Using a case study of how Honda retooled itself to succeed in the fast-growing Vietnamese motorcycle market, they demonstrate that reexamining the antecedents of past successes and revamping them are critical for success in the newly emerging markets of Asia. Historically, Japanese firms in many industries, ranging from consumer electronics to automobiles, have succeeded by systematically augmenting their quality image and adding more features for less cost or at a cost comparable to that of their rivals' products with fewer features. These opportunities in emerging markets, however, are in the rapidly growing middle markets that require good but not exceptional quality and at the same time look for relatively lower prices compared to developed country markets. To its credit, Honda adapted its mind-set to meet the new global reality.

Finally, Rangan and Hariharan demonstrate how firms such as Bharat Forge and Bharti Airtel from India and Lenovo and Geely from China are starting to move into the global arena with a flexible global mind-set. Unencumbered by past commitments and past learning that need to be unlearned, these firms from emerging markets are able to forge ahead with new business models and new globalization approaches with relative ease. They pose significant challenges to incumbent multinationals from developed countries.

# Notes

## Chapter One

1. T. Leavitt, "The Globalization of Markets," *Harvard Business Review*, May 1983. (Reprint 83308.)
2. For an extensive discussion of what is globalization, see A. K. Gupta, V. Govindarajan, and H. Wang, *The Quest for Global Dominance* (San Francisco: Jossey-Bass/Wiley, 2008), chap. 1.
3. See A. K. Gupta, P. Tesluk, and M. S. Taylor, "Innovation at and Across Levels of Analysis," *Organization Science*, 2007, 18, 885–897.
4. See W. Elfrink, "Executive Perspective: Virtualizing the Corporation," *ThoughtLeaders*, Cisco Systems 2008; also, the authors' personal discussions with Wim Elfrink during January and February 2008.
5. "IBM Shifts Global Procurement Headquarters to China," IBM Corporation press release, Oct. 12, 2006.
6. See F. Cairncross, *The Death of Distance* (Boston: Harvard Business School Press, 1999); "A Survey of Business and the Internet," *Economist*, June 26, 1999, pp. 1–25.
7. S. Spear and H. K. Bowen, "Decoding the DNA of the Toyota Production System," *Harvard Business Review*, Sept.–Oct. 1999. (Reprint 99509.)
8. All three quotes are from "The Past, Imperfect," *Time*, July 15, 1996, p. 54.

9. Quoted in T. Eisenmann, S. Bakshi, S. Briens, and S. Singh, *Google Inc.*, Harvard Business School Case No. 9–804–141, 2004.

10. Authors' personal discussions with Wim Elfrink during January and February 2008.

## Chapter Two

1. A 2010 study by McKinsey (D. Court and L. Narasimhan, "Capturing the World's Emerging Middle Class," *McKinsey Quarterly*, July 2010, http:/www.mckinseyquarterly.com /Capturing_the_worlds_emeging_middle_class_2639#), found that the total consumption in twenty-four emerging economies (including the BRIC countries) is estimated at $9.7 trillion in PPP terms. But much of the spurt in domestic consumption over the next decade is coming from a middle class of almost 2 billion people with a combined consumption spend of over $5.5 trillion (PPP adjusted).

2. The Hyundai India case study uses data from ICRA's India Passenger Vehicle Industry Report, 2010; KPMG's India Automotive Study, 2007; and company Web sites of Hyundai Motor India, Maruti Suzuki, Ford India, GM India, Toyota Bharat; and Honda India.

3. The Society of Indian Automobile Manufacturers (SIAM) reports years in April-to-March annual cycles. The data come from Industry Statistics (Domestic Sales), SIAM, 2011, http:// www.siamindia.com/scripts/domestic-sales-trend.aspx.

4. Hyundai Motor India Ltd, "Profile–R&D Center," 2011, http://www.hyundai.com/in/en/CompanyInformation/ HMIL/RDCenter/RND.htm.

5. This section is adapted in part from N. Dawar and A. Chattopadhyay, "Rethinking Marketing Programs for Emerging Markets," *Long Range Planning*, 2002, 35, 457–474.

6. The P&G case study referred to CBS's BNet (Interactive Business Network), a media article in January 2010:

M. Frazier, "How P&G Brought the Diaper Revolution to China," CBS/BNET, Jan. 7, 2010, http://www.cbsnews .com/8301–505125_162–51379838/how-pg-brought -the-diaper-revolution-to-china/. See also and P&G China's Web site http://www.pg.com.cn/jon/Overview/Introduction .aspx.

7. The McDonald's case study data are based on A. Kulkarni, W. Lassar, C. Sridhar, and A. Venkitachalam, "McDonald's Ongoing Marketing Challenge: Social Perception in India," 2009, ojica.fiu.edu.

8. Unilever's India case study uses data from Unilever India's Web site and a case study by Social Market Place: "Hindustan Unilever: Building a Rural Distribution Model," Social Marketplace, n.d., http://thesocialmarketplace.org/casestudy/ Hindustan-unilever/. Also see "India: Creating Rural Entrepreneurs," Unilever, n.d., and Hindustan Unilever Limited, "Investor Presentation, June 2010, http://www.hul .co.in/Images/HUL_MorganStanleyJune2010_tcm114 –219373.pdf.

## Chapter Three

1. C. Bartlett and S. Ghoshal, "What Is a Global Manager?" *Harvard Business Review*, Aug. 2003. (Reprint R0308F.)

2. P. Ghemawat and J. Nueno, "Zara: Fast Fashion," Harvard Business School Case No. 9–703–497, 2006.

3. A. Farhoomand, "Wal-Mart Stores: 'Every Day Low Prices' in China," case HKU590, Asia Case Research Center, University of Hong Kong, 2006.

4. Another articulation of the coevolution perspective without the notion of tension-embracing structure is given in Y. Sugiyama, *The Evolution of Global Strategy* (Tokyo: Yuhikaku, 2009). (In Japanese.)

5. M. Feldman, "Resources in Emerging Structures and Processes of Change," *Organization Science*, 2004, 15, 295–309.

6. The notion of structure here follows Giddens's dynamic view of the concept. In his view, "Structure exists only in and through the activities of the human agents." A. Giddens, "A Reply to My Critics," in D. Held and J. B. Thompson (eds.), *Social Theory of Modern Societies: Anthony Giddens and His Critics* (Cambridge: Cambridge University Press, 1989), p. 256. Thus, this dynamic notion of structure is intrinsically equipped with a self-renewing force that expresses itself through "the activities of the human agents." In the context of "tension-embracing structure," tension-embracing activities represent the engine of the coevolution of the two competing themes of local adaptation and global integration.

7. More precisely, these "business units" were called "product divisions" within Panasonic until the large-scale reorganization in 2003 led by its CEO at that time, Kunio Nakamura.

8. This insight into the role of the Lifestyle Research Center is discussed in K. Shiramomo, "On the Localization Pathways of a Japanese Home Appliances Firm: A Study of the Firm in the Chinese Market" (degree-completion thesis, University of Tokyo, 2007). (In Japanese.)

9. J. Immelt, V. Govindarajan, and C. Trimble, "How GE Is Disrupting Itself," *Harvard Business Review*, Oct. 2009. (Reprint R0910D)

10. C. Bartlett and S. Ghoshal, "Matrix Management: Not a Structure, a Frame of Mind," *Harvard Business Review*, July–Aug. 1990. (Reprint 90401.)

11. For an in-depth discussion on mind-set in the context of global strategy and organization, see Chapter Five in A. Gupta, V. Govindarajan, and H. Wang, *The Quest for Global Dominance: Transforming Global Presence into Global Competitive Advantage*, 2nd ed. (San Francisco: Jossey-Bass/Wiley, 2008).

## Chapter Four

1. The original argument of this chapter is from J. Shintaku and T. Amano, "Emerging Market Strategy of Japanese Firms," *Keizaigaku-ronshu*, 2009, 75(3), 40–62. (In Japanese.) It is largely revised in this English version.

2. S. L. Hart and C. M. Christensen, "The Great Leap: Driving Innovation from the Base of the Pyramid," *Sloan Management Review*, 2002, 44(1), 51–56; S. L. Hart and M. B. Milstein, "Creating Sustainable Value," *Academy of Management Executive*, 2003, 17(2), 56–69; T. London and S. L. Hart, "Reinventing Strategies for Emerging Markets: Beyond the Transnational Model," *Journal of International Business Studies*, 2004, 35, 350–370; and C. K. Prahalad, *The Fortune at the Bottom of the Pyramid* (Philadelphia: Wharton School Publishing, 2010).

3. A. Delios and W. J. Henisz, "Japanese Firms' Investment Strategies in Emerging Economies," *Academy of Management Journal*, 2000, 43(3), 305–323, and H. Sugawara, "The Origin of BOP Business and Possibility of Japanese Firms," *Journal of International Business*, 2010, 2(1), 45–67 (in Japanese), empirically analyze Japanese firms' investments in emerging countries.

4. See C. M. Christensen, *The Innovator's Dilemma* (Boston: Harvard Business School Press, 1997).

5. See K. Nakagawa, T. Amano, and K. Oki, "Recognizing the Role of Basic Marketing 4P in Asian Markets: The Case of Epson Indonesia," *Akamon Management Review*, 2009, 8(10), 625–634. (In Japanese.)

6. See M. Fujiwara, "Strategies and Resources of Diversified Firms," in H. Ito and T. Numagami, *Modern Management Theory* (Tokyo: Yuhikaku, 2008). (In Japanese.)

7. The market share of Epson's laser printers is relatively small. Instead, it is competitive in ink-jet printers.

8. OEM is a contract for outsourcing all or some of the production functions to mass production companies.

9. ODM is a contract for outsourcing all or some of the design and production functions to specialized companies in design and production.

10. See D. G. McKendrick, R. F. Doner, and S. Haggard, *From Silicon Valley to Singapore: Location and Competitive Advantage in the Hard Disk Drive Industry* (Stanford, Calif.: Stanford University Press, 2000).

11. T. Amano, *East Asia's Linkage and Japanese Firms: A New Perspective of Corporate Growth* (Tokyo: Yuhikaku, 2005) (in Japanese); and J. Shintaku and others, "International Division of Labor in the Japan and the U.S. Hard Disk Drive Industries," *Akamon Management Review*, 2007, 6(6), 217–242. (In Japanese.)

12. See T. Fujimoto, T. Amano, and J. Shintaku, "Comparative Advantage and International Division of Labor Based on Architecture Theory: Reexamination of a Multinational Firm's Theory from a Manufacturing Management Perspective," *Organizational Science*, 2007, 40(4), 51–64. (In Japanese.)

13. J. Otahara, "Motorcycle Industry: Long-Term Competitive Advantage with Low-Price Integral Products," in J. Shintaku and T. Amano (eds.), *International Management Strategy for Manufacturing Management: Industrial Geography in Asia* (Tokyo: Yuhikaku, 2009) (in Japanese), and K. Mishima *Motorcycle Industry in Southeast Asia*, Minerva-Shobou, 2010) (in Japanese) also look at the ASEAN motorcycle industry and Honda's strategy of offering low-priced products. The case description here is based on our field survey in 2003, 2009, and 2011.

14. Based on our interview in Honda R&D Southeast Asia and Honda Indonesia.

15. Motorcycle design and development started in Thailand in 1988, and in 1997, Honda R&D Southeast Asia Co. Ltd. was established in Thailand; it became a design and develop-

ment base. Honda invested 800,000 baht in this center in 2003, strengthening its motorcycle design activities for the ASEAN market. The center performs full-scale R&D activities, including market surveys, product planning, design, mockups, prototyping, and inspections.

16. Original platform designs of driving units come from Japan. Honda R&D Southeast Asia, together with the Asaka R&D center in Japan, modifies and recreates the ASEAN platforms. Most development and modification of upper bodies is accomplished in Thailand.

17. See T. Amano, "Indonesia's Motorcycle Market and Manufacturing Operations, *Akamon Management Review*, 2007, 6(9), 451–458. (In Japanese.)

18. Interviews in Honda Vietnam and Honda Thailand in 2009 and 2011 each.

## Chapter Five

1. T. Marukawa, "Jidosha Sangyo" [Automobile Industry: Failure of National Industry] in T. Marukawa (ed.), *Ikoki Chugoku no Sangyo Seisaku* [China's Industrial Policy in Transition] (Chiba: Institute of Developing Economies, 2000).

2. The policy aimed to group more than one hundred car manufacturers into eight to ten groups by 2000 and three or four groups by 2010.

3. R. P. Dore, *Taking Japan Seriously* (Stanford: Stanford University Press, 1987).

4. T. Nishiguchi, *Strategic Industrial Sourcing: The Japanese Advantage* (New York: Oxford University Press, 1994).

5. C. L. Ahmadjian and J. R. Lincoln, "Keiretsu, Governance and Learning: Case Studies in Change from the Japanese Automotive Industry," *Organization Science*, 2001, *12*, 683–701.

6. M. L. Gerlach, *Alliance Capitalism* (Berkeley: University of California Press, 1992).

7. S. R. Helper and M. Sako, "Supplier Relations in Japan and the United States: Are They Converging?" *Sloan Management Review*, 1995, 36, 77–84; M. Sako, *Prices, Quality and Trust: Inter-Firm Relations in Britain and Japan* (Cambridge: Cambridge University Press, 1992).

8. In August 1997, the Tianjin Mini-Auto Works, which had been producing Xiali since 1986, combined with the Tianjin Municipal Engine Works and the Tianjin Municipal Automobile Research Institute to form the first joint stock company in the group, Tianjin Xiali.

9. In reality, companies other than joint venture companies, such as sales companies and import and export companies, were functioning as part of the internal organization of GC as far as decisions on strategic planning and daily business performance are concerned. It is even questionable whether they have any independence as profit centers. There is reason to suspect that the main reason these companies took on an independent legal entity separate from the parent company was to facilitate negotiations with other companies.

10. In the case of Toyota, which has the most highly developed supply chain management in the Japanese car industry, its monthly production plan is almost purely order based, including orders from dealers that have no confirmation from the final customers.

11. For Japanese cars, production is minutely synchronized by employing a three-part system for information technology. First is assembly line control, where the production order plan is based on the final design. The information necessary for finished car assembly over the following three days is sent online from the assembly factory to the parts factory once a day. Second is tele-mail, which reports on parts delivery to the assembly factory online. And third is withdrawal *kanban*, attached to the parts. This online synchronization ultimately decreases the stock and production buffers.

12. Moreover, the bill market was not fully developed, and cash settlements (with no deadlines) were commonly made. This means suppliers' credit was extremely insecure and was based largely on verbal agreement. This was a serious issue, as suppliers' dependence on group sales was extremely high.

13. B. Asanuma, "Manufacturer-Supplier Relations in Japan and the Concept of Relation-Specific Skill," *Journal of the Japanese and International Economies*, 1989, 3, 1–30.

14. TAG often had to overvalue the physical assets to make a fifty-fifty joint venture, though much of the old machinery and equipment was replaced immediately.

15. That society was named after Kyoho Kai in Japan, which included Toyota's major suppliers, to enhance efficiencies for the entire supplier network. *Kyoho* means "supporting Toyota" in Chinese character.

16. The virtues for factory management are *Seiri* (sifting), *Seiton* (sorting), *Seiso* (shining), *Seiketsu* (standardizing), and *Shitsuke* (sustaining).

17. This change is explained by the fact that China had entered the World Trade Organization, and Chinese consumers were waiting for prices to drop as a result.

18. Sichuan Automobile Group was Toyota's partner in the Sichuan Toyota Motor Corporation, established in 1998 to produce a small bus known as Coaster.

## Chapter Six

1. United Nations Conference on Trade and Development, *World Investment Report 2009* (New York: United Nations, 2009) and *World Investment Report 2006* (New York: United Nations, 2006).

2. P. M. Thomas and S. Sen, "Tata Steel Gives India a Pound of UK," *Economic Times*, Feb. 1, 2007.

3. R. Ramesh and M. Millner, "Tata Celebrates Costly Victory in Corus Chase," *e Guardian*, Feb. 1, 2007, http://www.guardian.co.uk/business/2007/feb/01/india.frontpagenews.

4. D. R. King, D. R. Dalton, C. M. Daily, and J. G. Covin, "Meta-Analyses of Post-Acquisition Performance: Indications of Unidentified Moderators," *Strategic Management Journal*, 2004, *25*, 187–200.

5. K. P. Anju Seth and R. Pettit, "Synergy, Managerialism or Hubris? An Empirical Examination of Motives for Foreign Acquisitions of US Firms," *Journal of International Business Studies*, 2000, *31*, 387–405.

6. J. Kelly, C. Cook, and D. Spitzer, *Unlocking Shareholder Value: The Keys to Success—Mergers and Acquisition: A Global Research Report* (London: KPMG, 1999).

7. N. Kumar, P. K. Mohapatra, and S. Chandrasekhar, *India's Global Powerhouses: How They Are Taking On the World* (Boston: Harvard Business Press, 2009). Also see N. Kumar, "How Emerging Giants Are Rewriting the Rules of M&A," *Harvard Business Review*, May 2009. (Reprint R0905K.)

8. My sample consists of all acquisitions above $500 million completed by Indian firms from 2000 to 2009. I end up with twenty-one acquisitions, seventeen foreign and four domestic, listed in Table 6.1. It is interesting to note that all acquisitions except one were initiated from 2006 to 2008, the boom years preceding the recent financial crisis. I measure the stock market performance of the acquiring firms from the day before the announcement of the acquisition to one year after the announcement (Table 6.2). The performance measure I use is simply the relative stock market returns, defined as shareholder returns of the acquiring firm minus the returns to a broad index of the stock market. I also repeat the research using risk-adjusted returns, but there is no significant change in the results. I supplement the small sample

study with clinical case study analysis of the three largest acquisitions and attempt to explain what factors led to value creation or destruction in these three cases.

9. "How Indian Companies Fund Their Overseas Acquisitions," *India Knowledge@Wharton*, Dec. 14, 2006, http://knowledge.wharton.upenn.edu/india/article.cfm?articleid=4131.

10. Ibid.

11. P. Kale, H. Singh, and A. P. Raman, "Don't Integrate Your Acquisitions, Partner with Them," *Harvard Business Review*, Dec. 2009. (Reprint R0912M.)

12. I exclude the ONGC-Imperial Energy acquisition because ONGC is a government-controlled company and its emphasis is on control of natural resources rather than on specialized firm-specific resources.

13. Kumar, Mohapatra, and Chandrasekhar, *India's Global Powerhouses*.

14. Joe Leahy, "Indian Pride Fuelled Tata's Push for Corus," *Financial Times*, Feb. 2, 2007.

15. Anand Rathi Financial Services, "Tata Steel," Jan. 4, 2010.

16. JM Financial Institutional Securities, "Tata Steel," Mar. 8, 2010.

17. Reuters, "Novelis Shares Soar 13.5 Per Cent on Hindalco Takeover," Feb. 12, 2007, http://www.reuters.com/article/idUSN1238635220070212.

18. There might be reasons for vertical integration among parts of the upstream production of primary aluminum, as Rio Tinto Alcan believes. Other firms have chosen to deintegrate within the upstream segment.

19. John Garen, C. Jepsen, and F. Scott, "Economic Forces Shaping the Aluminum Industry," July 2009, http://www.secat.net/docs/resources/Economic_Forces.pdf.

20. http://www.alcan.com.cn/news_links/News/Alcan_news (accessed Mar. 25, 2010).

21. Alcan presentation, "Novelis Spin-off," http//www.novelis com/NR/rdonlyres/EADBB839-FD67–41B0–96AE -51488C56C1E3/0/NovelisPresentation_toInvestors_092904 .pdf (accessed Mar. 25, 2010).

22. Myra Pinham, "Novelis—Six Months On," *All Business*, July 1, 2005. http://www.allbusiness.com/primary-metal -manufacturing/alumina-aluminum/518421–1.html.

23. The company, Novelis, ended fiscal year 2010 with a net income of $405 million, but in fiscal year 2011, it had a lower net income: $115 million. http://www.novelis.com/en-us/ Pages/PressReleases.aspx?nvlhei=8000&Link=http:// novelis.mediaroom.com/index.php?s=43&item=29.

24. Sharon Carty, "Maybe Tata, Jaguar/Land Rover Is Not Such an Odd Couple," *USA Today*, May 29, 2008.

25. Ibid.

26. Dominic O'Connell, "Interview: Ratan Tata, India's Humble Business King," *Sunday Times*, May 10, 2009.

27. ICICI Securities, "Tata Motors," Feb. 5, 2010.

28. "Gone Shopping," *Economist*, May 28, 2009.

29. "Tata Steel: A Decade of Transformation," Sept. 18, 2008, http://www.tata.com/article.aspx?artid=nyykc7TJFnQ=.

30. Kale, Singh, and Raman, "'Don't Integrate Your Acquisitions."

31. Kumar, "How Emerging Giants Are Rewriting the Rules of M&A."

32. Ibid., p. 4.

33. S. de Smedt and M. Van Hoey, "Integrating Steel Giants: An Interview with the ArcelorMittal Postmerger Managers," *McKinsey Quarterly*, Feb. 2008.

34. Kumar, "How Emerging Giants Are Rewriting the Rules of M&A," p. 8.

35. Indiatimes News Network, "Industry, Politicos Hail the Deal," *Economic Times*, Jan. 31, 2007.

36. P. Thillaivarothayan, "India a 'Global Player,'" Ocnus.Net, Apr. 25, 2007, http://www.ocnus.net/artman/publish/article_28749 .shtml.

37. J. Leahy, "Indian Pride Fuelled Tata's Push for Corus."

38. A. Krishnamoorthy, "Jaguar Purchase Drives Tata Motors Shareholders to End Holdings," Bloomberg, Feb. 20, 2008, http://www.bloomberg.com/apps/news?pid=newsarchive& refer=india&sid=aYHS5AD.zR5c.

39. Kumar, Mohapatra, and Chandrasekhar, *India's Global Powerhouses*, p. 202.

40. Ibid.

41. T. Khanna and K. Palepu, "Why Focused Strategies May Be Wrong for Emerging Markets," *Harvard Business Review*, July–Aug. 1997. (Reprint 97404.)

42. Kumar, Mohapatra, and Chandrasekhar, *India's Global Powerhouses*.

43. G. de Jonquieres, "Asian Companies Should Not Rush to Go Global," *Financial Times*, Nov. 9, 2006.

44. For example, R. Chung, "The Cemex Way: The Right Balance Between Local Business Flexibility and Global Standardization," Case IMD-3–1341, International Institute for Management Development, Switzerland, 2005.

45. S. Chatterjee, "UB Group Buys Whyte & Mackay for £595 Million," *International Business Times*, May 16, 2007.

46. "Mallya's Spirits Run High," *Financial Express*, May 19, 2007.

47. "Vijay Mallya's United Spirits May Sell 49% of Whyte & Mackay," *Business Standard*, Feb. 9, 2009.

48. K. Giriprakash, "Whyte & Mackay Sees a Turnaround," *Business Line*, June 14, 2008.

49. "India's Marauding Maharajahs," *Economist*, Mar. 31, 2007.

50. M. Srivastava, "India's Ranbaxy Gives Headache to Japanese Drugmaking Parent," *BusinessWeek*, May 27, 2009.

## Chapter Seven

1. See, for example, K. P. Sauvant, "FDI in Emerging Markets: How Are They Doing—and What Should They Be Doing?"

(paper presented at a conference on FDI, Technology, and Competitiveness, UNCTAD, Geneva, Mar. 2007). http://www.unctad.org/sections/dite_dir/docs/dite_dir_03–07_Sauvant_en.pdf.

2. See, for example, L. T. Wells, *Third World Multinationals* (Cambridge, Mass.: MIT Press, 1983), and S. Lall, *The New Multinationals* (Hoboken, N.J.: Wiley, 1983).

3. "Cometh the Dragon," *Economist*, Nov. 13, 2010, pp. 81–83.

4. M. Wilkins, *The Maturing of Multinational Enterprise* (Cambridge, Mass.: Harvard University Press, 1974).

5. R. Caves, *Multinational Enterprise and Economic Analysis*, 2nd ed. (Cambridge: Cambridge University Press, 1996); B. Gomes-Casseres, "Ownership Strategies of Multinational Enterprises" (unpublished doctoral dissertation, Harvard Business School, 1985).

6. S. Hymer, *The International Operations of National Firms: A Study of Direct Foreign Investment* (Cambridge, Mass.: MIT Press, 1976).

7. P. Buckley and M. Casson, *The Future of the Multinational Enterprise* (London: Macmillan, 1976).

8. See Wells, *Third World Multinationals*, and Lall, *The New Multinationals*.

9. U. S. Rangan and J. D. Parrino, "Going Abroad Through Acquisitions: An Exploratory Analysis of Indian Companies' Recent International Expansion," *International Journal of Indian Culture and Business Management*, 2008, *1*, 335–353.

10. U. S. Rangan and S. Cao, "Going Abroad Through Acquisitions: An Exploratory Analysis of Chinese Companies' Recent International Expansion" (working paper presented at the Academy of International Business Conference at San Diego, June 2009).

11. See ibid.

12. M. Porter, *Competition in Global Industries* (Boston: Harvard Business School Press, 1986).

13. Y. Tsurumi and H. Tsurumi, "Fujifilm-Kodak Duopolistic Competition in Japan and the United States," *Journal of International Business Studies*, 1999, 30, 813–810.

14. Rangan and Parrino, "Going Abroad Through Acquisitions."

15. Ibid.

16. F. Knickerbocker, *Oligopolistic Reaction and Multinational Enterprise* (Boston: Harvard University, Graduate School of Business Administration, 1973).

17. Global pharmaceutical industry firms have been flocking to India since 1994 mainly because India signed the Trade Related Intellectual Property Rights protocol relating to intellectual property rights as part of the World Trade Organization agreement in 1994.

18. IBM left India in 1977 because of the country's strict indigenization laws.

19. M. Yoshino and U. S. Rangan, *Strategic Alliances: An Entrepreneurial Approach to Globalization* (Boston: Harvard Business School Press, 1995).

20. See Wells, *Third World Multinationals*, and Lall, *The New Multinationals*.

21. Much of the information on Indian capital control regulation comes from India's Ministry of Finance.

22. The information on China's capital control regime comes from various sources, such as PRS Group, *China Country Report*, July 1, 2009; "OECD Investment Policy Reviews: China 2008: Encouraging Responsible Business Conduct," Dec. 2008, http://www.oecd.org/document/40/0,3746,en_2649_34893_41735656_1_1_1_1,00.html; and UNCTAD, Investment Policy Monitor, no. 1, Dec. 2009, UNCTAD/WEB/DIAE/IA/2009/11.

23. See, for example, J. Harford, "What Drives Merger Waves?" *Journal of Financial Economics*, 2005, 77, 529–560, and M. Rhodes-Kropf, D. T. Robinson, and S. Viswanathan, "Valuation Waves and Merger Activity: The Empirical Evidence," *Journal of Financial Economics*, 2005, 77, 561–603.

24. McKinsey & Company, "Mapping Global Capital Markets: Fifth Annual Report," McKinsey Global Institute, Oct. 2008, p. 11.

25. N. Kumar, P. K. Mohapatra, and S. Chandrasekhar, *India's Global Powerhouses* (Boston: HBS Press, 2009).

26. Ibid., p. 9.

27. D. R. King, D. R. Dalton, C. M. Daily, and J. G. Covin, "Meta-Analyses of Post-Acquisition Performance: Indications of Unidentified Moderators, *Strategic Management Journal*, 2004, 25, 187–200.

28. A. Karnani, "Dubious Value of International Acquisitions by Emerging Economy Firms: The Case of Indian Firms," University of Michigan, Ross School working paper no. 1140, Apr. 2010.

29. Kumar, Mohapatra, and Chandrasekhar, *India's Global Powerhouses*.

30. Ibid.

31. Bharat Forge, "Dual Shore Manufacturing," n.d., http://www.bharatforge.com/company/dual_shore.asp.

32. V. Sehgal, K. Dehoff, and G. Panneer, "Frugal Engineering: A Powerful Approach to Develop Products and Services," *Economic Times*, May 7, 2010.

33. P. Cappelli, H. Singh, J. Singh, and M. Useem, *The India Way* (Boston: HBS Press, 2010).

34. Ibid.

35. "IBM Gets $80 Million Outsourcing Deal in Bangladesh from Bharti Airtel," *Wall Street Journal*, Dec. 7, 2010.

36. "Bharti and Vodafone Struggle to Make Money in Africa," *Telecom Africa*, Nov. 11, 2010, http://telecomafrica.blogspot.com/2010/11/bharti-and-vodafone-struggle-to-make.html.

37. M. Cox, "Lenovo Climbs to Second in PC Shipments," *Daily Channel News*, Oct. 16, 2011, http://www.echannelline.com/usa/story.cfm?item=27213.

38. J. Quelch and C. Knoop, "Lenovo: Building a Global Brand," Harvard Business School Case Study No. 9–507–014, 2006.
39. "A Bigger World," *Economist*, Sept. 18, 2008.
40. Ibid.
41. Quelch and Knoop, "Lenovo: Building a Global Brand."
42. Ibid.

## Chapter Eight

1. "Tata Swach Water Filter," tataswach.com, 2011, http://www.tataswach.com/TsrfTechnology.aspx.
2. "Accenture Will Increase India Market Focus, Says New MD," economictimes.indiatimes.com, Feb. 19, 2011, http://articles.economictimes.indiatimes.com/2011–02–19/news/28615144_1_global-delivery-network-identity-related-de-duplication-and-verification-core-biometric-identification-system.
3. "Mindtree Decides to Leave Cash-Sucking Android Phone Biz," androidos.in, Oct. 2010, medianama.com, 2009/10, http://androidos.in/2010/10/mindtree-decides-to-leave-cash-sucking-android-phone-biz/.
4. "How a Software Pro Sasken Turned Satphone Star," http://articles.economictimes.indiatimes.com/2010–10–12/news/28388378_1_sasken-inmarsat-low-cost-phone2010; "Sasken to Work on New Inmarsat," livemint.com, Nov. 2010, http://www.livemint.com/2010/11/19211111/Sasken-to-work-on-new-Inmarsat.html?atype=tp.
5. "India's Working-Age Population Growing Faster Than China's," euromonitor.com, Nov. 17, 2010, http://blog.euromonitor.com/2010/11/indias-working-age-population-growing-faster-than-chinas.html.
6. "Indian IT-BPO Industry," NASSCOM, 2011, http://www.nasscom.in/indian-itbpo-industry.

7. We have played executive, intrapreneurial, or entrepreneurial roles in the IT industry in both the United States and India. As participants and observers in this industry, we are keenly interested in how companies leverage India for innovation and what the future might hold. Our working definition of *innovation* is "the practical application of new ideas or inventions in industry or society." Our methodology draws on interviews, personal experiences, industry buzz, and research literature to uncover patterns of innovation, leading to practical recommendations for leaders.

   For the interviews in this study, we focused on IT companies in Bangalore in three broad categories: multinational companies (MNCs), small and medium enterprises (SMEs), and early-stage companies (start-ups and young companies). From a short list of ten, we picked three companies, one in each category: IBM as an MNC, Sasken as an SME, and Strand Lifesciences as an early-stage company. We chose these companies because of a demonstrated innovative streak, with recognition by professional peer groups or industry accolades.

   We sifted through in-depth interviews of many executives of the companies we selected, gained the perspectives from other industry professionals, participated in local IT industry meetings, monitored current industry buzz, reviewed business literature, and reflected on our own professional experiences in industry over the past two decades.

8. "The Lines Between Prepaid and Postpaid Are Blurring," cxotoday.com, Jan. 19, 2011, http://www.cxotoday.com/story/the-lines-between-prepaid-and-postpaid-are-blurring.

9. "IT Firms Gear Up to Strong Background Checks," currentitmarket.net, July 4, 2009, http://www.currentitmarket.net/2009/07/it-firms-gear-up-to-strong-background.htm; "IT Firms Have No Place for a Fake Resume," business-standard.com, July 13, 2008, http://www.business-standard.com/india/news/it-firms-have-no-place-forfake-resume/42021/on.

10. "A Special Report on Innovation in Emerging Markets," *Economist*, Apr. 15, 2010.

11. J. G. March, "Exploration and Exploitation in Organizational Learning," *Organization Science*, 1991, *2*, 71–87.

12. A. K. Gupta, K. G. Smith, and C. E. Shalley, "The Interplay Between Exploration and Exploitation," *Academy of Management Journal*, 2006, 49, 693–706.

13. J. R. Immelt, V. Govindarajan, and C. Trimble, "How GE Is Disrupting Itself," *Harvard Business Review*, Oct. 2009, 56–65.

14. The IBM executives interviewed were P. Gopalakrishnan, Kalpana Margabandhu, and S. Sugandha; the Sasken executives were G. Venkatesh and T. K. Srikanth; and the Strand Lifesciences executives were V. Chandru and S. Manohar. All interviews were conducted in 2010. In addition to these interviews and our personal experience, we consulted the following: R. M. Kanter, "IBM in the 21st Century: The Coming of the Globally Integrated Enterprise," Harvard Business School Case Study No. 9–308–105, Oct. 7, 2009; D. John, "Offshoring Industry in India—Moving Up the Value Chain?" CBS *Business Review*, June 2010; "Make Global M&A Successful the Daksh Way!" moneycontrol .com, Oct. 27, 2007, http://www.moneycontrol.com/news/ management/make-global-ma-successfuldaksh-way_310187 .html; O. M. Bjelland and R. C. Wood, "An Inside View of IBM's 'Innovation Jam,'" *MIT Sloan Management Review*, 2008, 50(1), 32–40: F. A. Martinez-Jerez and V. G. Narayanan, "Strategic Outsourcing at Bharti Airtel Limited: One Year Later," Harvard Business School Case Study No. 9–107–004, Dec. 4, 2007. See also "Bharti's $750 Mn IBM IT Deal Touches $2.5 Bn Mark," economictimes.indiatimes.com, Apr. 7, 2009, http://articles.economictimes.indiatimes .com/2009–04–07/news/28390916_1_bharti-and-ibm -outsourcing-deal-mtn; "IBM to Handle IT for Bharti Airtel's Africa Operations," economictimes.com, Sept. 18, 2010, http://articles.economictimes.indiatimes.com/2010–09–18/

news/27582116_1_african-operations-zain-manoj-kohli, "IBM Wins Vodafone Contract, Its Fourth Telecom Deal in India," livemint.com, Dec. 10, 2007, http://www.livemint .com/2007/12/10221309/IBM-wins-Vodafone-contract-it .html; and "Maxis Mobile Signs 5-Year IT Deal with IBM," cellular-news.com, Feb. 15, 2009, http://www.cellular-news .com/story/36033.php.

15. Kanter, "IBM in the 21st Century"; John, "Offshoring Industry in India—Moving Up the Value Chain?"

16. Ibid.

17. "Make Global M&A Successful the Daksh Way!"

18. Bjelland and Wood, "An Inside View of IBM's 'Innovation Jam.'"

19. John, "Offshoring Industry in India—Moving Up the Value Chain?" Martinez-Jerez and Narayanan, "Strategic Outsourcing at Bharti Airtel Limited."

20. Martinez-Jerez and Narayanan, "Strategic Outsourcing at Bharti Airtel Limited." See also "Bharti's $750 Mn IBM IT Deal Touches $2.5 Bn Mark."

21. "Bharti's $750 Mn IBM IT Deal Touches $2.5 Bn Mark."

22. "IBM Wins Vodafone Contract, Its Fourth Telecom Deal in India"; "Maxis Mobile Signs 5-Year IT Deal with IBM"; "IBM to Handle IT for Bharti Airtel's Africa Operations."

23. Interviews with P. Gopalakrishnan, Kalpana Margabandhu, and S. Sugandha.

24. Interviews with G. Venkatesh and T. K. Srikanth.

25. Interviews with V. Chandru and S. Manohar.

## Chapter Nine

1. See O. Shenkar, *Copycats: How Smart Companies Use Imitation to Gain a Strategic Edge* (Boston: Harvard Business Review Press, 2010), for an in-depth, comprehensive, and excellent discussion of the use of imitation as a competitive strategy.

2. Apple has received widespread media attention in many public sources. See, for example, "Chinese Authorities Find

22 More Fake Apple Stores," Reuters, Apr. 11, 2011. http://
www.reuters.com/article/2011/08/11/us-apple-china-fake
-idUSTRE77A3U820110811.

3. "Apple Incorporated," *New York Times*, Dec. 19, 2011, http://
topics.nytimes.com/top/news/business/companies/apple
_computer_inc/index.html.

4. K. Hannaford, "Two NYC Stores Selling Knock-Off Apple
Gadgets Under Attack by Apple," *Gizmodo*, Aug. 19, 2011,
http://gizmodo.com/5832504/two-nyc-stores-selling-knock
+off-apple-gadgets-are-under-attack-by-apple.

5. "Apple Moves Against Knock-Offs in New York," Reuters,
Aug. 18, 2011, http://www.reuters.com/article/2011/08/18/
apple-knockoffs-idUSN1E77H1Y920110818.

6. See A. K. Gupta and H. Wang, "China as an Innovation
Center? Not So Fast," *Wall Street Journal*, July 28, 2011, and
Shenkar, *Copycats*, for discussions of the limitations of
Chinese companies' innovation capabilities.

7. See J. Simone, "Criminal Enforcement Against Counterfeiters," *China Business Review*, 2002, 29(6), 22–23;
and S. Li, "Why Is Property Right Protection Lacking in
China? An Institutional Explanation," *California Management Review*, 2004, 46, 100–115, for a discussion of this
theme.

8. "Pfizer Sues China Company over Alleged Copyright
Infringement: A Report," Forbes.Com, Nov. 17, 2006, http://
www.forbes.com/feeds/afx/2006/11/16/afx3183866.html; J.
Edwardes, "What Will Happen When Viagra Goes Generic?"
AccessRx, n.d., http://www.lockelord.com/files/news/ab9ebdd4
–621f-4432-a383–1cae37df9ea1/presentation/newsattachment/
c5a9d67e-bdd9–4c7e-97e9–1d6efb6314dc/andrews
_pfizers%20viagra%20patent.pdf.

9. See M. M. Keupp, A. Beckenbauer, and A. Gassmann, "How
Managers Protect Intellectual Property Rights in China
Using De Facto Strategies," *R&D Management*, 2009, 39,
211–224.

10. See Gupta and Wang, "China as an Innovation Center?"

11. For additional discussions of the limitations of Chinese companies' innovation capabilities, see ibid.; Shenkar, *Copycat*; and D. F. Simon and C. Cao, *China's Emerging Technological Edge: Assessing the Role of High-End Talent* (Cambridge: Cambridge University Press, 2009).

12. See K. Lane and F. Pollner, "How to Address China's Talent Shortage," *McKinsey Quarterly*, 2005, 3.

13. Lego received widespread media attention from many public sources, including "Dual Protection for Industrial Designs Confirmed by Court," *News*, n.d., http://www.ccpit-patent.com.cn/News/2003041001.htm.

14. "Renault-Nissan Lands in China, Obama Buys Hybrid Cars," *Green Light*, Apr. 10, 2009, 1.

15. "Nissan Increases China Production, BBC, Sept. 2010, http://www.bbc.co.uk/news/business-11368125 retrieved 9–02–2011.

16. See C. O'Reilly, "Corporations, Culture and Commitment: Motivation and Social Control in Organizations," *California Management Review*, 1989, *31*(4), 9–26, for an excellent, in-depth treatment of this topic.

17. C. Andreadis, "Michigan Couple Charged with Selling GM Secrets to Chinese," *ABC News*, July 23, 2010, http://abcnews.go.com/TheLaw/Business/michigan-couple-charged-corporate-espionage/story?id=11236400.

18. "Ex-Ford Engineer Sentenced for Trade Secrets Theft," Reuters, Apr. 13, 2011, http://www.reuters.com/article/2011/04/13/us-djc-ford-tradesecrets-idUSTRE73C3FG20110413.

19. M. Humphries, "AMD Employee Charged with Intel IP Theft," geek.com, Nov. 11, 2008, http://www.geek.com/articles/chips/amd-employee-charged-with-intel-ip-theft-20081111/.

20. D. Kravets, "Former VP for HP Guilty of IBM Trade Secret Theft," *Wired*, July 11, 2008, http://www.wired.com/threatlevel/2008/07/former-vp-for-h/.

21. "China: Land of Opportunity and Challenge," *HR Magazine*, Sept. 2007, http://www.shrm.org/Publications/hrmagazine/EditorialContent/Pages/0907cover.aspx.

## Chapter Ten

1. Central Intelligence Agency, *The World Fact Book*, 2011, https://www.cia.gov/library/publications/the-world-factbook/rankorder/2001rank.html.

2. J. Immelt, V. Govindarajan, and C. Trimble, "How GE Is Disrupting Itself," *Harvard Business Review*, Oct. 2009. (Reprint R0910D.)

3. A quick glance at recent articles in the *Wall Street Journal* and *Financial Times* should confirm the validity of this statement.

4. This is the point made by Dawar and Bagga in Chapter Two in this book where we saw how Hyundai outflanked firms such as Toyota, GM, Ford, and Honda in the Indian automobile market.

5. C. M. Christensen, *The Innovator's Dilemma* (Boston: HBS Press, 1997).

6. N. Kumar, P. K. Mohapatra, and S. Chandrasekhar, *India's Global Powerhouse* (Boston: HBS Press, 2009).

7. Dual Shore Manufacturing, Bharat Forge, n.d., http://www.bharatforge.com/company/dual_shore.asp.

8. This formulation harkens back to the seminal work by P. R. Lawrence and J. Lorsch, *Organization and Environment: Managing Differentiation and Integration* (Boston: HBS Press, 1967).

# About the Editors and Contributors

## The Editors

*Anil K. Gupta* (agupta@umd.edu) is the Michael Dingman Chair in Strategy and Entrepreneurship at the Smith School of Business, the University of Maryland at College Park, and a visiting professor of strategy at INSEAD, where he served as the INSEAD Chaired Professor in Strategy until the end of 2010.

The author of over seventy papers and several books, Gupta received a doctorate from the Harvard Business School, an M.B.A. from the Indian Institute of Management at Ahmedabad, and a B.Tech. from the Indian Institute of Technology at Kanpur. He has been recognized by *Economist* magazine as one of the world's "rising superstars" in a cover story on innovation in emerging economies. His book *Getting China and India Right: Leveraging the World's Fastest-Growing Economies for Global Advantage* (2009) received the 2009 Axiom Book Awards' Silver Prize as one of the world's two best books on globalization and international business. He is also the coauthor of *The Quest for Global Dominance* (2008), one of the world's most widely referenced books on global strategy.

The recipient of numerous awards for excellence in research and teaching, Gupta is an elected lifetime fellow of the Strategic Management Society, as well as the Academy of International Business. He has been inducted into the *Academy of Management Journal's* Hall of Fame and ranked by *Management International Review* as one of the "Top 20 North American Superstars" for research in strategy and organization. He received the 2010 Best Professor in Strategy Award from CMO Asia. He serves regularly as a keynote speaker at conferences organized by corporations and industry associations, as well as leading institutions such as the World Economic Forum, *Economist* magazine, and *Bloomberg BusinessWeek*.

**U. Srinivasa Rangan** (rangan@babson.edu) holds the Luksic Chair Professorship in Strategy and Global Studies at Babson College. His teaching, consulting, and research focus on competitive strategy, globalization, and alliances. His current research deals with the globalization of Indian, Chinese, and Brazilian companies; their use of acquisitions and alliances; the evolution of industries and firm-level strategies; and the impact of national business systems on them.

After serving as a manager in industrial and international finance in India and England, Rangan held research and faculty positions at IMD, Harvard Business School, and Tulane University. He holds graduate degrees from IMD, London School of Economics, and Harvard University. An accomplished case method teacher, he is the recipient of several teaching awards. He has been a consultant as well as a designer and deliverer of executive programs for several firms. He has taught at Babson, Helsinki School of Economics, Stockholm School of Economics, Amos Tuck School at Dartmouth, Rotman School at the University of Toronto, Indian School of Business, and Indian Institute of Management, working with senior managers from several industries in North America, Europe, and Asia.

Rangan has coauthored two books. His first book, *Strategic Alliances: An Entrepreneurial Approach to Globalization* (1995), was named one of the top thirty business books of the year in both the United States and Europe and was translated into several languages. His second book, *Capital Rising* (2010), deals with how entrepreneurial ecosystems of countries and global capital flows interact to change the global competitive landscape. The author of several case studies on strategic management, Rangan has also published articles in academic journals. He has presented scholarly papers at academic gatherings and has been a speaker at several practitioner-oriented forums.

*Toshiro Wakayama* (wakayama@iuj.ac.jp) is a professor of strategy and innovation at the Graduate School of International Management, International University of Japan. He received his Ph.D. from Syracuse University and has worked for Xerox Corporation in the United States.

Wakayama's research focuses on the irreducible nature of business and strategy through interview-based fieldwork and system-theoretic perspectives. One strand of research is to give a mathematical characterization (using a formal extension of multi-relational networks) for a system of interacting, sometimes conflicting, strategic themes that a firm must manage as an integrated whole, with the aim of laying theoretical foundations for executives' insights into managing increasingly complex business organizations. Pairing this theoretical inquiry with empirical studies, he also pursues interview-based field studies on how firms cope with dual strategic agendas such as local adaptation versus global integration, mainly in manufacturing and retail sectors. In addition to M.B.A. teaching in the areas of competitive strategy, global strategy, and innovation-driven new business creation, he designs and manages highly successful executive education programs with participants from over twenty-five global firms in Japan. He has given industry talks and workshops at various organizations such as the Bank of Japan, IBM (USA), Fuji Xerox, Mitsubishi Research Institute, Oracle Japan, SAP Japan, Mitsui Shipbuilding, Fujitsu Laboratories, and Deloitte Tohmatsu Consulting.

## The Contributors

*Tomofumi Amano* (amano@e.u-tokyo.ac.jp), until his recent untimely demise, was an associate professor at the Graduate

School of Economics, University of Tokyo, Japan. He received a Ph.D. from Hitotsubashi University and served as a lecturer at Toyo University and an associate professor at Hosei University.

Amano's research focused on multinational enterprises' global strategy in Asia and emerging markets through interview-based fieldwork and system-theoretic perspectives. He applied manufacturing management theory to examine the relationship between comparative advantage structures among the countries in the region and the corporate strategy of international specialization with a look at manufacturing industry. His research focused not only on the empirical analysis of international specialization and industry structure in Asia but also on the economic and managerial impact of foreign direct investments by foreign firms in Japan.

**Charan Bagga** (cbagga@ivey.ca) is a doctoral candidate in marketing at the Richard Ivey School of Business, University of Western Ontario. His research interests include emerging markets, branding, behavioral pricing, and the marketing of durables. Prior to joining the Ph.D. program at Ivey, Bagga worked or consulted for leading global corporations like HCL, ITC, Standard Chartered, Fidelity National Financial, Progressive Insurance, and CSC. His work in different geographies (the United States, Canada, Singapore, Europe, and India) and different industry sectors (financial services, technology outsourcing, and consumer goods) gives him a good perspective on the challenges corporations face as they work in the globalized economy. In his more recent role before joining Ivey, Bagga was a senior business development manager with CSC's global outsourcing business unit. He holds an M.B.A. from the Indian Institute of Management, Bangalore, and an undergraduate degree in industrial engineering.

**Niraj Dawar** (ndawar@ivey.uwo.ca) is the Barford Professor of Marketing at the Richard Ivey School of Business, University of

Western Ontario. His research interests lie in the areas of marketing strategy, brand strategy, and cross-cultural consumer behavior. His publications in these areas have appeared in *Harvard Business Review, Journal of Marketing Research, Journal of Marketing, M.I.T. Sloan Management Review*, and other academic and managerial outlets.

Dawar has worked in Europe, North America, and Asia. Previously he was on the INSEAD faculty as an associate professor until 1998 and was also a visitor there in 2005 and 2010. In 1994 and again in 1995, he was a visiting scholar at the Hong Kong University of Science and Technology. In 2000, he was the Davidson Research Professor at the University of Michigan Business School.

Dawar has worked extensively with senior management teams of companies including Algorithmics, Asahi Glass, BMW (AG), Cadbury-Schweppes (Global), DeBeers (South Africa), HSBC (Asia), Microsoft (C.E.E.), J. Walter Thompson (International), and the McCain group (Worldwide). He has served as program director for Microsoft, McCain, and HSBC senior management programs.

**Sam Hariharan** (shariharan@babson.edu) is a member of the faculty in strategy and international business of the Management Division at Babson College in the United States. He received his Ph.D in corporate strategy from the University of Michigan.

Hariharan's teaching, consulting, and research focus on business and corporate strategy, global strategic management, and how companies innovate and create new competitive spaces. His current research deals with the globalization of Indian, Chinese, and Brazilian companies and their use of acquisitions and alliances. He has held faculty positions at the University of Michigan, the Marshall School of Business at the University of Southern California (USC), Purdue University, and GISMA (Leibniz University, Hannover, Germany). He is the winner of multiple teaching awards at Purdue University and USC.

In addition to his role as a consultant to businesses, Hariharan has designed and delivered customized executive programs for several companies and organizations in North America, Europe, and Asia. An author of several case studies on strategic management, Hariharan is the author of articles published in academic journals and book chapters. In addition to presenting scholarly papers at academic conferences, he is an active speaker at many corporate retreats, executive seminars, and conferences.

*Srikanth Kannapan* (smkannapan@yahoo.com) has more than twenty years of international experience in the United States and India working with technology companies such as Xerox, IBM Global Services, and Symphony Services. He has also founded and nurtured significant intrapreneurial and entrepreneurial ventures in Bangalore.

Earlier in the United States, Kannapan directed and engaged in research, consulting, and teaching at Cornell University and Xerox PARC in Palo Alto, California. On his return to India in 1998, he was the founding practice head for business intelligence at IBM Global Services, India, where he led some of the early business intelligence and analytics system implementations in India. He was the founder and CEO of eKnowVenture Technologies, a specialized decision analytics company that was later acquired by Symphony in 2002. At Symphony Services, he helped seed new analytics businesses, synergizing both targeted acquisitions and organic business development. Since 2005, he has focused on incubating technology-enabled start-ups and advising other early-stage companies.

Throughout his career, Kannapan has developed business strategies, driven marketing and sales, developed and implemented technology solutions, and managed customer relationships in application areas such as analytics, business intelligence, and software development for clients in manufacturing, retail, and telecom. He earned a master's degree and a Ph.D. from the

University of Texas at Austin, specializing in applications of artificial intelligence in engineering. He has a bachelor's degree in mechanical engineering from the Indian Institute of Technology, Madras.

*Aneel Karnani* (akarnani@umich.edu) is a faculty member in the strategy group at the Stephen M. Ross School of Business, University of Michigan. Prior to joining the University of Michigan's faculty in 1980, he obtained his doctoral degree from the Harvard Business School.

Karnani's interests are focused on three topics: strategies for growth, global competition, and the role of business in society. He studies how firms can leverage existing competitive advantages and create new ones to achieve rapid growth. He is interested in global competition, particularly in the context of emerging economies. He studies both how local companies can compete against large multinational firms and how multinational firms can succeed in these unfamiliar markets. Karnani researches poverty reduction and the appropriate roles for the private sector, the state, and civil society. He is interested in how society can strike the appropriate balance between private profits and public welfare in tackling major societal problems. He has published in and is a member of the editorial boards of several professional journals. He is the author of the book *Fighting Poverty Together: Rethinking Strategies for Business, Governments, and Civil Society to Reduce Poverty* (2011).

Karnani is also actively involved in executive development programs both in companies and through the University of Michigan. He consults with firms on strategic planning systems and strategy analysis and formulation. He is currently on the board of trustees of GreenPath. He has served a number of organizations as a consultant or management educator, including GE, IBM, Singapore Airlines, Singapore Technologies, Temasek, Acer, Whirlpool, Masco, Total, Holcim, Neopost, Abbott Laboratories, and Dow Corning.

*Takafumi Kikuchi* (kikuchi.takafumi@jp.panasonic.com) is a senior executive at Panasonic Corporation, where he is responsible for corporate global strategy planning as well as marketing strategy, especially for emerging markets and leading corporate transformation projects. He earned a master's degree in electrical engineering from Keio University Graduate School of Science and Technology in 1999. He then joined Panasonic Corporation, where he worked for network system development at its corporate R&D division. He successfully led new business creation such as smart card systems and an IPTV system as a project leader. In 2009, he received an M.B.A. from the International University of Japan. In his thesis, he explored how excellent global companies create structural competitive advantages by managing contradictory strategic themes such as local adaptation versus global integration.

*Kuruvilla Lukose* (k_lukose@yahoo.com) is the CTO of Altair Engineering's India Development Center, where industry-leading advances in scientific and engineering simulation are in constant creation. He focuses on the development of technical talent as well as extending Altair's technology footprint through collaborations with the rapidly expanding technical ecosystem in India.

Lukose has more than twenty years of international experience in the United States and India working with technology companies. He has an M.S. in structural engineering from Cornell University and a B.Tech. from the Indian Institute of Technology, Madras.

Lukose has worked as a professional engineer in the nuclear power industry. He has played key software development and engineering roles in U.S. corporations, including Structural Dynamics Research Corporation in Cincinnati. He led the technical marketing team in Silicon Graphics Computer Systems in India through which innovative applications of high-performance computing and visualization were made available to Indian industry. He has held a senior executive role in a leading discovery-oriented life sciences organization in India. He has worked as an independent consultant to national-level Indian government organizations in the domain of high-performance computer-based scientific simulation. He has significant expertise in marketing and competitive positioning of technical and scientific applications in global markets.

*Andreas Schotter* (andreas.schotter@thunderbird.edu) is an assistant professor of strategic management at the Thunderbird School of Global Management in Arizona and a visiting professor at the University of Aarhus in Denmark. He is a Wall Street Journal Distinguished Professor of the Year.

A dual German and Canadian citizen, Schotter received his Ph.D. from the Richard Ivey School of Business at the University of Western Ontario. He taught at the University of Western Ontario and at McMaster University, before joining Thunderbird, where he teaches core and custom courses in the M.B.A. program. In addition, he is the academic director of several custom executive education programs and a member of the *Thunderbird International Business Review* editorial board.

Schotter's primary research interests are multinational corporate development and subsidiary evolution, management of the headquarters-subsidiary interface, corporate strategic change, global innovation and technology management, emerging markets, social enterprises, and the role of boundary spanners in global firms.

Before embarking on an academic career, he was a senior executive with several multinational corporations in the automotive, industrial equipment, and luxury consumer goods industries in Europe and in Asia, where he lived for almost a decade.

*Junjiro Shintaku* (shintaku@e.u-tokyo.ac.jp) is an associate professor of corporate strategy at the Graduate School of Economics, University of Tokyo. He earned a Ph.D. in economics from the University of Tokyo.

After a period of research and teaching as a lecturer and an associate professor at Gakushuin University, Shintaku moved to the University of Tokyo. He is also a research director at the Manufacturing Management Research Center, University of Tokyo; an executive director of the Academic Association for Organizational Science; an executive director of the Japan Academy of International Business Studies; and cofounder and executive director of the Global Business Research Center, a nonprofit organization for industry-academia collaborative studies. He has been a key guest speaker in various events held by enterprises and Japanese government.

Shintaku's research is mainly on technological innovation and corporate strategies. He has written and edited many books in Japanese, including *Management Text: Introduction to Corporate Strategies* (2011), *Global Strategy of Manufacturing Management: Industrial Geography in Asia* (2009), and *Architecture-Based Analysis of Chinese Manufacturing Industries* (2005).

**Akira Tanaka** (tanaka@econ.nagoya-cu.ac.jp) is a professor on the Faculty of Economics at Nagoya City University, Nagoya, Aichi-ken, Japan. He has also been a visiting scholar at the University of New South Wales, Sydney, Australia, and Sapporo University, Hokkaido, Japan.

His primary field of research is contemporary Japanese economic and business history. He has been interested in the historical development of worldwide interfirm coordination systems in modern Japanese industry, especially the role of *sogo shosha* (Japanese general trading companies) in the iron and steel and automobile industries. He has visited several countries, including China, Korea, Taiwan, Australia, the United States, and the United Kingdom, for his research. His recent publications appear in *Journal of Business Research* and Japanese domestic journals such as *Organizational Science*. He is the author of the Japanese-language book *Postwar Japan's Mineral Industry: A Comparative History of Its Procurement System and Sogo Shosha*.

*Mary B. Teagarden* (mary.teagarden@thunderbird.edu) is a professor of global strategy at the Thunderbird School of Global Management, visiting professor at the University of Aarhus in Denmark, and editor in chief of *Thunderbird International Business Review*. She received her Ph.D. from the University of Southern California. She is recognized and sought after in academic, corporate, and government sectors for her teaching, executive training, and consulting. Her research focuses on global competitiveness, the strategic management of technology and innovation, talent management in emerging markets, and the development of global mindsets in high-technology industries around the world, including the People's Republic of China and India. Teagarden is principal coinvestigator on Thunderbird's Global Mindset Project, as well as faculty associate at the Global Mindset Institute and the Nordic Network for Climate Adaptation, Mitigation, and Economic Policy.

She is an active international consultant with global reach who has trained and advised more than sixty technology-intensive manufacturing and service firms in China, India, Malaysia, Mexico, and Brazil. She has published more than 127 articles, books, chapters, and case studies in *Harvard Business Review*, *Academy of Management Journal*, *Human Resource Management*, *Thunderbird International Business Review*, and *Organizational Dynamics*, among others. Top media outlets, including CNN, MSNBC, Fox Business, CCTV, ABC, the *Financial Times*, Harvard Business School Working Knowledge, CIO, and IEEE Spectrum call on her expertise regularly. Teagarden serves as an advisor or director on seven international boards.

*Haiyan Wang* (hwang@chinaindiainstitute.com) is managing partner of the China India Institute, a research consultancy with a focus on creating winning global strategies that leverage the transformational rise of China and India. She has also served as an adjunct professor of strategy at INSEAD.

Wang serves as a regular columnist for *BusinessWeek*, a contributing editor for *Chief Executive* magazine, and a blogger for

*Harvard Business Review*. She is the coauthor of two highly acclaimed books: *Getting China and India Right* (which received the 2009 Axiom Book Awards' Silver Prize as one of the world's two best books on globalization/international business) and *The Quest for Global Dominance*. Her opinion pieces have appeared in top international media such as the *Wall Street Journal*, *BusinessWeek*, *Chief Executive*, the *Economic Times*, *China Daily*, and *Times of India*. She has been frequently interviewed by CNBC, the *Wall Street Journal*, *Fox Business*, *India Today*, CNN *Expansión*, *Shanghai Daily*, and other prominent business media.

A native of China, Wang has spent the past twenty years consulting for and managing multinational business operations in China and the United States in several industry sectors. She serves regularly as a keynote speaker at major conferences and corporate forums in the United States, Europe, Asia, and Latin America.

**Yue Wang** (yue.w@unsw.edu.au) is a senior lecturer in the School of Organization and Management at the University of New South Wales, Sydney, Australia. He received his Ph.D. degree from the University of Melbourne.

Wang has been a visiting scholar at Nagoya City University and Doshisha University in Japan, Shanghai Jiaotong University in China, and Korea University Business School. His current research interests focus on alliance strategies of multinational enterprises in China and internationalization strategies of emerging market multinationals. His recent publications appear in journals such as *Management International Review, Journal of International Management, Advances in International Management, Journal of Business Research, Asia Pacific Journal of Management*, and *Thunderbird International Business Review*.

He is the author of *Contractual Joint Ventures in China: Formation, Evolution and Performance* and the lead editor of the book *Thirty Years of China's Economic Reform: Institutions, Management Organizations and Foreign Investment*.

# Index

Page references followed by *fig* indicate an illustrated figure; followed by *t* indicate a table.

Christensen, C., 90–91, 97, 99

Cisco: decentralizing into global hubs, 19, 26; strong one-company culture of, 22; TelePresence of, 21

CNPC (China), 141

Coca-Cola: catering to consumptions habits in China and Russia, 52; counterfeiters of iconic bottle of, 242; robust strategy staying within beverage domain of, 7; value chain leverage through acquisition of Thums Up brand, 182

Coevolution: cultivating a mind-set for, 83–85, 277; establishing strategic outposts for, 81–82; jump-starting through adaptation-intended acquisition, 82–83; moving from spontaneous to deliberate, 79–80; Panasonic China adoption of, 68–79

COKO Toy Company, 248–249

Collaborative innovation: disaggregation of value chains driving, 15–16, 278; emergence of intellectual property driving, 17; outsourcing driving, 15–16. See also Global innovation; Innovation

Communication strategy: broad messaging appealing to large segments, 50–51; mass media suited to reach EM-MC consumers, 51; for selling users and nonusers on product benefits, 51–52

Competitive advantage: global integration's competitive value for, 63; strategies in emerging Asia for, 265–284

Competitive positioning strategies: fostering a global mind-set for, 267, 282–284; globalizing through alliances and acquisitions for, 267, 278–282; reconceptualizing strategy for, 266, 267–271; reinventing the global organization for, 267, 276–278; rethinking innovation strategy for, 267, 271–276

Consumers: BOP (bottom of pyramid), 88, 205; EM-ME (emerging market–middle class), 35, 44, 46–48, 51, 53; MOP (middle of the pyramid), 88

Controls discipline norm, 255–257

Cooperation value, 63

Copyright. See Intellectual property (IP)

Corporate culture: IP through controls discipline tendency in, 255–257; moving toward strong one-company, 21–23

Corporate headquarters: network of global hubs instead of, 17–20; "virtualization of the corporation" replacing, 18

Corporate leadership guidance: for agility and patience, 230t–231t; agility and patience contradictions in, 213; emerging economies' innovative patterns and, 230t–231t; leadership psychology factor of, 214–215; unbalancing agility and patience, 215–216

Corporate mind-set, 24–27

Corporate social responsibility (CSR), 261–262

Corus Steel: EBITDA earnings of, 143; Tata Steel's acquirement of, 141, 143, 150–153. See also Tata Steel-Corus Steel case study

Court, D., 34

Cross-border acquisitions: announcements on, 169–170; by Asian countries (excluding Japan), 174t; competitive advantage through, 278–282; competitive threat posed by emerging market firms through, 198–199; financing, 145, 148–149; by firms from Asian countries, 174t–175t; formula for successful, 164–166; global capital markets thesis on, 185; global industries in which Indian acquisitions have occurred in tandem, 179t–180t; global players in industries engaging in, 178t; globalization thesis of, 176, 181–182; implications of emerging economy firms engagement in, 185–189; increasing number of emerging economy firms making, 170–173; increasing rates of, 141–142; by Indian firms (2000–2009), 145, 146t–147t; by industry, 175t; motivations and thesis of, 144–145, 173, 176–185, 189; Oriental approach versus Western approach to, 158, 159; poor outcomes for Indian firms, 162–164,

IBM's innovation in, 225–227, 274–275, 278; IBM's potential for innovation in, 217–220; as IT (information technology) outsourcing destination, 203–204; Kellogg India, 48–49; largest corporations' headquarters in, 3; McDonald's in, 49; P&G hair care market segment in, 46; pattern for innovation in, 204–207; percentage growth of key consumption indicators (2000–2009) with PPP adjusted, 33t; ranking economy and GDP (2010) of, 4t; retail outlets in, 55; Sasken's potential for innovation in, 220–222; sociocultural character of, 205–206, 211–212; Unilever's distribution system used in, 56. *See also* BRIC (Brazil, Russia, India, China) countries

Indian auto industry: changing landscape (2000–2010) of the, 43fig; competitive positioning in the, 268; growth of Hyundai market share of, 40–42, 44, 268, 276; Suzuki's Maruti Alto as best-selling car in, 47

Indian business experience: business infrastructure factors underlying, 210–211; corporate leadership guidance contributing to, 212–213; leadership psychology contributing to, 214–215; market factors underlying, 207–209; pattern of innovation in, 204–207; potential of innovation in the, 216–217; sociocultural factors underlying, 205–206, 211–212; talent factors underlying, 209–210; unbalancing agility and patience, 215–216

Indian firms: created value through international acquisitions by, 144–145, 146t; how easy capital is a weakness in acquisitions, 162–164, 279; increasing rates of cross-border acquisitions by, 171–173; stock market returns impacted by acquisition announcement, 148t; three unique traits leading to successful acquisitions, 162. *See also* Chinese and Indian (C&I) firms; Cross-border acquisitions case studies; Emerging economy companies

Indian Institute of Science (IISc), 222, 224

*India's Global Powerhouses: How They Are Taking On the World*, 145

Indonesia: motorcycle market of, 106, 107fig; ranking economy and GDP (2010) of, 4t

Indonesian motorcycle market: Honda's division of labor in development of, 107fig; Honda's motorcycle design for the, 106

Information technology (IT): cultivating a one-company culture role of, 23; India as outsourcing destination for, 203–204; Indian business infrastructure for, 210–211; Indian talent factors in, 209–210; Lenova Group's acquisition of IBM's personal computer business, 141, 169, 194–195. *See also* Technology

Infosys, 19, 181

Innovation: competitive positioning by rethinking, 271–276; examples of new and revitalized, 225–229; by IBM in India, 225–227, 274–275, 278; India and pattern for, 204–207; insights and recommendations for enterprise, 229, 232–233; patterns of leadership guidance in emerging economies, 230t–231t; Sasken's Inmarsat-linked satellite phone, 227–228; shifting perspective of, 203–204; Strand Lifesciences' AVADIS platform, 228–229; the Swach, 203; two examples of IBM's, 225–227. *See also* Collaborative innovation; Global innovation; Research & development (R&D)

Innovation potential: IBM's, 217–220; Sasken's, 220–222, 274; Strand Lifesciences', 222–224, 274; unlocking Indian business, 216–217

Innovator's dilemma: description of, 87; description of the, 90; HDD (hard disk drive) industry's experience with, 91; Japanese firms' responses to the, 87–88, 91–93; SIDM printers illustration of, 91–93. *See also* Emerging market dilemma

*The Innovator's Dilemma* (Christensen), 90, 99

Intel, 258

Tiajin Xiali Automobile Co. Ltd.,
121–122
Tianjin Automobile Industry (Group)
Corporation (General Corporation
[GC or Zong-Gongsi]), 121, 122, 123,
126, 128, 130
Tianjin Automobile Industry Sales Co.
Ltd., 122, 125
Tianjin Huali Automobile Ltd., 122
Tianjin Kyoho Society, 129, 130, 131
Tianjin Mini-Auto Works, 128
Tianjin Toyota Motor Corporation,
135
Tianjin Xiali Automobile Co. Ltd.,
133–134
Toyota: comparing Hyundai and, 41–44;
export from home strategy of, 8;
interest alignment approach of Nissan
versus, 252; *kanban* system used by,
124, 125; organizational
transformations required of, 18; parts
supply practices in Japan by, 118–119;
strategy toward China by, 117–136;
strong one-company culture of, 22.
*See also* Auto industry; Japanese
firms
Toyota Group-TAG joint venture (JV):
exclusiveness in parts transactions,
126–127; 5S (series of virtues)
introduced during, 130; globalizing
through, 281–282; *Jishu Ken* (self-
improvement) activities held during,
130; outcomes and lessons learned
from, 136–138; phase I (1990s)
transferring supplier management in
TAG, 128–132; phase II (2000s)
transferring supplier management in
TAG, 132–136; production
differences between Toyota and
TAG, 122–125, 281–282; renewal
negotiations for parts prices, 126;
restructuring Tianjin Xiali
Automobile Co. Ltd., 133–134;
settlement of TAG's parts payment
during, 125–126; TAG's interfirm
system impacting, 127–128; Toyota's
proposal to Chinese government for,
119, 121–122
Toyota Motor Technical Center
(China), 129–130
Trademark. *See* Intellectual property
(IP)

Trust-Mart (China), 83
Turkey, ranking economy and GDP
(2010) of, 4t
"2009 Manufacturing White Paper"
(Japan), 88

U

Unilever: distribution system used in
India by, 56; Lifebuoy soap sold by,
52; mass media used to reach
consumers by, 51; serving directly
through account managers, 55
United Breweries Group, 165
United Kingdom, 4t
United Phosphorous Limited (UPL),
57
United Spirits Limited (USL), 165–166
United States: Human Genome Project
of the, 222; no longer the top-
trading nation in the world, 35,
36fig; P&G hair care market segment
in the, 46; percentage growth of key
consumption indicators (2000–2009)
with PPP adjusted, 33t; ranking
economy and GDP (2010) of, 4t
U.S. Federal Reserve, 185

V

Value chain: atomization of the, 8–9;
collaborative innovation and
disaggregation of, 15–17, 278–279;
cross-border acquisition to increase,
144–145, 146t, 182–183; poor
outcomes of acquisitions made by
Indian firms, 162–164, 279;
traditional approach to, 8
Venezuela, 4t
Venkatesh, G., 228, 233
Viagra patent violation, 240
Vietnamese motorcycle market: China's
declining exports to, 101–104;
examining Honda's entrance into
the, 101–104, 269, 277; Honda's
division of labor in development of,
107fig; Honda's share (1998–2003) in
the, 101fig, 281
Vijay Mallya, 165
"Virtualization of the corporation," 18
Volvo-Geely acquisition, 169, 196–198,
283